The Darker Vision
of the Renaissance

Published under the auspices of the
CENTER FOR MEDIEVAL AND RENAISSANCE STUDIES
University of California, Los Angeles

Contributions of the

UCLA CENTER FOR MEDIEVAL AND RENAISSANCE STUDIES

1: Medieval Secular Literature: Four Essays. Ed. William Matthews.

2: Galileo Reappraised. Ed. Carlo L. Golino.

3: The Transformation of the Roman World. Ed. Lynn White, jr.

4: Scientific Methods in Medieval Archaeology. Ed. Rainer Berger.

5: Violence and Civil Disorder in Italian Cities, 1200–1500. Ed. Lauro Martines.

6: The Darker Vision of the Renaissance: Beyond the Fields of Reason. Ed. Robert S. Kinsman.

UCLA Center For
Medieval And Renaissance Studies
Contributions: VI

The Darker Vision
of the Renaissance

Beyond the Fields of Reason

Edited, with introduction, by
Robert S. Kinsman

University of California Press
BERKELEY • LOS ANGELES • LONDON 1974

University of California Press
Berkeley and Los Angeles, California

University of California Press, Ltd.
London, England

Copyright © 1974
by The Regents of the University of California
ISBN: 0–520–02259–9
Library of Congress Catalog Card Number: 72–78939

Sept 16, 1975

Printed in the United States of America

CONTENTS

INTRODUCTION   1
ROBERT S. KINSMAN,
University of California, Los Angeles

I.

DEATH AND THE DEVIL   25
LYNN WHITE, JR.,
University of California, Los Angeles

II.

RENAISSANCE WORLD-ALIENATION   47
DONALD R. HOWARD,
The Johns Hopkins University

III.

THE GENTLEMAN IN RENAISSANCE
ITALY: STRAINS OF ISOLATION IN
THE BODY POLITIC   77
LAURO MARTINES,
University of California, Los Angeles

IV.

HERMETISM AS A RENAISSANCE
WORLD VIEW   95
JOHN G. BURKE,
University of California, Los Angeles

V.

STRUCTURES OF RENAISSANCE MYSTICISM   119
KEES W. BOLLE,
University of California, Los Angeles

VI.

THE HIDDEN GOD: REFORMATION AWE
IN RENAISSANCE ENGLISH LITERATURE   147
PAUL R. SELLIN
University of California, Los Angeles

VII.

THE IRRATIONAL AND LATE
MEDIEVAL MUSIC   197
GILBERT REANEY,
University of California, Los Angeles

VIII.

MODES OF PERCEPTION OF REALITY
IN THE RENAISSANCE   221
MARC BENSIMON,
University of California, Los Angeles

IX.

FOLLY, MELANCHOLY, AND MADNESS: A
STUDY IN SHIFTING STYLES OF MEDICAL
ANALYSIS AND TREATMENT, 1450–1675   273
ROBERT S. KINSMAN

INTRODUCTION

Robert S. Kinsman

Sic omnes pii, ingredientes cum
Abraham tenebras fidei,
mortificant rationem, dicentes:
Tu ratio stulta es.

"THUS," REMARKS Martin Luther in his commentary on Galatians 3:6, "all the devout believers enter with Abraham into the darkness of faith, and put reason to death, saying, 'Reason, you are besotted.' "[1]

Twenty years ago Luther's comment would ill have functioned as the opening statement to a symposium. By its very tone it would have precluded further discussion and by its content have produced such discord that rational discourse could or would not then have taken place. In the years intervening, however, we have ourselves become so used to a heightened rhetoric of dissent that we adjust for hyperbole and coarse aphorism, or we have been so familiarized with the realm of unreason—abnormal, irrational and chemomystical—that we are inclined to heed, rather than ignore, Luther's attack on reason.

This collection of essays is not primarily addressed to a problem of cultural or historical periodicity, although we have chosen to stay more or less within the chronological limits of the years 1300 to 1675; nor does it concern itself with the much bruited "problem of the Renaissance," even though we can perhaps detect within our period certain basic shifts in the modes of apprehension and in the basic metaphors in which these

[1] The translation is my own; the Latin quotation may be found in *D. Martin Luthers Werke*, XL (Weimar, 1911), 362.

1

modes expressed themselves. We have, moreover, seen fit to
include certain thinkers traditionally assigned to the Reformation on the ground that they are products of a complex background not in itself bifurcated into artful distinctions such as
"Renaissance" and "Reformation." Our contributions, then, are
written as attempts to explore certain political, literary, social,
religious, medical, and artistic phenomena—irrational, nonra-
tional, and suprarational—which are observable within the confines of the chosen years.

It will not do, nevertheless, to let Luther's statement stand
unqualifiedly as indicative either of his own crucial position or
of that of the era itself. It is true that much has been written
about the influence of the late medieval nominalists upon Luther's view of the limits of reason. In many ways, it now seems,
Luther rejects rather than follows their notions, specifically
spurning the key dictum *facere quod in se est* as enunciated by
Ockham's follower, Robert Holcot (d. 1349).[2] Holcot had
argued in essence that man should do what is in him to do (*facere quod in se esse*); that is, if he would use his natural powers,
he could gain sufficient knowledge about the articles of faith
necessary for his salvation. By their very nature such supernatural articles of faith as the Incarnation or transubstantiation
go beyond reason rather than contradict it. One does not therefore deny reason if one holds that "reason cannot reach beyond
itself into the realm of supernatural faith which transcends the
realm of the senses."[3] Thus, *facere quod in se est* is to involve
the whole man, reason not excluded: "sine discursu rationis et
perceptione voluntaria veritatis, fides non habitur."[4]

To put the argument in a slightly different way, man can obtain sufficient knowledge of God from nature, the Book of
God's Creation, and sufficient enlightenment through reason

[2] See Heiko A. Oberman, " 'Facientibus quod in se est. Deus non
denegat gratiam,' Robert Holcot, O.P. and the Beginning of Luther's
Theology," *Harvard Theological Review*, LV (1962), 317–342. My
remarks on Holcot's position are essentially a summary of Oberman's
argument.

[3] *Ibid.*, p. 323.

[4] Cited in *ibid.*, p. 323 n. 30, from Sap. lect. 28.

or through the fullest use of his natural capacities combined, even though the ultimate and transcendental sovereignty of God is not only posited but also preserved beyond the reach of man's knowing. Admittedly, without grace, man would be helpless; without the use of his natural power, nonetheless, the offer of grace might be useless. Holcot's notion of the hobbled but still useful powers of reason came down to Luther's time in the teachings of Gabriel Biel (c. 1415–1495), rector of the University of Tübingen in 1485 and 1489: "... iste facit quod in se est qui illuminatus lumine rationis naturalis aut fidei vel utroque cognoscit peccati turpitudinem et proponens ab ipso resurgere desiderat divinum adiutorium quo possit a peccati mundari et deo suo creatori adherere."[5] After such preparations, God will extend grace. The point, again, is that God's love or His grace is within the reach of natural man without the preliminary assistance of grace.

With such a position Luther violently breaks. In 1517, in his *Disputatio contra scholasticam theologiam*, he explicitly rejects the nominalist position, early and late, of *facere quod in se est* as a liaison, whether between reason and revelation or between human will and grace.[6] Scholastic logic or nominalist special logic will not help; the proper disposition for the reception of grace is utterly beyond reason, for it is an effect of God's eternal election and predestination. Hence Luther's dictum: "It is wrong to say that without Aristotle, one does not become a theologian; to the contrary, these days, one does not become a theologian unless he does so without Aristotle." In fine, Aristotle is to modern theology as the dark is to the light: "Breviter, totus Aristotelis ad theologiam est tenebrae ad lucem."[7]

---

[5] "... he does 'what is in him' who, illuminated by the light of natural reason or of faith or by both, acknowledges the foulness of his sin and, determining to rise from himself, desires divine assistance by which he can be cleansed from sin and adhere to God his creator" (my translation). Cited from Biel, Lect. 59, by Heiko A. Oberman, *The Harvest of Medieval Theology, Gabriel Biel and Late Medieval Nominalism* (Cambridge, Mass., 1963), p. 133 n. 44.

[6] Oberman, in *HTR*, LV, 335.

[7] Cited in *ibid.*, p. 335 n. 79.

True, it is difficult to determine what the medieval view of irrationality is. It is almost as vexing to determine what the medieval view of reason is. Making allowance for ad hoc posturings and rhetoric of the occasion, we find that Luther is not against philosophy in its place (as he sees it) or against reason in its sphere (as he would define it) but against their presumption and blindness. Man may know *that* God is, but cannot know *what* God is. Reason generally operates within the realm of this world —it can build houses and cities, manage servants and estates, show how one can lead an honest, decent life—but not infallibly and certainly not omnisciently.[8] Valuable, even indispensable, though reason may be for *regnum mundi*, it is nothing but darkness in *regnum Christi*:

> The words of Christ could never be grasped or fathomed by reason, but only as the Holy Spirit reveals them to simple believers. The apostles themselves were of this sort: ignorant fishermen, for the most part, who learned to understand the Scriptures, not in the "schools," but through revelation. . . . Christ's conversation with Nicodemus shows clearly "what reason can do." Reason belongs to the flesh: it is so blind that it can neither see nor know the things of God.[9]

When reason overreaches its mundane limits it promotes incredulity on the one hand and attenuates belief on the other. It seems to be offended at Christian simplicity or, as Erasmus might have put it, "Christian folly." " 'Believe in Christ' and 'Love thy neighbor as thyself' are not enough: reason is offended at such simplicity and wants to do some great thing."[10] Thus it presumes to pry into the majesty of the hidden God, to seek to comprehend his will through the judgment of reason alone, without recourse to his word. The terrible danger of speculative thought is to seek God without a proper frame of reference:

> To seek God elsewhere than in Christ is to find a God whose

[8] For a clear exposition of Luther's position on reason, see B. A. Gerrish, *Grace and Reason: A Study in the Theology of Luther* (Oxford, 1962). I am here summarizing his statements on pp. 13–17.

[9] *Ibid.*, p. 18.

[10] *Ibid.*, p. 76; citation from D. *Martin Luthers Werke*, XL, 70. 40² 70.27.

glory is not His grace, a God who can only be approached in the terror of a burdened conscience. . . . For the anxious sinner, not knowing God as He really is in Christ, resorts frantically to good works of his own invention in the forlorn effort to *make* God propitious. What may begin with the arrogance of superior wisdom and virtue may end with the torments of afflicted conscience. "Shutting out the Mediator Christ" cannot but lead to a fall like proud Lucifer's.[11]

When reason encroaches on the bounds of faith, the results are attenuation of belief, skepticism, or unbelief. Faith is the omnipotent thing, for it grants God his glory, takes him at his word, believes him to be true to his promise. Reason does not comprehend that to hear God's voice and to believe are perfect worship. It would contend with belief as the two grappled in Abraham. What could be more foolish or irrational than for God to have told Abraham that he would have a son from the aged and barren womb of Sarah or to offer His own Son for sacrifice. Thus, all the pious must enter with Abraham the *tenebras fidei* and slay reason, saying "Tu ratio Stulta es."[12]

II

We shall admittedly not find that the term *ratio* is all that readily defined, and we cannot expect that the contrary of *ratio* will be *irratio*, for Luther makes obedience the desirable alternative to reason and Melancthon, like many an earlier commentator talking about ordinary reason in an earthly situation, supplies *malum* (evil) for the desired contrast. As Gerrish points out, there are in Luther's *Commentary on Galatians* (1535 ed.) approximately 230 references to *ratio* and, in some instances, the word is not "directly concerned with anything

[11] Gerrish, *Grace and Reason*, p. 78. Cf. Paul Sellin's analysis of Christopher Marlowe's *Dr. Faustus* (see pp. 177–187, below).

[12] For other remarks of Luther on this subject, compare the following: "For faith speaks as follows: 'I believe Thee, God, when Thou dost speak.' What does God say? Things that are impossible, untrue, foolish, weak, absurd, abominable, heretical, and diabolical—*if you consult reason*" (italics mine). See *Luther's Works*, ed. Jaroslav Pelikan and Walter A. Hansen, XXXVI (Saint Louis, 1963), 227.

that we could translate by 'reason.' "[13] At times it means "proof" or "argument" or "cause" or "motive" (when used in relation to conduct). As Gerrish further notes, it appears thrice in the idiom *exigere rationem* ("to demand an account") and several times in the idiom *rationem habere* ("to take account of," "to be concerned for").[14] Basically, however, *ratio* signifies a faculty of the human mind, the power that forms judgment or understanding based on materials referred to it by the imagination, intermediary between it and the senses, for, as Robert Burton remarks a century after Luther, "there is nothing in the understanding which was not first in the sense."[15]

It is tempting to digress here, quite in Burton's manner, on the anatomy of the soul, at times considered "the perfection or first act of an organical body," having the power of life and divided into three (or sometimes five) principal faculties: *vegetal, sensitive,* and *rational,* in their separate powers distinguishing vegetal plants, sensible beasts, and rational men, and in man alone combined. We shall not completely succumb, however, for we shall ignore the vegetal soul whose chief office is to turn nutriment into bodily substance by "natural head" and only briefly discuss the sensible soul, although we shall give ourselves a bit more time to explore the concept of the rational soul.

The sensible soul, located in the brain (the vegetal soul Burton locates in the liver), is divided into two parts, the "apprehending" power and the "moving" power. The first enables men to perceive the sensible things, whether present or absent, says Burton, "and to retain them as wax doth the print of a seal."[16] The second provides the body with locomotion outwardly and furnishes it circulation within, as moved by "spirits and pulse." The apprehensive power, the first, is further broken down into two parts: outward (the five senses) and inward

---

[13] *Grace and Reason*, p. 65.

[14] *Ibid.*, p. 65; see note on p. 66 for the conclusions to be reached about the use of *ratio* in Rörer's manuscript of Luther's commentary.

[15] *Anatomy of Melancholy*, ed. Holbrook Jackson (Everyman ed., 1964), I, 165.

[16] *Ibid.*, p. 157 (Pt. I, sec. 1, mem. ii, subsec. 6).

(the three "inwits": common sense, phantasy and/or imagination, and memory). Phantasy (or "fantasy," "fancy") is conceived of as an analytical and combinative power which more fully examines the materials that have been crudely synthesized from the senses by the "common sense." Located in the middle of the brain, it can review the "species" communicated to it by the common sense "by comparison of which [it] feigns infinite other unto [itself],"[17] or, if presented with some terrible object by the memory, the third "inner wit," phantasy, thus stirred, can produce prodigious things. "In men, it is subject, and governed by reason, or at least it should be; but in brutes it hath no superior, and is *ratio brutorum*, all the reason they have," Burton declaims.

It is of significance to the argument of our essays that "fancy" or "fantasy" as applied to a type of musical construction is first encountered as a meaningful term in the late fifteenth and early sixteenth centuries. It continued as a favorite form among English composers for the lute and keyboard until the early or mid-seventeenth century. The Elizabethan composer Morley set down in 1597 that

> The most principall and chieftest kind of musicke which is made without a dittie [i.e., without words] is the fantasie, that is, when a musician taketh a point [a fugal subject] *at his pleasure, and wresteth and turneth it as he list, making either much or little according as shall seeme best in his own conceit* [italics mine]. In this way more art be showne than in any other musicke, because the composer is tied to nothing but that he maye adde, diminishe, and alter at his pleasure.

We are here involved not only in a definition of something that is freely formed and impulsive, thus touching on the unconscious and hence "irrational," but also in a narrow and technical definition of the rational.

Although it may at first seem a mere quibble, *ratio* in the sense of established proportions, a discipline of relationships, turns out to have been the primary physical basis of musical intervals. As Gilbert Reaney points out in his essay (see pp. 217–219),

[17] *Ibid.*, p. 159 (Pt. I, sec. 1, mem. ii, subsec. 7).

to impose a different system of relationships, a duple rhythm, considered "lascivious" in the late fourteenth century, was to provoke a response that was unreasonable.

At any rate, "fancies" incorporated functional improvisational practices, a noticeable flexibility of style, and reflected a tradition of improvisation of a "creative fancy" that freely ranges or searches out tone or function (cf. the Italian *ricercare*, "that which is sought after," a musical synonym for *fantasia*). The appropriateness of the form to the inner ear, to the "Inward, Secret and Intellectual Faculties of the Soul," is attested to at the end of our period by Thomas Mace in *Musick's Monument* (1676). To him and, he adds, to many others, fancies were "like Divine Rapture, Powerfully Captivating all our unruly Faculties and Affections (for the time) and . . . making us capable of Heavenly and Divine Influences."[18] It is surely of interest that a form acknowledging the force of fancy, that skittery inward sense so frequently rebellious to reason, should have ultimately tamed unruly affections as it added its own entrancing "free" vigor to the restraints of a musical *ratio*.

To shift to a more somber and major note, the role of unruly imagination in the pathology of emotional or mental disease is fully noted in Burton's *Anatomy of Melancholy*. Although phantasy in the normal function of the sensitive soul is subject to reason, "in many men, through inward or outward distemperature, defect of organs, which are unapt or hindered, or otherwise contaminated,"[19] it is defective or damaged and produces deleterious or irrational imaginings, especially in dreams where unconscious fancy is freest of the reins of conscious reason. Hence sleepwalking is caused, says Burton, by vapors at night which move the phantasy, the phantasy in turn arousing the faculty of motion, that locomotive power of the sensitive soul which, "moving the animal spirits causeth the body to walk up and down as if they were awake."[20] Melancholy and sick men, whose phantasy is overactive and damaged, conceive ab-

[18] This quotation and that from Morley are taken from *Grove's Dictionary of Music and Musicians*, 5th ed. (1954), III, 21, 20.
[19] *Anatomy of Melancholy*, I, 253.
[20] *Ibid.*

surd apparitions or suppositions and hence claim they are kings or lords, cocks, bears, apes, or owls, or that they are transparent, senseless dead—all out of a "corrupt, false and violent imagination."[21]

We can further relate the question of fancy and the irrational more closely to these essays when we find "fancy" figuring in the witchcraft trials of the seventeenth century. Arthur Wilson, in the *Account of his Life by Himself*, testifies that at the Chelmsford trial of 1645 (the Chelmsford of Essex, England) he saw nothing in the evidence brought against eighteen women accused of, and later executed for, witchcraft which could persuade him that the defendants had other than "poore, mellenchollic, envious, mischievous, ill-disposed, ill-dieted, atrabilious constitutions, whose fancies working by grosse fumes and vapors, might make the imagination readie to take any impression."[22] Envious or irascible, they vented their grudges in such a way as to convince their listeners that they were the people they conceived themselves to be. By the strength of fancy they had thus brought things to pass. "And if there be an opinion in the people that such a bodie is a witch, their own feares (coming where they are) resulting from such dreadful apprehension, do make everie shaddow an apparition; and everie ratt or catt, an imp or spirit."[23]

We have seen nonetheless that normal human rational activity springs out of an awareness of the senses and their perceptions, distorted at times by fancy but filtering through to reason. The senses seize on "singularities," the understanding comprehends "universalities"; or, in other words, the understanding shapes changeless concepts from the changeable phenomena flowing to it from the senses. In its higher activity it is less and less dependent upon images passed to it through the unreliable lens of the fancy and recorded in the imagination or image-making receptacle of the mind. Its object, to repeat Bur-

---

[21] *Ibid.*, p. 255.

[22] Cited from *Peck's Desiderata Curiosa* (London, 1779), II, pt. xii, chap. xvi, p. 476, by K. M. Briggs, *Pale Hectate's Team* (London, 1962), p. 13.

[23] *Ibid.*

ton's phrase, is "God, *Ens*, all nature, and whatsoever is to be understood: which successively it apprehends"—or might apprehend if it were not confused in its powers and if it had an unimpaired will to move it.

Although the mystic purpose and method are variously defined, in the terms we have been following here they are the outreach of the soul to a union with God through the desire of love, or an affect of the sensitive soul (not the rational soul). Mysticism is a search for a way of unknowing, a deliberate attempt to turn away from the world of the senses, of space and time, through a denial of what is commonly valued in the sensory world, ordinarily the ultimate base of human knowledge. It is thus subrational in a strange way as well as suprarational. In either instance the mystic way lies clearly outside the fields of ordinary reason, even though it proceeds through its dark night of the senses to grace and to the vision of the Godhead.

The question of the mystical way and its relation to the rational soul, or the intellect, is not so far removed as it may at first seem from a discussion of the problems in exercising rational control over the fancy. To the power of fancy, Fracastorius would attribute all ecstasies, remarks Burton, or trances endured for whole days together "as that priest whom Celsus speaks of, that could separate himself from his senses when he list, and lie like a dead man, void of life and sense."[24] Be that as it may, it has not been our intention in these essays to stress the parapsychological aspects of mysticism. Kees Bolle, in "Structures of Renaissance Mysticism," has chosen rather to examine the rational forms that are deeply embedded in the methodology of the suprarational mystical experience—liturgical forms, for example.

We are thus brought to the third and "superior" soul of the tripartite soul—three in one—the rational soul. It includes the powers and performs the duties, Burton reminds us, of the vegetal and sensible souls and contains them within itself, inorganic and "uncorporeal." It, too, is subdivided into two parts "differ-

[24] *Anatomy of Melancholy*, I, 253–254.

ing in office only, not in essence": *understanding*, the rational power apprehending; and *will*, the rational power moving. The ultimate object of understanding is whatsoever is to be understood—nature, existence, God—all of which it "successively apprehends," moving from some sensible object through its corporeal substance and thence to the spiritual. It apprehends through the sensible soul, analyzes or synthesizes through the imagination, summons up memory, and depends upon reasoning in the process. The active or "agent" understanding, man's wit or acumen, is "invention," which fits things together in fresh insight or learns them anew. Once the understanding has abstracted an "intelligible species" from the phantasy or imagination or has judged whether what the imagination has recorded from the senses be "true or false," it commits such an evaluation to the passive understanding, a storage area for future collation.

Will, the other power of the rational soul, like *appetite* in the sensitive soul, "covets or avoids such things as we have been before judged and apprehended by the understanding." Whereas sensible appetite is governed by instinct, the will, or "rational appetite," is governed by reason. And here is the rub. Since the fall of Adam, in which all mankind sinned, the will is flawed; it is tempted to disregard or disobey the commands of reason. Like unaided reason it usually gets along in this world although with greater stumbling, but it is as unstable as fancy and almost as unreliable. In this state of disequilibrium or ataxia ("a confusion of our powers") man's weakened will can lead his vegetable or natural and especially his rational soul astray. In things of the will, man is "bad by nature, by ignorance worse," permitting bad habits in "art, discipline," and custom to dominate and tyrannize him.

III

With the more mundane and the terrible, diffuse "irrationalities" of the day we have still to grope. The larger manifestations can be understood in their own massiveness, as it were, the acute group anxieties and perhaps mass psychosis, as Lynn White suggests in "Death and the Devil" (esp. pp. 31–37). What to do with the less overt disturbances: "anxiety" as we more or less know it; psychic estrangement, that sense of estrangement from one's fellows about which one dare not comment for fear of being thought mentally abnormal; psychological isolation, or the individual's disinclination to participate in a group, his aversion to, or fear of, makng contact with another member of a group? And what about alienation, that deeper estrangement? Or anxieties over time and space?

To try to suggest that these states were known in one form or another, under one terminology or another, and were scanned from different points of view or discussed in changing metaphors, let us explore the notion that anxiety as an acknowledged psychological malaise was rather widely recognized in the Middle Ages and was labeled as an "irrational" state. Let us further examine its degrees of severity and its development from a cenobitic into a scholastic "sin" whence it passes into humoral psychology (note its association with "melancholy"), a mutation that will carry us to the end of our span of years down to 1675.

The noun *anxietas* can be found in the Latin writers of the Golden Age: in Cicero (*Tusc* 4.27), in Ovid ("anxietas animi," *Pont* 1.4.8.), in Seneca, and in Tacitus. Caelus Aurelianus (5th cent. A.D.) employs the noun several times in *Chronicarum passionum*, using it, for example, as a synonym for *maestitudo* (which ranges in meaning from "sadness" through "melancholy" to "dejection") in *Chron* 1, 5, 14.8. The verb *anxio, -are*, with the past participle *anxiatus*, can be twice found in the Vulgate translation of the Bible:

> *A finibus terrae ad te clamavi, dum*
> *anxiaretur cor meum.*   (Vulg., Ps. 60:3)
> "From the end of the earth will I cry unto thee,
> when my heart is overwhelmed." (AV, Ps. 61:2)
> *Et anxiatus est super me spiritus meus;*
> *in me turbatum est cor meum.*   (Vulg., Ps. 142:4)
> "Therefore is my spirit overwhelmed within me;
> my heart within me is desolate." (AV, Ps. 143:4)

The first repeated use of the word *anxietas* to define a psychological illness seems to occur in the writing of John Cassian (c. 366–c. 430), chiefly in the treatise *De octo principalibus vitiis* ("Concerning the Eight [*sic*] Principal Sins"). Whereas Cassian labels six of his items "sins," he employs the noun *morbus* (illness or disease of body or mind) for the other two, *tristitia* and *acedia* (defining the latter as *anxietas*: "quam nos taedium sive anxietatem cordis possumus nuncupare").[25] In two other places Cassian, discussing weariness or distress of the heart, defines it in Greek as ἀκήδεια, follows this with the Latin form *acedia*, and then defines the word in the phrase "anxietas sive taedium cordis."[26] The same wording may be found in a twelfth-century manuscript (Aed. Flor. Eccl. 37) in the Bibliotheca Laurenziana, and a remarkably similar phrase is in a late twelfth-century dictionary, compiled by Huguitius of Pisa: "*Acci* grece, cura Latine. Unde hec accidia, -e, id est *tristitia* ... *anxietas*, vel tedium." In fact the *Catholicon* of Johannes Balbus of Genoa (d. 1278), published in 1485 at Venice, also defines the more generic term *acedia* (there spelled *accidia*) as "taedium animi vel *anxietas*."

To be sure, following Saint Paul's distinction between "tristitia 'secundum Deum' " and "tristitia 'saeculi' " (2 Cor. 7:10), Cassian distinguishes between two types of *tristitia*. The one makes for humility, obedience, and patience; the other, for rancor, instability, and impatience.[27] Two centuries later, Isidore of Seville likewise divides *tristitia* into two kinds: the first, temperate and rational; the second, "perturbata et irrationalis."[28]

---

[25] Cited by P. Alphandéry, "De quelques documents médiévaux relatifs à des états psychasthéniques," *Journal de Psychologie*, XXVI (1929), 764.

[26] Cited by Siegfried Wenzel, *The Sin of Sloth: Acedia in Medieval Thought and Literature* (Chapel Hill, 1967), pp. 20, 211 n. 81.

[27] Cited from Cassian's *De inst.*, ix, 9–11, by Susan Snyder, "The Left Hand of God: Despair in Medieval and Renaissance Tradition," *Studies in the Renaissance*, XII (1965), 21 n. 6.

[28] Cited from Isidore's *Differentiarum*, II, ii, 40, by Snyder, "The Left Hand of God," p. 21 n. 8.

In a translation from John of Damascus's *De fide orthodoxa* made by Burgundio of Pisa in 1150, *acedia* is defined as *tristitia aggravans* ("depressing sorrow"); in the same Burgundio's translation from the fourth- or fifth-century work on the passions of man by Nemesius occurs the same phrase inversely defined, "anxietas vero est tristitia aggravans." For a last reference to the use of "anxiety" in the early and high Middle Ages, let us note that Caesarius of Heisterbach (c. 1170–c. 1240), in *De fructibus carnis et spiritus*, uses the noun *anxietudo* to indicate a mental state that springs "Ex frustrato rebus contrarius voto turbatae mentis."²⁹

The point to this series of illustrations is that *anxietas*, often coupled with *tristitia*, (1) denotes a stage of psychic depression of minor to intermediate severity; (2) constitutes an element of a larger, generic complex termed *acedia* or "sloth," a serious monastic "vice" which by the twelfth century had become incorporated (3) into the standard systems of moral or psychological analysis. In the progress through various associated conditions, as we shall see, *anxietas* could lead to severe depression, despair, and suicide. In making this chronological leap and symptomatic oversimplification, we are, to be sure, avoiding the complicated intervening processes by which Gregory the Great had reduced the eight chief vices to seven, using *tristitia* as the major term for the affliction that Cassian had termed *acedia*, and had linked the vices in a sort of linear progression.

What next concerns us is the manner in which the capital vices, specifically the capital vice of *acedia* (which did reestablish itself as a dominant term by reabsorbing *tristitia*, so to speak, and thus reestablishing the Cassianic analysis), were incorporated into the psychological systems of the time. Cassian had distributed a certain number of the vices among the three Platonic parts of the soul. Alcuin, in the eighth century, had established a schema in which *tristitia* and *acedia* (which he, at least, considered distinctive but connected afflictions) were related to irascible inclination of the appetitive power of the sensible

²⁹ Cited by Wenzel, *The Sin of Sloth*, p. 216, n. 17e.

soul, while gluttony and fornication, for example, were related to the concupiscent inclination of the appetite.[30]

Alexander of Hales (c. 1170 or 1185 to 1245) introduced and developed an even more elaborate scheme in which the vices result from a misuse of the three powers of the soul in accordance with the objects of the will. Thus *acedia* is listed as misdirection of the rational soul whose object is inward with respect to oneself (as distinguished from envy, a misdirection of the rational soul *with one's neighbor* as the "interior object," or pride, which stems from the same faculty, with an "interior object," but this time God).[31] By the second half of the thirteenth century, then, "the idea that the vices are corruptions of the *soul* gives way to the more restricted notion that they are misdirections of our *will*."[32]

At about the same time, what Wenzel terms the "cosmological" or "symbolic" model for the seven deadly sins developed as a third and psychosomatic explanation for these troublesome states.[33] Based on the notion that man is, after all, a composite of the four elements that make up the flesh, together with the three powers of the soul, it proposed that the three cardinal sins of pride, envy, and wrath arose from deformities of the tripartite soul, while the remaining four vices were said to spring from the properties of the individual elements. Thus *acedia* was associated with the element of earth: "*Acedia*, because Greek *melan* is *terra* or *nigrum* in Latin [*sic*], whence the *malencoli*, who are very much troubled by *acedia*." Then, remarks Wenzel, follows a statement that *acedia* actually belongs to both body and soul.[34] Thus the essential connection has been made between the scholastic intellectual dissection of sin and the humoral psychological analysis which allows for the interplay of body and soul in

[30] I base my summary of the development of systematic scholastic analysis of the sins on Siegfried Wenzel, "The Seven Deadly Sins: Some Problems of Research," *Speculum*, XLIII (1968), 4–6, 8.

[31] *Ibid.*, p. 6.

[32] *Ibid.*

[33] See *ibid.*, p. 8.

[34] *Ibid.*

the symptomology of psychic and physical malaise or disease. William Peraldus, Grosseteste, and Servasanctus, to whom the *liber de exemplis naturalibus* is attributed, adopted this rationale; William of Auvergne acknowledges the existence of this "combined explanation" when he mentions the fact that *acedia* is sometimes increased and strengthened by the melancholy humor. And priests, in accordance with the new directions in the practice of confession and penance authorized by the Fourth Lateran Council (1215–16), were instructed to consider the whole man and to recognize that some individuals were predisposed to certain vices by their physical makeup: "complexio etiam consideranda est, secundam quod signis exterioribus perpendi potest."[35]

By the fourteenth century *acedia* had become a term of considerable complexity and wide range of meaning, as it became popularized and itemized in the handbooks of the day. However attenuated or aggrandized its meaning, it never shed its sense of disquietude and instability. Alvarus Pelagius, a contemporary of Petrarch, whose own character Franciscus is marked in the *Secretum* by *acedia* in the sense of grief and depression produced by his reflection on the instability and misery of the human condition, divides *acedia* into sixteen fractions.[36] He begins with *tepiditas* and *mollities* (irresolution) and works through *dilatio, tarditas, negligentia,* and *imperseverantia* to the more severe aspects of the larger sin, those of *tristitia, tedium vitae,* and *desperatio.*

A contemporary account of the causes underlying the tortuous death in 1482 of Hugo van der Goes, the Flemish painter, may in itself most convincingly demonstrate how the syndrome of psychological disease now represented by *acedia* had attached itself to the humoral affliction of melancholy. As chron-

[35] Cited from Alain de Lille, *Liber poenitentialis,* by Wenzel, *The Sin of Sloth.* p. 194. Although Alain issued his caveat in 1200 or so, prior to the Fourth Lateran Council, his injunction accurately anticipates later handbook precepts for priests.

[36] See Siegfried Wenzel, "Petrarch's *Accidia,*" *Studies in the Renaissance,* VIII (1961), 41 n. 20, for Pelagius's complete list as published in the 1517 edition of his *De planctu eccelesiae,* written 1335–1340.

icled by the monk Gaspar Ofhuys, the painter, himself a monastic, was stricken with a mental illness while returning from a journey to Cologne. He babbled that he was condemned to eternal damnation. He would have injured himself bodily and cruelly (*corporaliter et letaliter*) had he not been forcibly restrained by those present.[37] On the analogy that Hugo was stricken with the same sort of affliction that had beset King Saul, the prior at Brussels, where Hugo had been hastily taken, had music played as part of a therapy and added other recreations of a sort that would subdue mental distress (. . . *quibus intendebat mentales fantasias repellere*). Despite these diversions, Brother Hugo did not improve. Persisting in his belief that he was a child of damnation (*filius perditionis*), within a short time he died.[38]

Gaspar, not entirely without malice, proceeds carefully to speculate on the causes for Hugo's death as advanced by the brethren. Frenzy? Demonic possession? Only God could tell. This fact notwithstanding, Brother Ofhuys posits two etiologies: one natural, the other divine. The first might be the distressed state brought on by ailments linked to the melancholy caused by alcoholism, as we might say, induced by the absorption of strong inflammatory wines offered at banquets given him even in the monastery by his distinguished visitors; or from perturbations of the mind as through "sollicitudine, tristicia, nimio studio et timore." And van der Goes, our chronicler goes on, had, moreover, been preoccupied to excess with the question of how he was to finish the paintings at hand or commissioned, which he could scarcely have finished in nine years!

Ofhuy's deepest conviction, however, is that Frater Hugo was afflicted by God as a means, first, of enabling the painter properly to meet his end by eschewing pride and, second, as a way of edifying the monks who thus learned that they too must restrain their passions lest their reason be overwhelmed. Finally, helpfully enabling us to complete the linkage of scholastic

[37] I draw upon the version printed in Joseph Destree's *Hugo van der Goes* (Brussels and Paris, 1914), pp. 214–218.

[38] *Ibid.*, p. 216.

penitential psychology with humoral psychology and with faculty psychology, Ofhuys reflects that when fantasy and imagination are too active and too troubled in revery, the delicate vein (*vena parva valde et gracilis*) that connects the imagination with the mind is tormented and breaks. Frenzy and dementia result. Thus in 1495, a dozen years or so after van der Goes's death, Hieronymus Münzer could, in consequence, set down his belief that the painter, fearing that he could not equal the achievement of his contemporary, van Eyck, became *melancolicus et insipiens*.[39]

IV

We must now attempt to penetrate the mystery of "alienation," another ecclesiastical term that has a dangerously modern ring but also has enough medieval particularities and peculiarities of usage to demand close inspection. As our colleague Gerhart Ladner has very nicely put it (and as our monkish chronicler Gaspar Ofhuys had already noticed),

> medieval thought had derived from its early Christian sources as in the instance of *tristitia* not one, but two ideas of alienation, and was to make them lastingly its own: estrangement from God and estrangement from the world. While alienation in the sense of a more or less radical detachment from the temporal terrestrial world was considered a Christian's duty and privilege, the necessity for it would not have arisen, had not in the Christian view a great calamity overtaken the universe at its very beginning and alienated it from the perfect order in which God had created it.... [T]heretofore St. Paul could say that, as long as he is in this body, man is an exile from the Lord.[40]

To be sure, as with Luther's attack on reason, or as in Cassian's identification of two types of *tristitia*, that larger synonym of

[39] For a full discussion of the sixteenth- and seventeenth-century syndrome of folly, melancholy, and madness, see the final essay in this volume.

[40] Gerhart B. Ladner, "*Homo Viator*: Medieval Ideas on Alienation and Order," *Speculum*, XLII (1967), 237–239.

anxietas and that somewhat more significant component of *acedia*, we must not rush to the conclusion that medieval alienation is to be identified with Gnostic or Manichean conclusions about the "all-pervasive estrangement and disorder of this world, conclusions which were over-spiritual and antinomian, exaggerated and desperate."[41] *Homo viator* in his peregrination through this life was journeying, crippled as he was, "within a universal order which was in itself good and which was made up of many more particular orders,"[42] if he could but clear his vision to perceive them.

Ecclesiastical or scholastic definitions, too, as we have seen with *anxietas-tristitia-acedia*, have their falls from grace. Again, as Professor Ladner has most perspicaciously noted,[43] in the high Middle Ages feudalism was driven ideationally to apply the notion of *peregrinatio*, wandering and search. Without that application, the chivalric ideals of the time, setting aside the question of their realization, would not have developed. For one things chivalry fused with the movements and motives of medieval pilgrimage in its "great pilgrimage in arms timed at recapturing Jerusalem, the ideal center of the Christian world."[44] For another, once the mass crusading spirit had died down, the individual notion of the knight-errant arose, the image of the Christian warrior "who must seek out the hostile forces of the world and find his own self in a ceaseless course of *aventure*."[45]

The moral significance of the knight-errant, isolated and alone, traveling through waste spaces and hostile environments, confronting dragons, wolves, trolls, bulls, bears, and giants, constitutes one of the important themes of the late Middle English romance *Sir Gawain and the Green Knight*, as Donald Howard argues in his essay, "Renaissance World-Alienation" (see esp. pp. 63–69). As Professor Howard claims (pp. 48–49), a sense of world-alienation had developed, practically speaking, in the late Middle Ages and became increasingly evident under

---

41 *Ibid.*, p. 239.
42 *Ibid.*
43 *Ibid.*, pp. 240–249.
44 *Ibid.*, p. 246.
45 *Ibid.*

certain guises in the Renaissance—the guise *de contemptu mundi,* for example—with the constant reminders of the world's mutability, misery, and vanity.

One could find other evidences of alienation in the exiles suffered by Tristram and Lancelot in Thomas Malory's encyclopedic recension, his *Le Morte Darthur* (finished c. 1470, copied down in the Winchester MS c. 1475, and printed 1485). Terribly agitated by love accusations, both men are driven into sheer, naked, stark madness. Tristram, significantly enough, is beaten with rods and clipped with shears as if he were a natural fool. When news of his madness reaches Mark and his court, they unanimously banish Tristram from the country for ten years. In similar fashion Lancelot, breaking down under Guinevere's harsh suspicions and accusations, leaps out of a bay window into a garden, whence, scratched on face and body by thorns, "he ranne furth he knew nat whothir, and was as wylde [var. "woode" or "mad"] as ever was man." For two years he wanders in care and pain and woe, "for," as Malory's litotes reads, "colde, hunger and thyrste he had plente!" Late in his wanderings Lancelot is given clothes at the gate to Corben Castle and straw and litter under the gate to lie in. Every day "they wolde throw hym mete and set hym drynke, but there was but feauw [few] that wolde brynge hym mete to hys hondys." And thus, with native details quite different from his French sources, Malory reduces Lancelot to the status of fool and outcast.

Related in kind to alienation but lesser in degree was the distance that a courtier imposed between himself and the vast body of men in his dedication to his lord, the self-enclosed center of a self-sustaining system. "The courtier has no being outside the service of the prince," argues Lauro Martines (see "The Gentleman in Renaissance Italy," p. 61, below), and was thus, so to speak, "condemned to live in exile . . . , the isolation of the political establishment itself, severed from the revitalizing forces of the larger human community" (p. 61, below). Charles E.

---

[46] Charles E. Trinkaus, Jr., *Adversity's Nobleman: The Italian Humanist on Happiness* (New York, 1940), p. 127.

Trinkaus[46] quotes Giovanni Corsi's account of Bernardo Oricel-lari's voluntary exile from Florence, in which that worthy, of his own will, left rather than remain in a city from which the "disciplines of all good arts as well as the best customs of the elders went into exile together with the Medici." Like many other Italian humanists, Baldassare Castiglione, author of *The Courtier*, shows signs of uncertainty and confusion over the role of fortune in Italian history, the political ineptitude of Italian rulers, and the fecklessness of Italian military forces. He seems aware of the mutability and worthlessness of this world, aware also of the laud and praise due man in his potentialities, and yet, trapped by his position, he seeks a third way out, that of *sprez-zatura* ("grace, ease"), and with that often either masks or avoids the primary questions.

In an important article written some fifteen years ago, Father Walter J. Ong drew attention to a series of Renaissance devel-opments within the arts of communication which related "shifts in symbolization and conceptualization" found in archi-tecture, painting, and the "new" science to "another series of shifts in the ways of representing the field of knowledge and intellectual activity itself."[47] For example, he noted the shift from knowledge conceived of in terms of discourse and hearing and persons to knowledge conceived of in terms of observation and sights and objects, a shift from argument in the hearing of a master to the drawing of conclusions to be disseminated by means of that Renaissance invention, the printing press. The differences of outlook were the differences between the older "audile culture" and the newer "visile universe." Within this outlook, whole concavities develop, so to speak: the shallow abstract space of Giotto, the symbolic space of early Flemish masters, the so-called rational space of fifteenth-century Ren-aissance art, the ideal space of Raphael and the High Renais-sance, and the compartmentation of the printed book, the inclusive world of the printed page. Whatever the causes for

[47] Walter J. Ong, "Systems, Space and Intellect in Renaissance Sym-222–239.
bolism," *Bibliothèque d'Humanisme et Renaissance*, XVIII (1956),

these two reorientations of outlook, Father Ong argued, the important thing was that the two worked in concert, that "man's view of the universe and his view of his own mind are in great part correlatives."[48]

A similar point can be made with respect to Renaissance Hermetism as a fairly well defined subject and with other Renaissance modes of perception, particularly as they relate to the primordial anxieties caused by the passing of time and the fear of death in its various forms. On the first topic, as John Burke indicates (see "Hermetism as a Renaissance World View," esp. pp. 97 n. 3; 98 nn. 5–9, below), scholarly investigations of the past two decades have convincingly shown that "in scope, substance, and intent, Renaissance Hermetism differs sharply" from the Hermetism of the late medieval period. Its lore had a deeper base among the educated, its views extended themselves more widely in religious and social attitudes, and its astrological, magical, and Cabalistic practices had some bearing (not always beyond the factitious) upon the development of modern science. In the interest of Pico, Reuchlin, Agrippa, and John Dee in number and number symbolism as a way of manipulating the angel names of the Cabala, we can perhaps find evidence that "Renaissance magic was turning towards number as a possible key to operation,"[49] ironically a kind of early development of applied mathematics to result in a changed approach to man's problem of mastery and rational control of the physical universe.

In analogous ways, in the literary and plastic arts, as Marc Bensimon's essay ("Modes of Perception of Reality in the Renaissance") illustrates, we are reminded that when neurotic man consciously searches for novelty, underlying the search "at the level of the instincts, [is] a compulsion to repeat."[50] The compulsion to repeat involves man in a theory of time and, one

[48] *Ibid.*, p. 224.

[49] Frances A. Yates, *Giordano Bruno and the Hermetic Tradition* (Chicago, 1964), p. 146.

[50] Norman O. Brown, *Life against Death: The Psychoanalytical Meaning of History* (Vintage Books, 1959), p. 92.

might add, space, for "time does not pertain to things in themselves out there but is a form of perception of the human mind."[51]

We may call to mind the drawings of Opicinus de Canistris, a Pavian monk languishing in papal Avignon in the second quarter of the fourteenth century. Like Nicholas of Cusa (Cusanus), in his sketches Opicinus relies on certain traditional astrological and ecclesiastical images such as circles, squares, and rectangles. More specifically, he overtly and simply manifests psychic strain in his sketches of a geographical world of sin in which geography is demonized and that sinful world is acknowledged as lodging in his sinful heart when he places a demonic map in a medallion over his own breast. Or, to end our discussion of the transmutation by anxiety of the painter's vocabulary, we call to mind Bosch's *Seven Deadly Sins*, a circular composition that represents the eye of God mirroring the seven mansions of sin. The wheel-like design of the picture leads the viewer's eye in an endless circle around the mansions, conveying a sense of futility, of destiny sensed as a wheel of fortune. As the inscription attached to God's eye really indicates—*Cave, cave, Deus Videt*—what God's eye sees as it looks at man is what man should see in a mirror: himself in all his distorted shapes and activities. It is in its own way a darker vision than any sun could ever fully dissipate.

[51] *Ibid.*, p. 94.

I

DEATH AND THE DEVIL

Lynn White, jr.

BECAUSE HISTORY is made of persons, and each of us
lives large parts of his life without much rational analysis,
every epoch of the past shows evidence of the irrational. As
some people, however, are more irrational than others, so also
some ages are more psychotic than others. This simply means
that the proportion of badly upset persons varies notably from
time to time and from place to place. The nature of, and the reasons for, such fluctuations have not yet been closely examined.[1]
Eventually, we must produce a history of hysteria as one of the
essential elements in the general history of culture.

It is a commonplace that insanity and genius are often closely
allied. The vast creativity of the Renaissance and its unrivaled
talent for innovation, its instinct for beauty and for intellectual
adventure, are glorious blossoms rooted in a slime stinking far
worse than anything that can be identified in the earlier centuries of the Middle Ages or in more modern times. No one will
ever be able to devalue Donatello or Dürer, Boccaccio or
Shakespeare, Valla or Copernicus, Luther or Saint Theresa.
Our understanding of them and of their insights, however, may
be advanced if we recognize the tragedy and ambivalence of
the world that was their context.

It is my quadruple thesis, first, that the period, roughly 1300

[1] See especially W. L. Langer, "The Next Assignment," *American
Historical Review*, LXIII (1958), 283–304.

to 1650, generally called the age of the Renaissance, was the most psychically disturbed era in European history;[2] second, that this irrationality was symptomatic of abnormal anxiety; third, that the anxiety arose from an ever increasing velocity of cultural change compounded by a series of fearful disasters; and fourth, that at last, in the seventeenth century, this spiritual trauma was healed by the emergence, in the minds of ordinary people, of an absolutely novel and relaxed attitude toward change.

This is not a happy sequence to expound. In many ways it is profoundly shocking. But the historian cannot be a sundial in a rose garden inscribed "I count only sunny hours." He must probe the dark as well.

All men know that they will die, and generally they accept death as integral to life. But Europeans of 1300 to 1650 had an obsession with death, because death in hideous forms descended about them so often.

In earlier centuries famine, pestilence, and war were occasional and generally local catastrophes, but the steady rise of population in all parts of Europe from at least the tenth century onward shows that life was tolerable. Huge new tracts of land were brought under cultivation, new villages were started everywhere, and cities expanded in size and activity. In the very early fourteenth century both this expansion and the accompanying mood of expansiveness changed suddenly.[3] An alteration of weather pushed pack ice so much farther south that the shipping route from Norway to Greenland had to be shifted. The new climate brought much greater uncertainty of harvests, with resulting hunger. In the years 1315 to 1317 there were universal crop failures in northern Europe, from Ireland to Hungary. In 1316 the records of Ypres in Flanders show that

---

[2] Its only rival is the late Hellenistic and Roman period, with its arenas, apocalyptic and messianic movements, and rapid spread of the concept of an afterlife of either bliss or eternal torture.

[3] Cf. Élizabeth Carpentier, "Autour de la peste noire: Famines et épidemies dans l'histoire du XIVᵉ siècle," *Annales: Économies, Sociétés, Civilisations*, XVII (1962), 1062–1092.

between May and October some 2,800 bodies, or roughly a tenth of the population, were buried at public expense. Especially in Germany, villages were abandoned wholesale, and many of them were never again resettled. With the labor force riddled, the revenues of the nobility collapsed and the tradition of the robber baron who lived by brigandage was reestablished and continued to trouble many regions as late as the seventeenth century. The famines of the 1330s and the 1340s were particularly severe in the south: in 1347 some 4,000 people are estimated to have starved in Florence alone.

Earlier generations had known war but, in general, hostilities had been fairly brief, save for the Crusades, which conveniently transported overseas many of the more belligerent. The fourteenth century opened a new and tragic era in European military history. The transition from feudal armies to mercenary troops was completed, but the supporting bureaucracies and tax-collecting agencies were not yet strong enough to assure that soldiers would be paid regularly. There was little notion of a standing army: troops were hired for a campaign and fired when it ended. During times of war these professional soldiers slew, burned, and looted by the nature of their task; but in peace, or when they were unpaid, necessity drove them to redoubled atrocities, especially on the population of the countryside and smaller towns, including systematic torture to discover hidden valuables.

This dreadful epoch opened in 1338 with the outbreak of the Hundred Years' War between England and France. The battlefield was France, which had been the heart of medieval Europe, and France was devastated and depopulated hideously. One reason that the cultural primacy in Europe passed briefly to Italy in the fifteenth century was the wrecking of the chief center of northern vitality. Similarly, large parts of Germany and eastern Europe were scorched by the Hussite wars that blazed for decades, anticipating in their brutality the religious wars that broke over Europe in the sixteenth century.

The wars of religion were not hostilities between regions; they were cruel civil wars in which neighbors murdered one another. Except in England, Catholics generally backed centralized government, whereas Protestants were fighting for local autonomy. In France, for example, a high proportion of the nobility and the self-governing burgher cities, fearing the growth of royal power, became Calvinist, as did the Netherlanders who resented Spanish Habsburg domination. In the long run, centralized government and Catholicism won most of the battles and lighted most of the fires of execution. Protestantism was not simply contained; it was exterminated over wide areas which it had once controlled. The culmination of the ghastly process was the Thirty Years' War, from 1618 to 1648, which reduced the population of Germany by at least one third. Only toward the middle of the seventeenth century did governments conclude that mercenaries must be replaced by highly disciplined standing armies, salaried in peacetime as well as during war. Not even in our own century have the terrors of war in Europe matched those of the Renaissance.

Famine and war: these were enough to transfix men of that time with the horror of death. But there was also plague.

Epidemics had come before—there were major visitations under Marcus Aurelius and again under Justinian. But the earlier Middle Ages had known nothing comparable to the Black Death, the bubonic infection that swept out of Asia late in 1347. Striking first at Caffa, a Genoese trading post in the Crimea, and carried thence by the rats infesting ships, it went swiftly to Constantinople, to Messina, along the coasts of the Mediterranean to Gibraltar, then up the Atlantic seaboard to the Baltic, arriving in northern Russia in 1350, leaving carnage in its wake. The Byzantine emperor, John VI Cantacuzenos, whose youngest son perished, has left us a remarkable clinical account of the disease, particularly noting that some few people who were stricken seemed to have a certain immunity: if they survived, they "were no longer possessed by the same evil, but were safe. The disease did not attack twice in order to kill them."[4] To modern eyes, this heritable immunity was the hope of the future, but to contemporaries it only emphasized the unpredict-

[4] C. A. Bartsocas, "Two Fourteenth-Century Greek Descriptions of the Black Death," *Journal of the History of Medicine*, XXI (1966), 396.

ability of grim fate. Complete animal panic swept Europe. Many fled the cities for the countryside, thus speeding the general infection. Even allowing for the absence of such refugees, a cautious study estimates the dead at Siena, for example, as at least 50 percent of the population and probably more.[5] Perhaps at Siena the death rate was unusually high. Mortality varied from place to place. But modern historians, burrowing into the masses of extant public records, seem increasingly agreed that with its first stroke the Black Death wiped out not less than a third of Europe's entire population.

This first sweep, however, did not end the disaster. Every few years an epidemic returned. By 1400 Europe's population was probably half what it had been in 1347, and less in some regions. Replacement was slow. Even as late as 1665 a city like London could be immobilized by such a disaster. But shortly thereafter, perhaps because a new species of brown rats ousted the black kind harboring bubonic-carrying fleas, the plague vanished. Abnormally high death by disease is a distinctive element in the age of the Renaissance.

What did it do to men's thinking? The social fabric was shaken because new personnel assumed functions for which they had had no adequate preparation. One must picture this difficulty in specific situations. In 1348, at the Collegiate Church of São Pedro de Almedina in Coimbra, the prior, the cantor, and all the canons died within a month. Their hastily inducted successors discovered themselves in charge of an institution about which they knew almost nothing, and they could find no regulations. So they held a meeting to decide how the corporation should be run and how the income for the prebends should be divided.[6] All over Europe, survivors were inheriting property and offices of the dead. It is indicative that in São Pedro the number of canons was apparently not reduced even though the labor force cultivating the fields that endowed the church had surely been cut severely. For some four centuries Europe had

[5] William M. Bowsky, "The Impact of the Black Death upon Sienese Government and Society," *Speculum*, XXXIX (1964), 18.

[6] Virginia Rau, "Un document portugais sur la Peste Noire de 1348," *Annales du Midi*, LXXVIII (1966), 331–334.

gradually been expanding its apparatus of church and secular government as population grew. But when, in the fourteenth century, population plummeted and economic production shrank, this apparatus was not notably contracted, at least at first. The result was that the established overhead costs of society had to be carried by a dwindling number of workers. This produced a vast discontent that often broke out in violence. Naturally lower productivity soon made itself felt: many an endowed post, whether in Church or state, could no longer support its occupant. The solution was plurality of benefices, that is, combining several inadequately supported functions (often in different places) to provide income for one man. But pluralism led to inefficiency and corruption. In all parts of Europe and at all levels of organization, the centuries of the Renaissance were marked by a decline in probity and an increase in disenchantment with the established order, traceable chiefly to a clumsy and reluctant adjustment of medieval superstructures to the suddenly reduced base of population.

Famine, war, and plague—of this last I have indicated only a part. In 1492, when the ravages of the older scourges seemed at long last to have been diminishing, Columbus's sailors brought back syphilis from the Caribbean. Once more, Europe had no accumulated genetic immunity and no cure. Since death from syphilis is less immediate than death from the plague, the effects of syphilis are harder to trace historically. But the sixteenth century was smoldering with it. Indeed, the effort to monasticize secular society which we call "Puritanism" was doubtless in part a social prophylactic against the dread new disease.

In his classic monograph on the subject, Alberto Tenenti[7] insists on "the new centrality of death" in the thought and emotions of the Renaissance. During its first thousand years, Christian art had felt no necessity to develop a symbol of death or to dwell on the fate of the physical body between the moment of death and the sounding of the Last Trumpet when mankind puts on incorruption. Then, in about 1225 (and, as we shall see, such a date in the thirteenth century is important for our think-

[7] *Il senso della morte e l'amore della vita nel Rinascimento* (Turin, 1957).

ing), the motif of three living men encountering three corpses appears in Italy. This theme is gradually elaborated until the three corpses illustrate three stages of decomposition. But only after the Black Death of 1347–1350 do we find artists depicting the destroying figure of Death descending like a hurricane on mortals to reap a grim harvest with his scythe. The theme develops further in northern Europe in the Dance of Death, which is first found at Paris in 1424, showing corpses leading emperor and pope, peasant and craftsman, burgher and scholar, to the grave. The evolution culminates in the middle of the sixteenth century in Pieter Brueghel's *Triumph of Death* in the Prado: it is a pageant of the annihilation of the human race, unrelieved by any hope for this world or another.

As one gropes through this unsavory phase of European art and the literature that accompanies it, the conclusion emerges that it is not simply a majestic symbolism of despair; it is a symptom of pervasive psychic derangement, one of the psychiatric perversions: necrophilia, the enjoyment of corpses. The Campo Santo at Pisa, with its fresco of the Three Living and the Three Dead, became a favorite place for promenades. In the fifteenth century, when François Villon wrote his ghastly *Ballad of the Hanged*, Parisians liked to go on picnics to the Montfaucon gibbet outside the city where they could revel under the shredding remains of the dangling dead. The sepulchral art of the time shows signs of pleasure in corruption. In earlier generations tombs had been covered with recumbent images of knights and ladies, abbots, bishops, and kings peacefully at rest awaiting the Day of Judgment in confidence that God is merciful. In the later fourteenth and fifteenth centuries, however, especially in northern Europe, tombs were not infrequently ornamented with nauseously realistic sculptures of disintegrating corpses, the hair and flesh dripping from the bones, with worms and crabs crawling from the eye sockets and exposed ribs. The age of the Renaissance was an epoch not only of human tragedy but also of widespread mental derangement accentuated by tragedy. Yet we must remember that the first, fairly mild, evidences of socially manifested necrophilia emerge about 1225, long before the catastrophes of the fourteenth century. Overt disasters therefore do not explain the psychotic phenomenon, except perhaps in degree.

The same may be said for many of the other usual Freudian categories of perversion. Masochism became epidemic among the Flagellants after the Black Death, but there was a notable flagellant movement in the 1260s. As for sadism: systematic torture of an accused person to extract confessions was not authorized until a decree by Pope Innocent IV in 1252. Thereafter it became habitual, and there was a gruesome elaboration of instruments of torture. That this practice was rooted in a social psychosis is indicated by the fact that, as Gustave Cohen has pointed out,[8] the popular theater of the fourteenth, fifteenth, and sixteenth centuries was filled with tortures and executions that lasted even longer on the stage than in actuality. But the actuality was relished likewise: Jan Huizinga[9] has noted that the city of Mons purchased a criminal from a better-stocked community so that the inhabitants might have the pleasure of seeing him quartered; "at which," says the contemporary account, "the people rejoiced." So profound and widespread was this perversity that protest against cruelty was regarded as immoral. When, toward the middle of the fourteenth century, a pregnant woman was convicted of stealing and selling two consecrated Hosts to Jews for obscene rites and was condemned to be burned alive, and before her execution the child was cut from her body for baptism, those who expressed sympathy for her were excoriated by one of the leading women mystics of the day, Margareta Ebner.[10]

It may be worth noting that, as with so much of the piety of this age, Margarita Ebner's religion found expression in incredibly sexual forms: in mystical experience, Christ was her bridegroom and not in any allegorical way; the infant Jesus was her own child, to whom she gave suck. We quail before the irrationality of that age. Gilles de Retz, one of the greatest nobles of France, a friend and battlefield companion of Joan of Arc,

[8] *Histoire de la mise en scène dans le théâtre français du moyen âge* (Brussels, 1906), pp. 148, 267, 275.

[9] *The Waning of the Middle Ages* (London, 1927), p. 15.

[10] Oskar Pfister, *Religiosität und Hysterie* (Leipzig, 1928), p. 44.

abducted, violated, tortured to death, and then dismembered scores of small boys; yet in entire sincerity, it would seem, he endowed a church in honor of the Holy Innocents.

With a sufficiently strong stomach one could go on endlessly exploring the derangements that affected so many individuals during the Renaissance that they achieved cultural acceptance. Costume offers its symbols. The most overt expression of schizophrenia is found in the fashion for clothing split in design down the middle, with each side of a different color and often of a different cut. This oddity first appears in the Sachsenspiegel manuscript at Heidelberg, produced a generation before the Black Death. And as for exhibitionism, no other civilized age anywhere in the world has made the male genitals so conspicuous as the sixteenth century with the codpiece.

A related phenomenon in the Renaissance was demonic possession. Every society has cases of possession. In most groups the possessing entity is a god or a totemic animal. In modern Western society entranced persons are called mediums and speak with the alleged voices of the dead. From the earliest times to about the eighteenth century, however, in our culture possessing entities were demons, and there were sporadic occurrences in every generation down to 1491 when suddenly demonic possession became occasionally epidemic, especially in nunneries. In one German cloister, for example, at three o'clock each afternoon the abbess and all the sisters simultaneously became possessed and started mewing and purring like cats. That some of the clergy recognized the subjective nature of this affliction is indicated by the actions of Cardinal Mazarin in 1638: he ended a serious epidemic of possession in southern France by ordering that no further publicity be given to it.[11]

---

[11] T. K. Oesterreich, *Possession, Demoniacal and Other* (New York, 1930), p. 189. That monastic medicine had at least a subordinate tradition of rational understanding of possession is indicated by a remarkably analytical contemporary description of the mental illness that seized the great Flemish painter Hugo van der Goes (c. 1433–1482) in his last years (see Karl Birnbaum, "Zur Psychiatrie des späten Mittelalters," *Deutsche medizinische Wochenschrift*, LIII [1927], 1058–1059 and also the Preface to this collection of essays, pp. xix-xxi).

Whatever its nature or cultural conditioning, the fact that demon possession for the first time seized groups, rather than simply individuals, in the late 1400s at the moment we generally regard as the peak of Renaissance creativity may throw some light on the sources of that creativity.

Equally significant of social psychosis were the group seizures of agonized and prolonged dancing called tarantism in Mediterranean lands and Saint Vitus's dance in the north. It is notable that its first appearance was in the Rhineland in 1347, a year before the Black Death reached that region, and that the mania quickly spread to Brabant and Lorraine. All ages and stations were affected; the *Chronicle of Metz* records that the "priest saying Mass, the judge on the bench, the plowman at the plow danced and leaped, but in grief."[12] Outbreaks of this choreutic plague continued deep into the sixteenth century. Yet, since it began before the Black Death in a region unaffected as yet by chronic warfare, one cannot blame this nervous disease entirely upon overt catastrophe. The causal trauma must have been covert.

The most spectacular and tragic Renaissance symptom of social psychosis was the witch mania. But once again the manifestation antedated the famines, pestilences, and wars of the fourteenth century. While the death penalty was occasionally visited upon sorcerers and witches in pagan antiquity and even in the early Germanic kingdoms, the Church taught that witchcraft was a superstitious delusion. Charlemagne, combating Teutonic paganism, made the execution of a witch a capital crime. About 906, in the *Canon Episcopi*,[13] belief in the possibility of witchcraft was declared heretical, and this view was incorporated into canon law about 1150 in Gratian's *Decretum*. While there are literary and general legislative references to witches, I find few indications of flesh-and-blood witches in

[12] Ernesto de Martino, *La terra del rimorso* (Milan, 1961), p. 238; see also Alfred Martin, "Geschichte der Tanzkrankheit in Deutschland," *Zeitschrift des Vereins für Volkskunde*, XXIV (1912), 113–134.

[13] Joseph Hansen, *Quellen und Untersuchungen zur Geschichte des Hexenwahns und des Hexenverfolgung im Mittelalter* (Hildesheim, 1963), pp. 38–39.

Europe during some seven hundred years between the late sixth[14] and the late thirteenth centuries. Even in 1258 Pope Alexander IV did not consider witchcraft a serious problem; to some inquisitors in the Rhineland who asked what they should do about charges of sorcery, he replied that their task was to extirpate heresy, and that they should not be diverted into hunting witches unless there was clear indication that heresy likewise was involved.[15]

During the next few years European opinion about witchcraft suffered a rapid and terrible mutation. Part of the blame must rest on no less an intellectual than Saint Thomas Aquinas, who, while regarding the invocation of demons as mere superstition rather than as heresy, nevertheless developed, on the basis of Saint Augustine, a doctrine of the possibility of a pact made by a witch with demons. This doctrine quickly enabled his fellow Dominicans, who largely ran the Inquisition, to identify witchcraft with heresy.[16] The first person in the later Middle Ages to be tried, convicted, and executed for witchcraft was an old woman of Toulouse, Angèle de la Barthe, who was burned in 1275.[17] Jean de Meun who, in the older tradition, considered the whole matter of witchcraft to be monstrous nonsense, tells us that about the same time in northern France it was being whispered that not less than a third of the entire population was practicing sorcery.[18]

The madness spread rapidly, especially after 1300, and to all parts of Europe. Indeed, it is of macabre interest to Americans

[14] Gregory of Tours, *Historia Francorum*, VI, 35, ed. B. Krusch, *Monumenta Germaniae historica, Script. rerum Merovingicarum*, 2d ed., I, fasc. 2 (Hannover, 1942), 305–306, tells how Queen Fredegund, about 584, tortured and executed some women of Paris accused of witchcraft. In 580 there had been a similar episode *ibid.*, V, 39, *ed. cit.*, I, fasc. 1 [1937], 246–247).

[15] Hansen, *op. cit.*, p. 1.

[16] Charles H. Hopkins, *The Share of Thomas Aquinas in the Growth of the Witchcraft Delusion* (Philadelphia, 1940), pp. 149, 177–178, 183.

[17] R. H. Robbins, *Encyclopedia of Witchcraft and Demonology* (New York, 1963), p. 208.

[18] *The Romance of the Rose*, trans. H. W. Robbins (New York, 1962), pp. 391–392.

that it infected even the medieval enclave in the New World: in 1407 a man named Kolgrim was burned for black magic in the Norse colony in Greenland.[19] Throughout the fifteenth century the hunt expanded, and in 1484 Innocent VIII gave it the complete backing of the Papacy. Hideous tortures were applied to all the accused in an effort not only to extort confessions but also to secure accusations of other witches, who were then arrested and tortured. It would seem that few of those accused escaped execution. Nor, after the Reformation, was there any less intensity among Protestants than among Catholics in the persecution of witches. While everyone recalls with horror John Calvin's burning of Michael Servetus as a heretic, few remember that in a single year, 1545, while Calvin was ruling Geneva, thirty-four women were burned or quartered for witchcraft in that city. Nor did the wars of religion from 1560 to 1648 bring any slackening; in fact, some historians believe that the slaughter of witches reached its furthest extension in those decades.[20] There are no reliable estimates of the total number of victims between 1300 and 1650, the age of the Renaissance, but it surely amounted to scores of thousands, each victim suffering torture and a dreadful death. In a single year the bishop of Bamberg is said to have burned some 600; that of Würzburg, 900. In 1514, in the tiny diocese of Como, 300 were executed. In Savoy a great festival was held at which about 800 were burned in a batch. It is not easy to think well of ourselves who come of a race capable of such generally approved brutality.

Then, as rapidly and unexpectedly as the witch mania had grown in the late thirteenth century, it evaporated in the later seventeenth, save in such marginal regions as Poland and Massachusetts. Hugh Trevor-Roper, one of the most recent historians to ponder the enigma, confesses that the reason for its erosion "is mysterious still."[21] In contemporary intellectual terms, the arguments against believing in witchcraft were inadequate;

[19] Gwyn Jones, *The Norse Atlantic Saga* (London, 1964), p. 66.
[20] H. R. Trevor-Roper, "Witches and Witchcraft," *Encounter*, XXVIII (June 1967), 13–24.
[21] *Ibid.*, p. 27.

nevertheless the belief vanished. The notion that people simply wearied of sadism does not explain why they had continued to delight in it for the preceding 350 years. Trevor-Roper inclines, but without strong conviction, to the view that the new scientific vision of nature and its operations made witchcraft irrelevant. But how deeply had the views of Copernicus, Galileo, and Descartes penetrated the popular mind by the time belief in witchcraft was abandoned by the average European? Scarcely at all.

To understand both the origins and the end of the witchhunt, we must put it into the context not only of all the social psychoses and emotional traumas of the age of the Renaissance, but also of those of the three centuries preceding 1300.

In this matter anthropologists can help historians. Among the Navahos the practice of witchcraft and witch persecution has fluctuated in relation to the psychic pressure of the white American culture upon traditional Navaho ways.[22] After the conquest of the Navaho tribe there was a great resurgence of witchcraft, which later subsided. Then, during World War II, thousands of young Navahos served in the armed forces of the United States or worked in California shipyards. When they returned to their tribal lands they were profoundly maladjusted to the old matriarchal society: they did not know what it was right to do, or to think, or even to feel. Some, clutching at supernatural powers to solve their problems, became sorcerers; others, unconsciously seeking a scapegoat for the confusions and frustrations of their lives, attacked the witches.[23] There were some savage executions of witches in the Navaho country during the early 1950s.

Among the Navahos, then, the practice of witchcraft and the hunting of witches have been mirror images of a single de-

[22] Clyde Kluckhohn, *Navaho Witchcraft* (Boston, 1962), pp. 65–128.

[23] Lynn White, jr., *Machina ex Deo* (Cambridge, Mass., 1968), pp. 169–179. Similar pressures appear to be producing similar results in contemporary African societies (cf. John Middleton and E. H. Winter, eds., *Witchcraft and Sorcery in East Africa* [London, 1963], pp. 20–25).

vice for coping with hostility and venting frustrations generated by intolerable external pressures upon the traditional Navaho way of life and by emotionally unassimilable change. Since the old Navaho pattern is woman-centered, it is not astonishing that in this tribe magic has been chiefly practiced by men. If this anthropological interpretation can be transferred to Europe, it would explain one of the most puzzling aspects of Renaissance witchcraft: the large number of witches as compared with wizards. Evidently in a time of cultural stress the marginal sex clutches more avidly for drastic expedients. And Western culture has always been, and remains today, overwhelmingly patriarchal.[24]

Yet we must be cautious: the situation of the Navahos has been very different from that of Europe in the period 1300 to 1650. While until about 1500 Western culture remained far more amenable to borrowing from other cultures than it has since become, and while terror of the Turk rose in steady crescendo during the fifteenth and sixteenth centuries, European ways of acting, thinking, and feeling have never been subjected to alien pressures in any way comparable to those suffered by the Navahos. If it is to be useful for understanding European history, the anthropological hypothesis must be modified to fit the European facts.

Anxieties produced by internally generated change may be as profound as those produced by external influences. Indeed, they may be even more traumatic because the source of the change is less identifiable; the threat is the more ominous because it cannot be so easily labeled.

Historians have found no static cultures. The more closely

[24] Quite different social patterns, however, may produce superficially similar patterns of witchcraft. Among the Lobedu of the northern Transvaal, women occupy a remarkably high status; yet most witches are women because, in Lobedu opinion, the practice of polygyny, resulting in rivalry among co-wives, is the chief incentive to witchcraft (cf. J. D. Krige, "The Social Function of Witchcraft," *Theoria* [Natal], I [1947], 10, 19). For difficulties in reconciling African with Oceanian data on the sociology of witchcraft, see Maxwell G. Marwick, "Witchcraft as a Social Straingauge," *Australian Journal of Science*, XXVI (1964), 263–268.

one looks at the history of any people, the more evident change becomes. It is clear, however, that the pace and the intensity of change vary considerably, not only within the development of a culture but between cultures.

In the Middle Ages and early Renaissance the West was in many ways very like the Near East; it was quite eager to adopt innovations from the more sophisticated societies of Byzantine and Islam, as well as from more distant regions. Yet we are beginning to realize that the medieval West rather early began to develop a cultural dynamism that greatly surpassed that of the Near East, and one that was essentially indigenous, even though borrowings provided some stimuli.

During the tenth and early eleventh centuries the last waves of invaders, the Magyars and the Vikings, were domesticated, and physical security sharply improved in Europe. A three-hundred-year boom in population, growth of cities, and economic prosperity commenced, and by the later eleventh century contemporaries were commenting on the rapidity of change in social relationships.[25] Moreover, the efforts of Cluny to reform monasticism and of Pope Gregory VII to reform the Church as a whole produced intense controversy because, in essence, the reformers were demanding a major revolution: the secession of the Church from the feudal system. The strife over lay investiture of clergy shook not only the social fabric of Europe but also its inherited assumptions. The twelfth and thirteenth centuries saw ever accelerated change; architecture, literature, piety, governmental structures, methods of industrial production—every aspect of life was in flux.

By the later thirteenth century, when the witch mania appeared, vast numbers of people seem to have been spiritually out of breath from running too fast. Their inherited axiom was that change was bad; Roman antiquity, or the age of the early Church, was their ideal. Any change, they thought, served only to put them further from that past Golden Age. Yet change was all about, and resentment of it was compounded by guilt

[25] Lynn White, jr., "The Life of the Silent Majority," in *Life and Thought in the Early Middle Ages*, ed. R. S. Hoyt (Minneapolis, 1967), p. 88.

because the person who hated it in principle often profited from it in detail.

And the world was chaos; the good old days were gone. The pope had exterminated the Hohenstaufen dynasty and was beginning to overreach himself with claims to universal power which would shortly bring the Papacy toppling and make the pope hardly more than chaplain to the king of France. Italy and Germany were slipping into anarchy because of the ephemeral papal triumph over the Holy Roman Empire. The feudal aristocrats, rapidly losing their military primacy to mercenaries and their governmental function to salaried bureaucrats, were growing cynical about themselves and their world. Merchants were squeezed in their consciences between the necessities of a new money economy and the old ethical condemnation of usury. In the early thirteenth century the Papacy had invented the institution of the university to cope with the waves of new learning raised by large numbers of philosophical and scientific works translated from Arabic and Greek. But both students and faculties were restless; soon the new learning was being criticized as vehemently as the old learning had been. In every area of life the once secure foundations seemed to be slipping. People feared the new, but were discontented with the old. It was an age of acute anxiety.

We know from the records that the practice of witchcraft was, at least in part, a means of escaping vague, unformulable anxiety. The Church was the heart of the old order, and the heart of the Church was the Mass. At times, at the sacred moment of the elevation of the Host, a woman would spit or make an obscene remark.[26] The accumulated tension in her would be

---

[26] *Malleus Maleficarum*, trans. Montague Summers (London, 1928), p. 98. The schizophrenic implications of the Black Mass as an inversion of the symbolism of the Mass are uncertain since, despite all rumors and charges, there seems to be no firm evidence of the Black Mass earlier than the notorious affair involving Mme de Montespan in 1679–1682 (see Robbins, *op. cit.*, pp. 50, 80). I incline, however, to accept the Black Mass as stylistically coherent with the fourteenth century, since in late thirteenth-century French literature the forms of Christian liturgy were increasingly used to celebrate anti-Christian attitudes (cf.

released, but this euphoria was clearly the work of Satan. She would try it at another Mass; it worked. Soon she would convince herself that she was in alliance with the devil and able to exercise demonic powers. The vast majority of her neighbors were subject in varying degrees to the same anxieties. Another way of coping with them was to be able to blame the state of things on witchcraft; it provided a focus of enmity, a formula for purging inner disquiets. Eventually the woman's neighbors would detect that she was a witch and would burn her amid general delight. The satisfaction could only be increased if, under torture, she accused quite innocent people, who also, under torture, confessed to sorcery.

But if this interpretation of European witchcraft is correct, why did not our ancestors develop into witches and witch-hunters in the early eleventh century, when the velocity of cultural change first began to induce serious concern? Our general hypothesis, drawn from anthropology, is confirmed by the fact that it was precisely in the early eleventh century that Western Christians began to burn heretics and attack Jews. After the execution of Priscillian and a few of his followers by the Roman authorities in 385, there followed a span of more than 600 years during which, in the West, many heretics were excommunicated, but they were not executed, tortured, or even imprisoned. It is psychologically significant that when, at Orléans in 1022, this era of decency ended, the bishop protected the heretics against the efforts of the mob to lynch them; the burnings occurred only after the king capitulated to popular demands and those of his wife. The next holocaust occurred at Milan in 1028. In 1048–1054 the bishop of Liège saved accused heretics from being seized and burned by the angry populace. Deep into the twelfth century many of the upper clergy were trying to moderate the vengefulness of laymen toward heretics.[27] Their efforts suggest that the roots of animosity were

---

Marcel Françon, "Jean de Meun et les origines de la Renaissance," *Publications of the Modern Language Association*, LIX [1944], 624–645).

[27] Jeffrey Burton Russell, *Dissent and Reform in the Early Middle Ages* (Berkeley and Los Angeles, 1965), pp. 250–256.

neither intellectual nor institutional: the mob needed scapegoats on whom it could vent a generalized hostility.

But heresy itself seems to have fed on the growing alienation, since by the early thirteenth century it was epidemic, especially in the culturally advanced areas of northern Italy and southern France. At that point Innocent III joined the mob, and the heretics were wiped out with fire, sword, and rack. Like the witch and the witch-hunter who emerged as the supply of burnable heretics dwindled, both the heretics and their executioners were coping with the same unendurable tensions.

The dismal history of anti-Semitism follows the same pattern. Despite antagonisms generated during the early years when Christianity, originally a Jewish heresy, was breaking away from the synagogue and sweeping into its fold a large number of the Hellenized Jews of the Diaspora, not for many centuries to come did Western Christian resentment of Jews express itself in violence with any frequency. Jews were subjected to inconveniences and pressures, but, as in Islam until our own day, the atmosphere was generally tolerant save for one bad period in the seventh century. By the middle of the eleventh century the Jewish communities of France and the Rhineland, abetted by those in Spain, were beginning to assume the intellectual leadership of cosmopolitan Judaism which had so long rested in the new declining centers in Mesopotamia.

But the Western context was changing.[28] In 1010 there were minor mob actions against Jews in Rouen, Limoges, and Mainz. In 1065 the bishop of Narbonne had to protect Jews against attacks by soldiers on their way to Spain to fight the Muslims. Catastrophe descended in 1096 when, despite the resistance of most bishops to the mounting hysteria, undisciplined bands of pilgrim-Crusaders marching to the Holy Land started to massacre Jews, especially in the Rhineland. The Crusades, incidentally, are one of history's most curious examples of mass aggression, since, to most of the thousands who took the cross, the infidels of Islam against whom they marched were somewhat more distant and shapeless than the imps of hell them-

[28] Cf. Salo Baron, *A Social and Religious History of the Jews*, 2d ed., IV (New York, 1957), 89–94.

selves. The Second Crusade saw renewal of pogroms, even though Saint Bernard of Clairvaux, the leading churchman of the day, tried to stop the slaughter. But gradually, as cultural anxiety increased, the Church succumbed to popular pressures, with the notable exception of the Papacy which consistently sheltered the Jews of Rome and Avignon. In 1144 the first charge that Jews had sacrificed a Christian child was recorded; a century later Jews were accused of desecrating the Host. Anti-Semitism became a normal attitude in Europe, and gradually the Jews were either murdered or expelled from almost all the West, culminating in their exile from Spain in 1492. A few communities huddled in scattered cities of Germany and Italy, but most of those who survived the recurrent atrocities fled to the less dynamic Slavic East which, from the late thirteenth to the twentieth century, remained the chief center of Jewry.

Heretics, Jews, and at last witches: a generalized hostility toward oneself and one's world must vent itself in torturing and slaying an identifiable and relatively defenseless group which it is culturally not only permissible but even necessary to hate. In 1321, in a wide region of Guyenne, the lepers momentarily served the same social purpose; they were accused of poisoning wells and practicing magic, and some dozens were burned.[29]

The scapegoat theory of such savage excesses is by no means novel. But this interpretation should be clarified by relating the origin and course of such agonies to the rising velocity of cultural change observable in Europe from about the year 1000 onward. In the eleventh, twelfth, and thirteenth centuries there was a vast increase of cruelty toward scapegroups, but there were not many signs that the personality structure of any large number of people was yet disintegrating.[30] By the late thirteenth

[29] G. Lavergne, "Le persécution et la spoliation des lépreux à Perigueux en 1321," in *Recueil de travaux offert à M. Clovis Brunel* (Paris, 1955), II, 107–113.

[30] As noted in the introduction to this volume, the chief evidence of personal alienation in these centuries is the vice then called *acedia*, which was most commonly found in a monastic context (see P. Alphandéry, "De quelques documents médiévaux relatifs à des états psychasthéniques," *Journal de Psychologie*, XXVI [1929], 763–787).

century, however, elaborate and calculated sadism, as contrasted with hot-blooded massacre, was appearing. So also we find masochism, necrophilia, and many other symptoms of inner personal derangement emerging at the level of social acceptance. The age of the Renaissance, 1300 to 1650, was a time of human tragedy unparalleled in Europe, and perhaps elsewhere in world history. Someday we may hope to know more exactly how such tragedy was related to the simultaneous creativity of that epoch.[31]

But why, about 1650, did all forms of scapegoatism decline so suddenly and so quickly in western Europe? Why did social manifestations of aggression and personal disorientation so markedly diminish?[32] Explanations in terms of religious indifferentism, rising compassion, popularization of a scientific world view, bourgeois capitalism, or the development of colonial outlets for agression will not withstand scrutiny.

Let me suggest that anxiety over the velocity of cultural change arises only in people who accept the myth of a golden past. We know little as yet about changes in the basic attitudes of ordinary Europeans in the seventeenth century, the kind of

[31] Alfred Gallinetk ("Psychogenic Disorders and the Civilization of the Middle Ages," *American Journal of Psychiatry*, XCIX [July 1942], 42–54) concludes that, in monastic circles, the Middle Ages cultivated mechanisms for inducing hysteria, and that this hysteria was often culturally creative.

[32] It may be significant that, for the first time since the ninth century, the Christian doctrine of eternal punishment of sinners in hellfire began to be questioned in the middle of the seventeenth century, although the conviction, even among skeptics, that the belief was a salutary deterrent to crime long prevented open criticism of it (see D. P. Walker, *The Decline of Hell: Seventeenth-Century Discussions of Eternal Torment*. [London, 1964]). While a belief in hell is found in Christianity from its beginnings, Christian art does not begin to emphasize the torments of the damned until the eighth and ninth centuries (cf. Beat Brenk, *Tradition und Neuerung in der christlichen Kunst des ersten Jahrtausends: Studien zur Geschichte des Weltgerichtsbildes* [Wiener byzantinische Studien, 3] [Vienna, 1966], pp. 212–213). During the later Middle Ages the punishments of hell, doubtless to the satisfaction of the righteous public, achieved astonishing levels of realism and sadistic ingenuity.

people whose anxieties had made scapegoats necessary. Because they were saturated in a Greco-Latin classical education, a high proportion of the upper classes continued to idealize the distant past until the very end of the century when the "quarrel between the Ancients and the Moderns" corroded ancestor worship in their thinking. It is my impression that somewhat earlier in the century less educated folk began to absorb an admiration for change largely because they came to realize that much of the gadgetry that was making daily living so much more convenient had been quite unknown to the ancients.

To offer one example: about 1580 a Flemish artist, Jan van der Straet, published in Antwerp an elaborate series of engravings intended for wall decoration. The captions are in Latin, but not very elegant Latin. These pictures, intended for popular consumption, were hawked widely. They sold well, and in 1638 they were reissued. One of their major themes is *Nova reperta*, the new discoveries made since antiquity: America, the mariner's compass, gunpowder, printing, clocks, distillation, the cultivation of silk and sugar, stirrups, water mills (here van der Straet was wrong), windmills, oil paints, eyeglasses, the astrolabe, water-powered metallurgical machinery, copper engraving.[33] I suspect that as we get deeper into the history of popular culture, we shall find further evidence that by about 1650 the novel idea of progress, which had had a long gestation in theological and apocalyptic forms, began emerging in the general thinking of Europeans, not as a philosophical concept, but simply as a happy recognition of the fact that people now knew a lot more, and could do a lot more, than any people in the past. Once such a notion was absorbed into the repertory of normal ideas, change and the prospect of further change lost their general power to terrify, since specific changes that one deplored could be identified and opposed. John Donne's lament for a vanishing order—"Tis all in peeces, all cohaerance gone" —succumbed to the vision of mankind's perfectibility. The idea of progress had vast therapeutic value because it enabled most

[33] Johannes Stradanus, *New Discoveries of the Middle Ages and Renaissance*, ed. E. Rosen and B. Dibner [Publication of the Burndy Library, 8] (Norwalk, 1953).

people to maintain personal psychic stability in the face of an ever increasing cultural velocity. Its advent marks the end of the Renaissance because it notably reduced the quantum of anxiety which had been the most characteristic feature of Western society in that age.

Our own century has seen one fearfully destructive hurricane of anxiety and scapegoatism: Nazi Germany. It grew out of the corporate psychosis of the German people after their defeat in World War I. The rest of the world localized and terminated it quickly, at great cost. One hopes that historians, anthropologists, social psychologists, and the whole guild of humanists may probe deeper into such phenomena so that we may all learn better how to control the vast potential for evil which lies within each of us.

RENAISSANCE WORLD-ALIENATION

Donald R. Howard

AT THE end of Chaucer's *Troilus and Criseyde*, we see the hero after his death standing in the "hollowness of the eighth sphere," looking upon the planets and hearing the music of the spheres:

> And down from thennes faste he gan avyse [to scrutinize]
> This litel spot of erthe, that with the se
> Embraced is, and fully gan despise
> This wrecched world . . . [1]

Troilus, it must be understood, is not in heaven. He is up somewhere in the Ptolemaic universe (the exact spot is in debate)[2] and, looking back, he turns his attention upon "this little spot of earth which is embraced by the sea." His reaction is stated quite explicitly: he wholly *despises the world*—he "held al vani-

[1] *Troilus and Criseyde*, V, 1814–1817; quoted from *The Works of Geoffrey Chaucer*, ed. F. N. Robinson, 2d ed. (Cambridge, Mass., 1957).

[2] See Morton W. Bloomfield, "The Eighth Sphere: A Note on Chaucer's *Troilus and Criseyde*, V, 1809," *MLR*, LIII (1958), 408–410. I regret that I did not have available when this essay was written, in 1967, the full discussion which has since appeared, John M. Steadman's *Disembodied Laughter: Troilus and the Apotheosis Tradition* (Berkeley, Los Angeles, and London, 1972).

te" in contrast with the "pleyn [full] felicite" of heaven. This last is probably Chaucer's own observation, for there is no reason why Troilus should know anything about heaven; he is a pagan, and even after this moment he is sent off in the charge of Mercury—where, we never know. What makes the passage paradigmatic, at least for my topic, is that Troilus seeks out as his last object of contemplation not the earth, and not the heavens, but the world; he learns from his new vantage point the medieval lesson of contempt toward the world; and then, seeing those who weep for his death, he laughs. It is an astonishing conception (it originated with Dante and Lucan): that the dead can laugh. And what it means, I believe, is that Troilus experiences here that noninvolvement with worldly things which I am going to call alienation from the world.

What does "world" mean in this sense? Obviously it does not mean the earth, the terrestrial orb: Troilus first sees the *earth*, but then despises the *world*. It can, and in part does, refer to the duration of earthly life and so is a temporal metaphor, like Latin *saeculum*; but by the late Middle Ages *saeculum* and *mundus* were used interchangeably, and English "world" translates both. When the medievals say "world," they have in mind not merely time or place but a sphere of activities. The world was renounced by monks in their vows and indeed by all Christians in baptism; it was coupled with "the flesh" and "the devil" as a source of temptations; and the "things of the world," according to an important biblical text, were "not of the Father but of the world." *Mundus*, used sometimes in opposition to *ecclesia*, referred also to secular government and the affairs of the organized laity.[3] In short, the world was all that stood between man and nature; it was the realm of made things, of human actions and institutions. We still use the word in this sense when we speak, for example, of "going out into the world," of "saving" the world or of destroying it. In various degrees we belong to this world and engage ourselves with it; and this en-

---

[3] On this meaning of "world" in medieval thought see Donald R. Howard, *The Three Temptations: Medieval Man in Search of the World* (Princeton, 1966), chap. 2 and *passim*.

gagement with the world is what I will call *worldliness*. If it were given to us to experience in full consciousness every condition of human life simultaneously, we would live in a state of unremitting worldliness. But human consciousness is selective, so that as we commune in one realm our consciousness is drawn away from others. If we commune with nature, or with God, or if we sink very deep into our own thoughts or into intimacy with others, we are drawn, as we say, "out of this world." And this noncommunion with the world is what I mean by *world-alienation*.

"Alienation" is not the happiest term, having become a tag for adolescent truculence and suburban ennui; but its etymological sense is just what I mean: it is otherness, estrangement. I do not mean "alienation" in its psychological sense of the lack of rapport with others or with one's self; nor in its sociological sense (which derives from Marx) of noncommitment to the values of a society.[4] And whether these various kinds of alienation are associated with one another remains for me an open question. The term "world-alienation" was used first, so far as I know, by Hannah Arendt[5] to describe the reaction of modern man to what she calls the "loss of the common world." She associates world-alienation primarily with the fact that the Renaissance voyages of exploration, although they set out to explore the vastness of the world, ended by making the world seem small; she considers the Protestant ethic and the invention of the telescope as influences. By world-alienation she means a sense of otherness with respect to man-made things—not to the globe, but to that experience of worldly life on the globe which men can claim to share; it is a sense of the meaninglessness and uselessness of the world, its ineffectiveness to unite men into communities or separate them out of a mass, to make men feel that "all's right with the world," that they know where they are and feel satisfied that they belong there. Of course such a

[4] On the meaning of "alienation" in contemporary thought see esp. Robert A. Nisbet, *The Sociological Tradition* (New York, 1966), chap. 7; Kenneth Keniston, *The Uncommitted: Alienated Youth in American Society*, repr. (New York, 1967), pp. 451–475.

[5] *The Human Condition* (Chicago, 1958), esp. pp. 248–257.

distinctly modern feeling did not exist at all during the Renaissance. How could it? Renaissance men had a different conception of the world from ours and different attitudes about belonging to it. I use the term "world-alienation" without meaning to equate the modern phenomenon with the medieval one. But I hope to show that something like the modern feeling existed then, and that there is some historical continuity between the two. I trust that I can show, too, that a "common world" was never really gained, that there was only a *search* for the world.

This world-alienation, which I believe was endemic to the Renaissance, deserves to be studied as an irrational feature of the age because it minimized reason's role. It did not reject the *conception* of reason as a faculty of the soul; reason, it agreed, imparted moral truths and recommended moral behavior. But it put little stock in reason's power to change nature or the world. It held that reason was enfeebled and nature corrupted by the fall; and it turned aside every hope that man's reason could understand or his efforts affect the corrupted currents of this world with reminders of the world's mutability, misery, and vanity. It fostered instead control over the inner man and commended the "art of dying." Then, too, world-alienation itself came much more from the heart than from the head. It ignored reason. It cannot therefore be charged to Christian doctrine; there were excellent reasons in theology for rejecting the world, but there were no less excellent ones for believing in man's dignity and in the active life. Nor can it be charged to monasticism; monastic orders fostered a Christian humanism and a Christian activism as well as prayer and contemplation. It was, as we shall see, an ideology, a complex of emotions; it might be called a sensibility. The bare-bones idea, which was reasonable enough, had its niche in Christian doctrine to be sure; but what gave the idea life was its emotional appeal.

In order to look for world-alienation I shall begin in the twelfth century; I happen to believe that almost nothing can be understood about the Renaissance without doing so. And to make the search easier, I am going to throw overboard the term "Renaissance." It carries too much weight of association. Everyone knows that such terms are arbitrary, yet "Renaissance" and "Middle Ages" do go on wearing tatters borrowed from Sir Walter Scott and Jakob Burckhardt. All of this I mean to shun. I shall treat the period from the twelfth to the seventeenth century very simply as one stretch of years and call it the Middle Ages just because it was in the middle, between the early Christian period and that more recent period when Christianity lost its hold upon European thought. The Renaissance was, from this point of view, an event, not a historic period, and similar events occurred in various nations during various centuries.[6] In turning my back on the Renaissance, I hasten to add, I do not claim that I can make it go away. My only claim is that the feeling or attitude I want to describe should be added to the whole *son et lumière* with which we create our understanding of that age: the dawnings, the wanings, the discoveries and the losses, the rises and the falls, and of course the dyings and the rebirths.

I

Throughout the Middle Ages alienation from the world, and even from other people, was considered desirable. The only undesirable alienation was the archetypal alienation of creatures from God: the casting of Satan out of heaven and the fall of man. Into the life of every individual came an element of this evil alienation, because one result of the fall was the obscuring of man's reason and hence ignorance of God's will. And in order to lessen his alienation from God, every Christian needed to alienate himself from the world. God and the world were understood to be in opposition. One of the great texts of the Middle Ages was 1 John 2:15–16: "Love not the world, neither the things that are in the world. . . . For all that is in the world, the lust of the flesh, and the lust of the eyes, and the pride of life, is not of the Father, but is of the world." The world was conceived as inimical to union with the Father; and

---

[6] Cf. C. S. Lewis, *De Descriptione Temporum* (Cambridge, Eng., 1956); Dietrich Gerhard, "Periodization in European History," *American Historical Review*, LXI (1956), 900–913.

the essence of the world was the three "lusts," which were equated with the temptations of Adam and Christ. As Gerhart Ladner has pointed out,[7] this medieval notion of a desirable alienation from the world was what made the image of *homo viator* so central. In earlier times the desert fathers, the gyrovagues, the hermits and anchorites, show the high value placed upon ascetic homelessness; and in later ages the isolation of monastic communities, or such institutions as the pilgrimage, the crusade, or knight-errantry, reflect the medieval predilection for voyaging, wandering, and homelessness as an expression of spiritual world-alienation.

But the world was not bad. From Saint Augustine the medievals inherited a careful statement of the world's nature. Augustine, a convert from the Manichean heresy, had a vested interest in explaining how the world could seem so bad and still be the creation of a god who is good. If God is good, Augustine reasoned, all that he creates must be good. But obviously no creature could be as good as God himself; so Augustine called God the immutable Good and his whole creation a mutable good.[8] In the fall of Adam the race experienced the ability of creatures to become less good; but Augustine believed that no creature, however he might wallow in evil, could ever escape the goodness of his created nature.[9] The Augustine we notice when we read him is the Augustine who dooms unbaptized infants and sees the awful corruptness of the mundane order; but pessimistic as he may seem to us now, he was exceedingly cautious always to avoid the pessimism that questioned the goodness of God and of God's creation. "One is at a loss to decide," he cries, "whether, in creating the body, greater regard was paid to utility or to beauty."[10] And in Augustine's thought the Christian life consisted in avoiding worldly things insofar as they might tempt us, but still using them well for our salvation.

During the twelfth century this carefully balanced view of

[7] Gerhart B. Ladner, "*Homo Viator*: Mediaeval Ideas on Alienation and Order," *Speculum*, XLII (1967), 233–259.
[8] *City of God*, XI, 10.
[9] *Ibid.*, XIV, 11.
[10] *Ibid.*, XXII, 24.

the world and this purposeful alienation from it came to be slightly altered. Everybody knows that during the twelfth century there was a great surge of energy; we do not know the reason for this phenomenon. The Gothic cathedral, courtly love, the chivalric ethos, the universities, the towns, the revivals of Roman law and Latin literature, translations from Greek and Arabic, vernacular poetry—almost everything we associate with the close of the Middle Ages gets under way in the twelfth century. But alongside this movement occurs a corresponding upsurge of pessimism and gloom.[11] This development, very often brushed under the carpet in histories of the period, is no easier to explain than are the worldliness and the optimism of the age. Perhaps it was a reaction. Or perhaps the age simply worked up an energy and an extremism which expressed themselves in all directions. Perhaps previously existing ideas came to be more carefully articulated and thus more distinctly polarized. At all events, at the end of the eleventh century we begin to find a tradition of writings that condemn the world in the most extravagant language. Implicit in them, and sometimes expressed, is the proviso that worldly things are not inherently evil and *may* be used to good purposes. But their spirit belies any such concessions: they are indeed very harsh.

The content of these writings on contempt of the world need not delay us, for they nearly all say the same things. They argue that worldly life is mutable and transitory, that its pleasures are vain and disappointing, that man is fallen, his nature corrupt, and his body infirm. They often depict human society as a

[11] This pessimism is, by its generic name, "contempt of the world" (cf. Howard, *Three Temptations*, pp. 68–75 and *passim*). On the background of the idea see Robert Bultot, *Christianisme et valeurs humaines: La doctrine du mépris du monde* (Louvain, 1963——), IV; when completed this history will cover the period from Saint Ambrose to Pope Innocent III. See also *Revue d'ascétique et de mystique*, XLI, no. 3, (1965), which contains a number of articles on the subject. In arguing that the tradition begins in the late eleventh century I have in mind the characteristic style of such works and the frequency with which they were written. The subject itself has of course a vast background in Christian thought; but in the eleventh and twelfth centuries we find the emergence of a literary genre with a characteristic style.

caldron of vices and hypocrisies, and a good many of them end
with apocalyptic passages describing the punishments of hell
and the joys of heaven. From more than 200 poems on the
subject, I choose for illustration two very short ones; neither
has been published and I doubt that either is known at all. They
are preserved in two fifteenth-century manuscripts at the Cambridge University Library. The shorter is this:

> Cur in hac miseria miserius moramini?
> Hac mundana gloria quare dilectamini—
> Vos qui moriemini, relinquentes omnia?
> Mors que parcit nemini vestra tollet gaudia.[12]

A similar ditty, attributed (I think wrongly) to Saint Bernard,
is probably drawn in part from a longer poem of the thirteenth
century; but it is hitherto unnoted in its present form:

> Dic homo mortalis, dic de putredine vermis;
> Dic caro, dic pulvis, quid prodest gloria carnis?
> Cur miser insanis, quare putredo superbis?
> Disce quod es, quod eris; memor esto quod morieris.

> Sperma prius, post factus olens, post vermibus esca,
> Post cinis, inde nichil; unde superbit homo?
> Ut rosa pallescit cum solem sentit adesse,
> Sic homo vanescit: nunc est, nunc defuit esse.[13]

---

[12] "Why in this wretchedness do you linger on more wretchedly?
Why do you take pleasure in this worldly glory, you who are going to
die, leaving everything behind? Death, who spares no one, will take
away your joys" (Cambridge University Library MS Ii, 4.9, fol. 69ʳ
[s. XV]). I am indebted to Mr. R. V. Kerr of the Cambridge University Library for his kind assistance and to the library itself for permission to print this poem and the following one.

[13] "Tell me, O mortal man, tell me about the putridity of the worm;
tell me o flesh, o dust, what good is the glory of Flesh? O mad wretch,
why do you take pride in putridity? Learn what you are, what you will
be; remember that you will die. First you were sperm, then stench, then
food for worms, then dust, and thence nothing; what then, does a man
have to be proud about? As the rose pales when it feels the sun draw
near, so man will vanish: now he is, now he has ceased to be." (Cambridge University Library MS Ee, vi.29, fol. 17ʳ [s. XV]). The first

There are as many prose works as poems on the subject between the eleventh and the sixteenth centuries. Among earlier writers are Saint Peter Damian,[14] Saint Anselm of Canterbury,[15] Hugh of St. Victor,[16] Saint Bernard of Clairvaux,[17] and the fifteenth-century biographer Johannis Trithemius.[18] The great classic of the genre, written about 1195, is the *De miseria humanae conditionis* of Pope Innocent III.[19] It was universally read well into the seventeenth century. It survives today in almost 500 manuscripts in the libraries of all European nations. It was printed in more than fifty editions before the eighteenth century and was translated into almost all European languages, even Irish.[20] Chaucer, in the *Legend of Good Women* (G Pro. 414–415), tells us that he had translated it, although his translation, if it ever existed, has not survived. In 1576, in the second

---

four lines begin an otherwise different poem in Brussels, Bibl. Roy. MS 1404 (II.2620), fol. 13–13ᵛ (s. XIII). See Hans Walther, *Initia carminum*, no. 4355.

[14] *Apologeticum de contemptu mundi* (in Migne, *Patrologia Latina* [hereafter *PL*] 145:251–292).

[15] *Exhortatio ad contemptum temporalium et desiderium aeternorum* (*PL* 158:677–686).

[16] *De vanitate mundi et rerum transeuntium usu* (*PL* 176:703–740).

[17] *Meditationes piissimae de cognitione humanae conditionis* (*PL* 184: 486–508). The attribution is disputed.

[18] *De vanitate et miseria humanae vitae liber* (Moguntina: Petrus Friedbergensis, 1495), fols. 172–192ᵛ. One should mention as well the *De Contemptu Mundi*, the great satirical poem of the twelfth century, 3,000 lines long, by Bernard of Morval, ed. H. C. Hoskier (London, 1929).

[19] *Lotharii Cardinalis (Innocentii III) De miseria humanae conditionis*, ed. Michele Maccarrone (Lugano, 1955). For a modern English translation, see *On the Misery of the Human Condition*, trans. M. M. Dietz, ed. with introd. by Donald R. Howard (Indianapolis, 1969). See also Robert Bultot, "Mépris du monde, misère et dignité de l'homme dans la pensée d'Innocent III," *Cahiers de Civilisation Médiévale*, IV (1961), 441–456.

[20] MSS and printed editions are listed in Maccarrone, *Lotharii Cardinalis* pp. x-xxii. Other MSS continue to come to light (see Michele Maccarrone and Keith V. Sinclair in *Italia Medioevale e umanistica*, IV [1961], 167–173; Donald R. Howard, in *Manuscripta*, VII [1963], 31–35; and Robert E. Lewis in *Manuscripta*, VIII [1964], 172–175).

decade of Elizabeth's reign, two English translations appeared: Humphrey Kerton's *The Mirror of Mans Lyfe*, which went through five or more editions in a decade, and George Gascoigne's "The View of Worldly Vanities," the first part of *The Droomme of Doomes Day*. In short, *De miseria* was one of the great books of the age.

What does Pope Innocent III say about the misery of the human condition? He divides his work into three books, one each on the *ingressus*, the *progressus*, and the *egressus* of human life. In the *ingressus* section he describes the indignity of birth and the helplessness and weeping of infants, their nakedness, the vileness of the body, the shortness of life, the discomforts of old age, the universal wretchedness of men. He explains why the body is called the prison of the soul and describes the brevity of human joy, the unexpected sorrows of human life, the perpetual nearness of death, the terror of dreams, and the suddenness of misfortune. The second book, "The Guilty Progress of the Human Condition," argues that "Riches lead to immorality, pleasures to shame, and honors to vanity." In the final book, called "The Damnable Exit from the Human Condition," Innocent describes the agonies of death, the putrefaction of corpses, the wretchedness of the damned, and the punishments of hell.

From the twelfth century to the seventeenth men wrote and read works like Pope Innocent's *De miseria*. It would normally be expected that such works disappeared gradually from the scene after the fourteenth century, replaced by works on the dignity of man; but this did not happen. There are some hundred prose treatises similar to Innocent's, and as many more shorter tracts, sermons, and meditations.[21] These go on being written and read in the sixteenth and seventeenth centuries. Many humanists wrote on the theme: Maffeo Vegio,[22] Poggio

[21] There is no bibliography of these works. As many as are known to me will be listed in a forthcoming collaborative repertory of incipits to Latin works of 1100–1500 on the virtues and vices, to be edited by Morton W. Bloomfield, Donald R. Howard, and L. B. S. Guyot

[22] *De felicitate et miseria dialogus*, in Luigi Raffaele, *Maffeo Vegio: Elenco delle opere, scritti inediti* (Bologna, 1909), pp. 83–116.

Bracciolini,[23] Aeneas Silvius,[24] Giovanni Conversino,[25] Ficino.[26] Some humanists, but not all, diverge from tradition: Aeneas Silvius wrote only on the misery of kings and their courts; Petrarch in his dialogue on the subject—the *Secretum*—did not quite let his opponent Saint Augustine have the last word; Erasmus[27] in later life backtracked from his earlier treatise *de contemptu mundi*; and Celso Maffei[28] had the participants in his dialogue interrupt their discussion and go off to dinner. It is true, too, that humanists wrote on the dignity of man, offering rebuttals to the arguments of *contemptus mundi*.[29] But treatises on the dignity of man were few in number, were written only in Italy, and were in vogue chiefly during the fifteenth century; treatises on contempt of the world, on the other hand, were written and read in all nations throughout Europe until the seventeenth century.

In the fourteenth and early fifteenth centuries there appeared also a number of works—an offshoot of the *de contemptu* tradition—which isolate a single theme, that of death as the universal leveler, the end of all life; death illustrates the mutability of all worldly things and alienates every man, whether he wishes it or not, from the transitory loves of this world. Late in the fifteenth century the old salutation "Ave Maria," the words of Mary at the Annunciation, had added to it the familiar response,

---

[23] *De miseria conditionis humanae*, in *Opera* (Basileae, 1538), pp. 84–131.

[24] Variously called *Tractatus de miseria curialium* and *De miseria et stulticia curialium* (Cologne, 1468, etc.)

[25] *De miseria humanae vite*, at Venice, Bibl. Querini-Stampaglia, Cod. IX, 11, fols. 55ᵛ–57ᵛ (s. XV) [frag.].

[26] *Stultitia et miseria hominum*, in *Opera*, 2 vols. (Basileae, 1576), I, 636–638.

[27] *De contemptu mundi epistola*, in *Opera omnia*, V (Leiden, 1704), 1239–1262. See Albert Hyma, *The Youth of Erasmus* (Ann Arbor, Mich., 1930), pp. 167 ff.

[28] *Dialogus de contemptu mundi* (Brixiae, n. d.)

[29] See Charles E. Trinkaus, Jr., *Adversity's Noblemen: The Italian Humanists on Happiness* (New York: Octagon Books, 1965), repr. of 1940 edition with a new preface.

"Pray for us sinners now and at the hour of our death."[30] The classic *Ars moriendi*, written early in the fifteenth century by an unknown author, exists in more than 300 manuscripts in Latin and the vernacular tongues, was printed more than 100 times before 1500, and continued to appear throughout Europe until the end of the seventeenth century.[31] But it is only one such treatise. There survive probably 200 or 300 Latin works on the subject—little doggerel verses, prose treatises, sermons—dealing with death, with the art of dying, with the last things, with the right preparation for death; among the authors one finds Erasmus and Saint Thomas More.[32] There are thirty or more such works in English.[33] I need not labor the point; it is very simple: the fifteenth, sixteenth, and seventeenth centuries were obsessed with death, with the vanity of earthly pursuits, with the mutability of the world itself. The final alienation of the dying man from the world was forever in their thoughts.

What is the quality of this obsession? Certainly it is more violent, more exaggerated, and more pictorial than the earlier ascetic and monastic spirit. The Dance of Death, the death's-head, the fascination with one's conduct in facing death—none

[30] *Catholic Encyclopedia* (New York, 1910), s. v. "Hail Mary," VII, 112, col. 1.

[31] Sister Mary Catharine O'Connor, *The Art of Dying Well: The Development of the Ars moriendi* (New York, 1942).

[32] Some of these, chiefly those found in MSS in German libraries, have been examined by Rainer Rudolf in *Ars moriendi:Von der Kunst des heilsamen Lebens und Sterbens* (Cologne and Graz, 1957). For Erasmus, *De preparatione ad mortem; quomodo se quisquis debeat preparare ad mortem* (1533), see O'Connor, *Art of Dying Well*, pp. 180–181. See also Thomas More, *Four Last Things* (c. 1522), ed. D. O'Connor (London, 1935).

[33] See Nancy Lee Beaty, *The Craft of Dying: The Literary Tradition of the Ars moriendi in England*, Yale Studies in English, 175 (New Haven and London, 1970), a selective study that does not mention all English works on the subject. See also Klaus Jankofsky, *Darstellungen von Tod und Sterben in Mittelenglischer Zeit: Untersuchung literarischer Texte und historischer Quellen* (Berlin, 1970); Rosemary Woolf, *The English Religious Lyric in the Middle Ages* (Oxford, 1968), chaps. 3, 9.

of these had been a convention of the earlier Middle Ages. The obsession with death does not really appear until the late fourteenth century, and doubtless the plagues were an influence. But the real vogue of these works began more than a generation after the great plague of 1348 and went on for two centuries. To explain this vogue as the dark underside of a new secular spirit should surprise no one, for surely fear of death goes hand in hand with love of life.

To me the interpretation of these tendencies which best fits the facts is that the new burst of energy in the twelfth century went in both directions. As secular feeling became stronger, the warning voice of *contemptus mundi* became more demanding. The age became at once more zestful and more despairing, more worldly and more otherworldly. The contrast between the two attitudes increased rather than abated. If there was a further rebirth of secular spirit late in the fourteenth century and in the fifteenth, that was exactly when the topos of death burst upon Europe. Gerhart Ladner thinks it was from this time, too, that in various persecutions the alienation of men from their fellowmen came to its full potential of horrors.[34] And, from the fourteenth century, there were witches.

I should like to make two observations about the idea of contempt of the world.

First, it was a moderate position. The language of Pope Innocent III's *De miseria*, and of all similar writings, sounds extreme; but at least by contrast such views are moderate. A far more extravagant pessimism in the twelfth century was the doctrine of the Cathars, the so-called Albigensians. This religion, apparently imported from the Near East, appeared in Europe during the 1140s and quickly gained an enormous following throughout southern France and northern Italy. Within a generation the Church felt it very profoundly as a threat and took every kind of measure against it. The Cathars wished ostensibly nothing more than a reform of Christianity; like puritans of all times—*cathar* indeed means "pure"—they were presumably sober and self-righteous. The perfecti among them—the monk-

[34] Ladner, "*Homo Viator*," pp. 255–256.

like initiates of the sect—practiced an elaborate abstinence from fleshly indulgences. The threat they posed was not in their asceticism, but in their hatred of matter. To them matter was inherently evil; it was created by the devil, and the devil was even seen by some of the Cathars as a universal force opposed to God. This belief made them see the world and the body as an unholy prison which housed the pure soul. Hence the soul's only object must be to flee all entanglements with matter and to free itself of the body. To them the worst of crimes was pro-creation, because it imprisoned another good soul in another evil body; hence they believed that the race should be allowed to become extinct. And at the extreme of their alienation from the material world was their occasional practice of the *endura*, ritual suicide by starvation. All these beliefs led the Cathars very far from orthodoxy. Because they believed matter is evil, they could not say the Mass in the prescribed way, for bread and wine are material things. They did not even recite the Lord's Prayer without the substitution "give us this day our supersubstantial bread." They could not accept the doctrine of the Incarnation, could not venerate the Virgin Mary, could not believe in the resurrection of the body.[35]

Writers dealing with contempt of the world naturally had to avoid any tendency toward this heretical pessimism. Hence Pope Innocent III says in his prologue that he could as easily write a corresponding treatise on the dignity of human nature; and Saint Bernard[36] begins by reminding us that man is made in the image of God. Writers on contempt of the world all argue that the world and the body are corrupted, transitory, and in-

[35] On the Cathars, see Steven Runciman, *The Medieval Manichee: A Study of the Christian Dualist Heresy* (Cambridge, Eng., 1960), pp. 116–170; Jeffrey Burton Russell, *Dissent and Reform in the Early Middle Ages* (Berkeley and Los Angeles, 1965), pp. 188–229. For recent studies, see Daniel Walther, "A Survey of Recent Research on the Albigensian Cathari," *Church History*, XXXIV (1965), 146–177.

[36] *PL* 184:485–486. The treatises of Innocent III and Bernard were intended to be or were actually accompanied by treatises on the dignity of man (see Lewis W. Spitz, "Man on This Isthmus," in *Luther for an Ecumenical Age*, ed. Carl S. Meyer [Saint Louis and London, 1967], pp. 23–66).

firm; but they never suggest that the body is inherently evil. They argue that human society is in a sorry state; but their corollary is that it needs to be improved, never that it should be abandoned or that the race should be allowed to die out. They argue that human life is full of misery, is transitory and vain; but they never suggest that there is an abstract principle of evil in the universe. They condemn abuses; but they never condemn earthly existence.

Second, contempt of the world itself really betrays and reflects the new worldliness of the twelfth century. I hope I will not be thought a paradox-monger if I say flatly that writers on contempt of the world only *seem* to represent man as desirably alienated from worldly things. Their attention is, first of all, focused wholly on this world. They may sound weary, disillusioned, even despairing; but they all betray a tacit interest in and attraction to the world. They tell us that all things pass away, that the great men and the illustrious civilizations of the past are turned to dust, that our little goals of pleasure, property, or reputation are mere vanities, like foam, like bubbles. But they are certainly not indifferent to those human wishes. They see them all in minute detail, can become anecdotal and specific: the old man, says Pope Innocent, makes silly gestures, his teeth decay, his nose runs, his ears get stopped up with wax.[37] Moreover, when they tell us to renounce the pleasures of the world one of their favorite arguments is that those pleasures are always disappointing and do not give us real satisfaction; riches breed anxiety, sexual gratification breeds desire anew, honors and reputation make men haughty and despised or envious and discontent.

In contempt of the world, then, we have a special style of worldliness. But it is very carefully boxed in. When these writers say that man is fallen and wretched they must be careful never to suggest that he was created evil or that his body is evil; hence they must add that he was created good and has dignity. But then they recoil from their own worldly attraction and remind themselves that the world is vanity and disappoint-

[37] *De miseria,* I, x.

ment. Every time they focus on the world, or comb Scriptures for its comments on the world, they are going to find something that will suggest otherworldly considerations. There is, they seem to feel, some important truth to be learned from contemplating the world itself, though (as it turns out) it is the old truth of Christian ascetic morality expressed with a new violence and with a new particularity. Still, in finding that truth they have already turned their thoughts to the world.

There is a whole phase of my topic which I must slight for want of time: the human body. Already in medieval thought the body and the world are associated, and man's lesser analogical world is called a microcosm.[38] To the Cathars, the body itself, composed of matter, was evil. To writers on contempt of the world it was not evil but vile. Pope Innocent reminds us in minute detail of our bodily woes: sickness, age, and pain are paraded for illustration. He informs us that while trees give off fruit and balms, man gives off dung and urine, harbors lice and tapeworms. (Writers on the dignity of man refute the point by describing the proportionableness of the body and the utility of its functions, echoing Saint Augustine.)[39] If the world is that which stands between man and nature, the body appears to be "of the world" and is among those things we must hold in contempt. But the medievals are always aware that we are connected to our bodies. They know that the "first movements of sense" are of the flesh and, with the world and the devil, a source of temptation; but they know, too, that sense energizes our actions, so that we can turn bodily impulses to good account by directing wrath against evil and desire toward God.[40] Their alienation from the body repeats in little their alienation from the world. They must not say the body is evil; but if they

[38] See Charles S. Singleton, "The Poet's Number at the Center," *MLN*, LXXX (1965), 8–9 and n. 6.

[39] See esp. Gianozzo Manetti, *De dignitate et excellentia hominis* (Basel, 1532), Bk. 4; Trinkaus, *Adversity's Nobleman*, pp. 72–76.

[40] See e.g., Saint Augustine, *De Genesi ad litteram* (PL 34:436–437). The two concupiscences, good and evil, are the basis of Augustine's no-

say it is beautiful and proportionable and reflects the wisdom tion of the two cities.

of its Creator, they must remind themselves that it is corrupted and vile. Anatomical studies of the Renaissance repeat this ambivalence toward the body by making the dissector an aproned butcher at a table while the professor of anatomy remains a robed figure on a dais, using words, not knives. The idealized sculpture of the Renaissance puts the body at a remove from actuality, making it an object to contemplate rather than a prison or mansion for the soul; and in mannerism we have a distortion of the body which hovers somewhere between the ideal and the grotesque. The body, men know, will end in death; throughout Europe in the fifteenth, sixteenth, and seventeenth centuries everywhere are found representations of dancing skeletons which leer at the living and mock them.

II

It can be objected that what I am proposing is dreadfully abstract, that I have extrapolated an intellectual construct from medieval writings and imposed it upon medieval culture. So far that is what I have done; but it is not at all what I want to do. On the contrary, I would like best to call attention away from abstractions like "secular feeling" and "worldliness" and "alienation" to something concrete, simple, and factual. I would like to find out from what the medievals wrote what it was they thought and felt. But of this we can never expect more than a glimpse. Think what we might discover if we could be set down even for a day in the fourteenth century, if we could see how people looked and talked, know how it felt *then* to read a work on contempt of the world; if we could walk the streets of a town and catch the spirit of the times, just as we now catch in Los Angeles or Rome or Copenhagen the distinctive spirit of each place.

I am going to try another way of accomplishing something at least faintly like this. I am going to put aside the tools I have been using—the terms and distinctions, the topoi, the unit ideas—and take from one poem a passage that seems to illustrate world-alienation. That poem was written in England during the late fourteenth century; it is the romance *Sir Gawain and the Green Knight*. The work is never associated with the Renaissance, and I choose it partly because it is so generally thought "medieval." The single manuscript of it passed through the hands of two Elizabethan collectors and came to rest on the shelves of the British Museum, to remain unpublished for almost 400 years. Discovered in the early nineteenth century, it attracted little attention as a work of art until the twentieth century. We might say we of the twentieth century invented it, that is, we conceived an idea of what to look for in it. And it may be, although I am not sure anyone has ever said so, that what has drawn it into our cultural life is its power to fulfill our expectations, its power to speak to us as many works of that age do not. Perhaps this power comes from a feeling about life in the poem which is really new, really postmedieval. How this power got into a poem written in the west Midlands of England late in the fourteenth century, I do not know. It came in part, I believe, from the kind of ideas and attitudes I have been describing; but I expect that it really came from the romances, and that this feeling in the romances reflected the worldly and the idealistic attitudes of the knights. I would be willing to argue that humanism itself was descended from these aristocratic or chivalric attitudes, and that it was largely an attempt by middle-class intellectuals to emulate them. But all of that is another problem.

The passage I focus on is the one where Sir Gawain rides through a wilderness seeking the mysterious adversary who will presumably chop off his head with an ax. He rides, we are told, "Fer floten fro his frendez fremedly"[41]—like a stranger or alien, wandered afar from his friends—and he is surrounded now at every turn by enemies (unless, the author comments, they are illusions). Sometimes (the poet says) Sir Gawain fights with dragons, sometimes with wolves, sometimes with trolls that live in the crags and sometimes with bulls and bears, and

[41] Line 714; quoted from *Sir Gawain and the Green Knight*, ed. J. R. R. Tolkien and E. V. Gordon, 2d ed., rev. Norman Davis (Oxford, 1968).

at other times with giants; from all these terrors he is saved (so the text states) because he has bravery and endurance *and* because he serves God.

But, the poet adds, winter was worse than his battles with these monsters. Cold, clear water falls out of the clouds and freezes in midair. Almost dead from the chill, Gawain sleeps in his armor, on bare rocks. The passage is a very powerful one, not just for its close, novelistic detail and its almost surreal selection of images, but for the texture of the verse, the variety of its movement, its clustering of harsh and clattering consonants, and its bleak repetition of vowels:

For werre [strife] wrathed hym not so much þat wynter nas wors,
When þe colde cler water fro þe cloudez schadde,
And fres [froze] er hit falle myȝt to þe fale [pale] erþe;
Ner slayn wyth þe slete he sleped in his yrnes [armor]
Mo nyȝteȝ þen innoghe in naked rokkez,
Þer as claterande fro þe crest þe colde borne [stream] rennez,
And henged heȝe ouer his hede in hard iisse-ikkles.   (726 732)

Most remarkable is the tactile nature of the images; it is something unusual in medieval literature for an author to make us so aware of cold metal, hard rocks, damp sleet, icicles. But the passage does more than describe another chilly trip through England; it figures the removal of the knight-errant from the world. He wanders aimlessly in a wilderness, in direct confrontation with nature and the supernatural. The figure is not so extreme as the "poor naked wretches" of *King Lear*; but nothing of the world is left to Sir Gawain except his armor, and we are made to feel the cold even penetrating that. The animals he fights off, according to one critic,[42] represent sins; but if they do, they represent them as dangers, not actualities, as what the medievals would have called the "first movements of sense" or what we might call id impulses. In his alienation from the world Sir Gawain comes into direct confrontation with external nature and (perhaps) with his own animal side, his fallen nature. He endures the adventure through courage and faith.

[42] Hans Schnyder, *Sir Gawain and the Green Knight: An Essay in Interpretation*, Cooper Monographs, 6 (Bern, 1961), pp. 51–53.

In the next stanza he rides into a deep forest. Mournful birds perched on bare twigs chirp piteously from the cold. The knight is, we are reminded, all by himself: "mon al hym one" (749). He prays aloud for "sum herber" (some shelter) where he might hear the Christmas Mass. And at once, no sooner than the prayer is off his lips, he sees a "won" (habitation) with a moat around it; it stands on a knoll, over a lawn, under the boughs of massive trees; and it is, we are informed, the most beautiful castle that any knight ever owned. It has a park all about it with a spiked fence; and the castle itself "shimmered and shone" through the oaks. It is described in such detail that it can be dated: it is in the architectural fashion of the late fourteenth century.[43] A brand-new castle, only just built in the author's lifetime, and it turns up in the old days of King Arthur, as the answer to a prayer! From its moat a wall of huge stones rises up, fortified under its battlements "in the best style." It has handsome turrets with loophole windows. Inside is a high "hall" with towers and ornamental pinnacles having craftily carved tops; on the roof chalk-white chimneys and painted pinnacles are scattered about. At first the castle had been called by the plain Old English word "won" (habitation) and then "holde" (fortified place); only once is it called a "castel," a Norman-French word. But now, when it is described in detail, we are given a whole flood of French words of such delicate connotations that it is possible to argue whether they are synonyms or are meant to denote minute architectural distinctions. What, for example, was the difference between a filiole and a pinnacle? Such is the language that conoisseurs talk. Nothing could be more worldly; the description reflects both in content and in language that most mundane of tendencies, the interest in fads. And the fad involved is opulent, ornamental, and indisputably high class. For indeed the castle *is* the world; the knight passes from wilderness to civilization just as soon as he knows it is there, this *won* or *holde* that will shelter him. I do not suppose anyone has ever read the passage without an extraordinary sense of relief and joy. But this reaction is something more than the

[43] See *Sir Gawain*, ed. Tolkien and Gordon, pp. 99, n. to 1. 794.

homely pleasure of coming in out of the cold: it is the pleasure
of anticipating shelter and comfort when we see it available; it
is that rush of hopeful delight any American would feel if he
were to discover far off in the distance (as, alas, one never does)
a luxurious hotel while driving across Kansas. And this rush of
joy, this delight in comfort and in safety, is what worldliness
really is.

It may be suspected that I am making the castle into a symbol
of the world. That is exactly what I am doing. The notion is
polemical, for one critic thinks it stands for the other world,
another that it is a symbol of the Heavenly City;[44] the rest do
not think it is a symbol at all. But first let us decide what we
mean by a symbol. The castle is after all very particular; we are
told all about its moat, its pinnacles, its chimneys. In it, Gawain
is entertained by a charming ironist, Bercilak, and by his beautiful wife. He is given excellent meals, is furnished with rich
robes and a mantle lined with ermine, is even provided a private
chamber to sleep in and a bed hung with silk on gold rings. It
is all overdecorated, even allowing for the usual superlatives of
romance; and to the extent that the description is idealized or
(as we should now say) "romantic," it is suspiciously unreal.
The newness of the place, the author's awed tone, the prodigious catalogue of luxuries—all these make us feel that here is no
ordinary castle. It is described with a slyboots realism that makes
it seem a caricature, a supercastle, perhaps a metacastle. If the
castle symbolizes the world it does so because real castles really
did epitomize the world, really were made objects that protected man from nature, and were of course walled towns. It
was just this meaning, which castles really had, that made them
so readily available as symbols: the author of *Piers Plowman*
figures the world as a tower in a wilderness, and a later drama-
tist shows earthly life as a "castle of perseverence." Hence the
author did not need to con over the interpreters of the Bible for
a precedent. It is the very castle-ness of the castle which gives

---

[44] Mother Angela Carson, "Morgain La Fée as the Principle of Unity
in *Gawain and the Green Knight*," *MLQ*, XXIII (1962), 3–16; Schnyder, *Sir Gawain*, pp. 55–57.

it a symbolical meaning. Moreover, this pairing of the castle up high on its knoll against the rough wilderness through which the hero has passed suggests a common motif in medieval and Renaissance art: the background landscape in which a wilderness on one side is juxtaposed against a civilized town or citadel on the other. And this motif, as Erwin Panofsky has shown,[45] echoed common ideas of world history, suggesting sometimes the progress of civilization from a harsh primitive state, sometimes its decadence from a golden age.

But is our castle to be viewed as a civilized world or a decadent one? My question is partly answered by a curious line that occurs at the end of the description. The poet tells us that there were so many pinnacles on the castle's embrasures "Þat pared out of papure purely hit semed" (802) (that it seemed as if it were cut out of paper). This image of a paper castle seems to undercut everything that has gone before; it seems to suggest that, in spite of its apparent magnificence, it is a mere house of cards, fragile and illusory. What is more, castles cut out of paper, so Professor Ackerman has discovered,[46] really existed in the fourteenth century. At elaborate feasts the main dishes were served with a paper cover over them cut in an elaborate design to simulate a castle. Since Chaucer's Parson inveighs against this practice when discussing "pride of the table,"[47] we can assume that moralists viewed it as overly luxurious and self-indulgent. The line suggests, therefore, that the world of the castle has about it something not merely unsubstantial and frail but something morally questionable. And that is, as everybody knows, the kind of world the castle turns out to be.

What happens in the castle bears me out. The hero is tempted, is indeed tempted three times, like Adam and Christ. And he succumbs, on the third try, by accepting a magic girdle which will save his life. Later he is told that "loving his life" was his weakness. Just why it was a failing, and how serious that failing

[45] *Studies in Iconology: Humanistic Themes in the Art of the Renaissance*, repr. (New York, 1962), chap. 2, esp. pp. 64–65.

[46] Robert W. Ackerman, " 'Pared Out of Paper': *Gawain* 802 and *Purity* 1408," *JEGP*, LVI (1957), 410–417.

[47] *Canterbury Tales*, X, 444.

is, need not concern us; I have had my say about the matter elsewhere.[48] The passage shows us a real feeling, at least one poet's feeling, about the world. When the knight is alienated, in direct confrontation with nature, he needs shelter and food; moreover, as a Christian, he must return to the world before he can hear Mass, for the Mass requires an altar, bread and wine, and a priest. But when the world of the castle appears, and as the hero comes to be so richly and amusingly at home there, it tempts him with its lures; and in some slight measure he succumbs to them by "loving his life."

There is something else we must notice. In the end, Gawain—in the teeth of his own shame—is accepted back at court amidst laughter and good cheer. He is still the best of knights, and while he wears the girdle in token of his shame his fellows adopt a similar baldric to commemorate his success. His whole journey seems viewed as a metaphor of worldly life; when he starts out on his return journey we are told "Wylde wayez in þe worlde Wowen [Gawain] now rydez" (2479). After this experience Gawain will presumably see the world in a truer perspective and will keep a certain alienation which he had lost by loving his own life. But it is all seen in a very gamelike spirit. The Round Table returns to its merriment, and the author, good-humored, draws us away from the ancient world of Camelot back into fourteenth-century England. Every reader would have understood that worldliness is a danger, that alienation from it is a safe position, that the ultimate world-alienation of eternity is safest of all; but in fact what the poem demonstrates is that the world cannot ever be wholly escaped, except in death. And this idea is viewed in a spirit of amused irony.

At the beginning of this essay we looked briefly at another moment of world-alienation in fourteenth-century English literature: the moment when Troilus looks down on the earth from the eighth sphere and begins to despise the world. That is a tragic, not a comic ending. It could be argued that it is really a happy ending, since the hero is released from life's pain and a just order is seen in the universe; but then the same could be

[48] Howard, *Three Temptations*, pp. 223–241.

said of *Hamlet* or *King Lear*. In their last moments tragic heroes are all going to learn this lesson about the world. But tragedy, whether Chaucer's or Shakespeare's, is experienced from the vantage point of worldliness, and what we come away with is a wisdom that is sad to have to know. I am ready to argue that this is Christian tragedy, that Christian tragedy is about the world and that we return from it with a new and chastened understanding of what life in the world is about.[49] This worldliness in Chaucer's *Troilus* has been the subject of sharp controversy; there is a whole school of thought which would have us believe that Chaucer wrote his work for no other reason than to illustrate the vanity of earthly loves. But even if that is true, he was himself lured by the world into making it seem, however fleeting, a profoundly beautiful thing. Compare the dreary tragedies of Chaucer's *Monk's Tale* and one sees at once what they lack; their stories are rehearsed in bare-bones abstract and their drab moral is uncompelling and dispirited. Turn to the *Troilus* and the same moral bursts upon us in its full truth and sadness because the world of the story has been made to live, to lure us into its mutable wonder.

The ending of the *Troilus* shares with the ending of *Sir Gawain* an ambivalent view of the world; the world is a thing of beauty, but inferior in a hierarchical Christian scheme. A while ago I tried to describe the world-alienation of the twelfth century, the boxed-in system of ideas which could be discerned in writings on contempt of the world. What I think I see in these two passages is something very similar, but now it has seeped into men's feelings about life and the world; it has be-

[49] The importance of "the world" as a controlling image in the Elizabethan theater has only lately been understood. It was no mistake that Elizabethan theaters themselves bore names like the Globe; indeed the theaters were in effect round as the earth is. See Thomas B. Stroup, *Microcosmos: The Shape of the Elizabethan Play* (Lexington, Ky., 1965); Frances A. Yates, *The Art of Memory* (Chicago, 1966), pp. 321–367; Frances A. Yates, *Theatre of the World* (Chicago, 1969); Jackson I. Cope, "The Rediscovery of Anti-Form in Renaissance Drama," *Comparative Drama*, I (1967), 155–171, expanded in *The Theatre and the Dream* (Baltimore and London, 1973).

come an unthinking response to the world. What had been a system of intellectual checks and balances now appears as an ambiguity felt about life itself. It becomes a kind of poise. We catch somewhat the feeling of that poise by grasping at literary effects; we can click our tongues about the comic irony of *Sir Gawain* and the tragic irony of the *Troilus*, but it was the ambivalence and the contrarieties in their culture which made these ironies take shape. Irony now becomes a way of accommodating worldly impulses to otherworldly ideas, and so becomes an instrument of cultural change. The writers have inched their way into a new feeling about life.

This feeling about life is embodied, I believe, in the form of literary art during the period, at least of narrative art: it becomes a creation of worlds. Certainly in *Troilus* Chaucer was at pains to build up in the utmost detail a full picture of ancient Troy, that doomed city in the last days before its fall; he uses what lore he knew—of pagan gods, temples, and rites—plus much anachronistic detail in order to immerse us in that world. Similarly, *Sir Gawain* depicts through elaborate descriptions the world of Camelot in the days of Arthur. Both authors begin by underscoring the historical distance of their settings, reminding the reader that it is from tradition and book learning that they have their stories; both also draw the reader away from this created world at the end, joining him in the present day as the time duration of the story recedes into time past. Moreover, both authors make a great to-do of their own presence as narrators; they refer to themselves, omit material and summarize, comment on the action, and thus engaging themselves with the reader seem alternately to become immersed in their stories and to hover about them at an ironic distance, from which they can be amused or skeptical (like the Gawain poet) or even (like Chaucer) pitying, regretful, envious, awed, chastened, and enlightened.

This possibility of the author's withdrawal from the world of his story corresponds to and perhaps imitates the hero's alienation; the alienation of hero and of author confers perspective and wisdom. Hence the writer's final withdrawal from his cre-

ated world is a return to the real world in which he communes
directly with his readers. Direct confrontation with the reader,
as it becomes an element of narrative art, makes storytelling itself a deliberate act of world-alienation first into a relationship
with an imagined reader, then into a fictive antiworld, then
back to the world of readers and books where the voyage becomes an illumination. The writer becomes a voyager; thus
Chaucer can address the reader:

> Owt of thise blake wawes [waves] for to saylle,
> O wynd, o wynd, the weder gynneth clere;
> For in this see the boot hath swych travaylle,
> Of my connyng, that unneth [with difficulty] I it steere.
> This see clepe [call] I the tempestous matere
> Of disespeir that Troilus was inne . . .   (II,1–6)

We, his readers, as we engage ourselves with him, move with
him into those imagined worlds and, at the last, return with him,
enlightened, to the quotidian world of pen and paper, bound
volumes, eyeglasses.[50] Chaucer's *Troilus* ends with an epilogue
and a concluding prayer; but it also ends with the author fussing
out loud about getting his work copied accurately, worrying
out loud about its place in a literary tradition, commending his
work to some contemporary fellow writers. In the very pro-
foundest sense, this fictive antiworld is a world made out of
paper. And what do we return with? A worldly experience, an
intellectual grasp of its nature, the aesthetic pleasure of getting
home safe, and the conviction that the enterprise confers spiritual advantages. This is the world-alienation of all those who
shuffle papers; and in it is the perennial character of humanism.

---

[50] It must be remembered that this private world of readers was itself a brave new one. Paper (which made reproduction of books cheap-
er and easier) was not introduced in Europe until the twelfth century;
eyeglasses were invented in the thirteenth. Owning bound volumes
and reading them by oneself was still a new experience in the fourteenth century; the possibility of doing so (which created the need for
the printing press) was an essential ingredient in the humanists' *vita soli-
taria*.

III

The writer with a thesis such as mine should by rights shuffle through his notes and produce more works and authors. If there were world enough and time, I would bring Petrarch from the wings and parade him as the author of a *de contemptu mundi* and a work about the solitary life, quote passages from his letters in which he equates learning and voyaging, follow him up Mont Ventoux. I would bring forth Rabelais, who figures his proposed new world as a monastery, and Montaigne, who centers his attention on the little world he knows best, himself. I would assign roles to Poggio, Ficino, Erasmus, More.

Instead, I will raise two speculative questions.

First: If there had been a "search for the world" after the twelfth century, was the search a success? My answer is equivocal. It was a success because all the arguments and rebuttals, and the emotions vested in them, generated a tension that gives to the period its ineluctable excitement. This electric quality of the age is what I find wanting in the familiar explanatory models applied to it, in "rebirth," thesis and antithesis, decline and rise; they grind so slowly, they are so measured and so stately. I propose "search" (but not "quest") as a model because, if you contemplate the experience of searching—after a fact, a library book, the button off your shirt—what characterizes every search is the niggling doubt that it is worth the trouble. We may go on searching with a dogged listlessness or with a certain zest, but we know all along that there *must* be better things to do. Who has not had, while poking for some lost object under a chair, a momentary sense of worldly vanity? That tension is the very essence of searching. The period from the twelfth to the seventeenth century successfully kept up such a search for the world. But I do not know any moment when we can say men of that time succeeded in finding it.

It may be thought that the discovery of the New World was an exception. But that is not so. As soon as men understood that there was a fourth continent they called it the New World; of course they were using *world* in its geographical sense as that part of the earth providentially given to man as a habitation. Hence they projected upon the New World their own imaginings; as O'Gorman shows, they invented it.[51] They saw it (1) as a physical entity—a continent—and (2) as a spiritual entity able to fulfill a providential mission; they invented it with a body and a soul, in their own image. They then projected upon the New World hopes and fantasies for a natural order, better than the civilized one they traditionally held in contempt. In these utopian fantasies they were really expressing their contempt for the world they knew; such dreams, Saint Thomas More concluded in the *Utopia*, were more to be desired than expected. And in another mood they projected upon the New World not their hopes but their fears; they imagined it the abode of "anthropophagi, and men whose heads do grow beneath their shoulders."

Neither did Renaissance men find the world in classical antiquity. From their "discovery" of the ancient world we normally date the rise of humanism; but in fact—as with the "new world"—they invented the ancient world. Take, for example, the ancient Greeks. They were, we now know, not at all " classical" but turbulent, litigious, quarrelsome. The golden mean is a noble ideal, but it was no more practiced by them than equality is by us; on the contrary, it was the ideal needed by a civilization that had the most violent passions in all phases of experience. In their extravagance and turbulence the ancient Greeks were probably more like modern Greeks than anything else. It is very nearly symbolic that they painted their statues and buildings in gaudy colors, so that the classical purity of conception and execution we admire would have seemed to them drab and incomplete. Renaissance men had some notion of this, for they saw the Greeks through Roman eyes.[52] But it

[51] Edmundo O'Gorman, *The Invention of America: An Inquiry into the Historical Meaning of the New World and the Meaning of Its History* (Bloomington, Ind., 1961), esp. pp. 138–141.

[52] See T. J. B. Spencer, " 'Greeks' and 'Merrygreeks': A Background to *Timon of Athens* and *Troilus and Cressida*," in *Essays on Shakespeare and Elizabethan Drama in Honor of Hardin Craig*, ed. Richard Hosley (Columbia, Mo., 1962), pp. 223–233.

was not what interested them. Humanism extrapolated from the ancient world what it most needed and wanted: a vision of purity in aesthetics, Latinity, and art; of idealism in philosophy; of "humane" letters; and of an ethics centered upon man. The ancient world the humanists liked was truly a world made out of paper: a world based on texts, conceived by those who studied and edited those texts and wrote about them in a great and loving act of the imagination. Their imaginative re-creation invented a world more noble and more "classical" than the great dead civilization that inspired it. But it was not a world in which they could be comfortable, for it had existed before the time of Christ; like their medieval ancestors, they had to allegorize it.[53]

My other question is: Does the search end? It can be argued that it ends with the Enlightenment, but I believe its more decisive ending occurs in the nineteenth century. It ends only when Christian eschatology becomes supplanted by an idea of infinite process operating in history and the universe. Given this idea, the world can no longer be felt as a duration from which men will be freed into another life. And if the world is part of a process stretching infinitely forward and backward in time, it cannot be renounced. Man "finds" the world, if at all, just at this moment when there is no longer any ideological reason to renounce it.[54] But it is one of the ironies of history that exactly then, when the world becomes man's permanent abode, the *idea* of the world is shaken. It is shaken by technology. The legitimate areas of worldly attention had always been the objectives of human endeavor and manipulation; beginning in the nineteenth century an improved technology turned the old objectives into actualities. I will give the most obvious example. The "search for the world" included a search after just government by just rulers; warfare in a just cause was traditionally one means to establish such a government. But when technology

[53] Don Cameron Allen, *Mysteriously Meant: The Rediscovery of Pagan Symbolism and Allegorical Interpretation in the Renaissance* (Baltimore, 1970).

[54] See Hannah Arendt, *Between Past and Present* (New York, 1961), pp. 63–75.

applied to warfare develops weapons of infinite destruction, the old ideal of power used in the service of justice has to be called into question; man is left to confront his own motives. Another example may be found in the traditional idea that reputation or fame is a just reward for worldly accomplishments, a measure of immortality in the successive stream of human lives. Technology applied to the making of reputation has discovered ways to manipulate public opinion, and the result is demoralization of the 1984 variety, or somber jargon about "images," or cynicism about the justice of reputations; man is left to contemplate the gap between what he is thought to be and what he is. The success of technology in realizing the ancient objectives of worldliness has thus turned man back upon himself. This confrontation with ourselves is not necessarily a bad thing, and it is not to be blamed on technology or the world. If it is our species of world-alienation, it is alienation from a traditional idea of the world. I am skeptical that we are more alienated from the world itself than men of former times; for all our freeways and our air travel, even our flights into space, most people seem no less in touch with the world of things than men were in previous ages. What we are alien to is an idea of the world appropriate to the actual world we experience and a feeling for ourselves adequate to our uses of technology in making and maintaining a world. Since Marx introduced into social thought the concept of self-alienation, alienation has everywhere been viewed as an evil; but it need not be so, and was not so even in Hegel. For it is only through mind in its abstraction from the world that we can understand the world and only in death that we can be fully alienated from it. Without mind we must be thrown utterly upon the world; and those who belong utterly to the world are aliens unto themselves.

THE GENTLEMAN IN RENAISSANCE ITALY: STRAINS OF ISOLATION IN THE BODY POLITIC

Lauro Martines

THERE ARE moments in history when the thrust of political power is such that it affords men few choices. They are either with the dominant wave or against it. To be different is almost akin to dropping out of the historical process.

The Renaissance—a great moment for the fortunes of power —made exhausting demands on the human spirit, particularly so in the sixteenth century. Personal integrity must have been doubly rare then. The principal historical stances were two, those of the exile and the gentleman. The gentleman stood for order, authority, privilege, and tradition. His badge was a particular grace and carriage. The exile, whether political or religious, stood for change of some kind, for a reshuffling of the forces and perceptions associated with the institutional establishment. While the one conformed, the other was a critic, an outsider, or at times a rebel. The gentleman conformed par excellence to the thrust of power; he ranged himself on the side that, at least initially, was strongest. In his supreme personification—and it is in this sense that I use the word *gentleman* in this essay—he served as counselor to the prince. He was one of the prince's most trusted servants: a courtier (*cortegiano*) or a governor.[1]

---

[1] As in Sir Thomas Elyot's use of the word in his *Boke Named the Governour* (1531).

The critic—the breath of discontent—was banished or voluntarily withdrew from the field. If his exile was self-imposed, he literally fled or carefully retreated into a prudent silence. He was often compelled to be an observer, but his condition guaranteed that he could not be indifferent.

Between the two roles of exile in forlorn absence and gentleman in serviceable presence there was movement or ambiguity, at times a startling and fruitful ambiguity. Machiavelli, who longed for a personal alliance with power, was in exile when he wrote *The Prince*. His most formidable intellectual opponent, Francesco Guicciardini, was a gentleman: a jurist, an adviser to Medici princes, and governor of Modena, Reggio, and finally of all Romagna. An ex-republican, Giucciardini was hated by the republican group in Florence but at the end of his life fell under the suspicion of his Medici patrons. One of the shrewdest critics of the age, Erasmus, refused to be a counselor to popes and princes. Suspected or hated by Protestant and Catholic alike, he lived far from his native ground, a voluntary exile who felt that he belonged to Europe and Christianity, rather than to one place or one church.

Often in sixteenth-century Europe the individual could not call his conscience his own. Men got at it by spying on him, by opening his letters, grilling him, rifling his notes, or by putting him on the rack. The whole man had to belong to one persuasion or another: to the prince or to the prince's enemies, to Christ or the Antichrist. Machiavelli, Giucciardini, More, Servetus, and Montaigne were to see or to suffer this dilemma in different ways. John Calvin, himself an exile, would have turned against the apostate and fugitive, Bernardino Occhino, ex-general of the order of Capuchins, if Occhino's views had been defective on the nature of the Trinity. Exiles thus dreamed of their own establishment where they, ironically, would then put on some of the trappings of the gentleman.

Exiles and gentleman, critics and conformists, raged or quarreled from high moral principles. There was no end to the flow of indignation and fine words. When dissenters were burned or drowned or mutilated for their views, the one thing we can be sure of is that each side ardently believed that its convictions made for a better life, material, spiritual, and social.

The pervasive effects of political power in Renaissance Europe may best be studied by fixing our attention on the Italian peninsula. Modern political exile has its beginnings there and it is there that the ideal of the Renaissance gentleman is first fully delineated.

Ever since the twelfth century the cities of Italy had exhibited intense energies and a genius for politics. When the imperial hold over the peninsula was loosened, owing partly to the conflict between Church and empire, the great Italian communes reached out and avidly grabbed for self-government. Before the year 1200 Milan, Florence, Pisa, Genoa, and some of the other major communes were already running their own affairs. They were miniature states. They had elaborate constitutions, citizen armies, parliaments, a body of statutory law, and a diplomacy. They soon had subject towns and territories.

The thirteenth century brought a host of urgent problems, the foremost of them growing out of one fundamental question: Were Italian cities to be ruled by oligarchies or was government to have a more ample and flexible social base?[2] A booming economy and the rising claims of new men put this question ahead of everything else. The cities were in trouble. Walled in and laid out in narrow streets, they were the ideal nurseries for political passion. Men were drawn into tight-knit associations: guilds, fraternities, military societies, and neighborhood companies. They armed themselves. They made and broke alliances. The richest and most ambitious citizens built towers and houses that looked like fortresses.

In the course of the thirteenth century, there ensued the most violent sort of political conflict. Civil war and the toppling of communal governments became everyday occurrences. When compromise was achieved, it was nearly always uncertain and

[2] This theme is developed in Lauro Martines, "Political Conflict in the Italian City States," *Government and Opposition: A Quarterly of Comparative Politics*, III (Winter, 1968), 69–91.

short-lived. Not infrequently the sides in conflict hankered for the physical elimination of political opponents. Exile and capital punishment became the common penalties. Men were often banished by the hundreds. On occasion, anticipating defeat, they fled noisily from the city or withdrew into exile quietly and almost secretly. Nearly all the major cities of northern and central Italy—Padua, Milan, Genoa, Pisa, Florence, Siena, and so on—were subject to sudden reversals of this type. By the fifteenth century exile was an old practice in Italy. Much, however had changed.

During the classical age of the commune, the thirteenth century, contending factions and groups were more evenly balanced. A larger sector of the population was drawn into the struggles, with the result that men in exile were often able to set up governments in exile. In the age of the Renaissance, criticism of the political establishment fell off sharply; it was less outspoken and more intellectualized; it tended to be increasingly isolated; and its effects were less likely to be turned into physical violence because the power of the establishment was now too great. The social struggles of the thirteenth century had long since been resolved. Signorial government (i.e., one-man rule) had triumphed in most cities. The exceptions (Siena, Lucca, Genoa) had been taken over by oligarchies. Confronted by a more integrated and powerful public authority, the exile or political critic of Renaissance times assumed more risks and faced more dangers.

The widespread use of exile reveals that governments were not prepared to suffer much criticism or opposition. Voluntary exile (e.g., that of Giannozzo Manetti, the humanist) was often chosen because the individual in question was afraid; at times it also signaled his keen discomfort in an isolation so intense that he could no longer bear his native ground. A tradition of tolerance was not developed. Public authority, even in the postcommunal age, persisted in feeling vulnerable. Politics was not so organized as to admit dissent; the dissenter was as likely as not to be looked upon as a criminal. Dissent became something very much like treason and Roman law was cleverly used to help establish this view.[3] Seldom, even in Florence and Venice, the leading oligarchies, was the political elite prepared to allow open debate to go on in the great legislative councils.

In this atmosphere, the political critic could not avoid carrying the effects of strain into his way of seeing and assessing events. Only in exile might he succeed in throwing off part of what weighed on him and thereby realize a modicum of liberation. Yet some tension always remained. For this reason the most acute political observers of the period betray not only a dark streak (accountable on other grounds) but also a note of exaggeration, an exaggerated view of clarity or vice, and occasionally even a mad note. Machiavelli, Giannotti, Varchi, and Guicciardini himself, who was bewitched by the force and distortions of ambition for political honors and power, were all prone to exaggerate.

The condition of the exile made possible the world of the gentleman. Not that one bred the other, but the ideal of the Renaissance gentleman (the courtier, the adviser to princes) could not be realized save in a setting where the power of the prince (or of the oligarchy) was absolute or nearly so. In such a setting the executive authority had no trouble silencing dissent or driving it into exile.

The ideal of the Renaissance gentleman was first fully described by a nobleman from Mantua, Baldasare Castiglione, in *Il Libro del Cortegiano* (The Book of the Courtier),[4] the age's most famous work of this genre. Conceived and written in Urbino and Rome between 1513 and 1518, the book was not published until 1528 and then swiftly went through numerous editions. Something in it immediately struck the upper-class reading public, some happy self-image and a certain drawing together of scattered or half-formed wishes.

Set in the court of a prince, the palace at Urbino, and divided

---

[3] See especially C. Ghisalberti, "Sulla teoria dei delitti di lesa maestá nel diritto comune," *Archivio giuridico*, CXLIX (1955), 100–179.

[4] I shall be relying on Bruno Maier's edition of *Il Libro del Cortegiano* (Torino, 1955) and drawing on the English translation by Charles S. Singleton (New York: Anchor Books, 1959).

into four parts, the book is presented in the form of a conversation. The participants are gentlemen and ladies of the court, most of them from north and central Italy. With two or three exceptions, all come from the nobility or urban aristocracy. In the opening pages of the dialogue, we find them casting around for a subject of conversation. Considering and then rejecting more frivolous topics, they finally agree to talk about the ideal or perfect courtier. With some digressions, the discussion goes on for four evenings. The interlocutors gradually draw a picture of the ideal courtier, though with no particular rigor or design in their discourse. Let us look at the finished portrait.[5]

The courtier should be born of noble blood and have "beauty of countenance" and a graceful carriage. Thoroughly schooled in Latin and Greek, he is to be at home with the *studia humaniora*: rhetoric, poetry, history, and moral philosophy. He should be conversant with the mysteries of painting and sculpture. In addition to writing verse skillfully, he should become an expert musician, dancer, and gamesman. His conversation will be light, amusing, rich, or serious, as the occasion demands, and his speech, in whatever tongue it may be, pure and fluent. These qualities and accomplishments belong to his social and humanistic endowments, but his professional skills are not neglected. There is emphasis on his dedication to the profession of arms. He is expected to show mastery in handling weapons of all kinds, in riding, leaping, wrestling, hurling stones, and hunting. The value of hunting is that it helps to keep him fit for war. He combines prudence and boldness; he is a man of great versatility; he is honor bound; in war he seeks glory; in politics, and ultimately at all times, he seeks the good of his prince.

This summary of the courtier's attributes does not convey the book's richness and subtleties but it provides a working context for the following analysis.

Rather early in the discussions much emphasis is put on the element of grace (*grazia*) in the manner and all the movements of the courtier. "And it seems to me," one of the speakers observes, "that you require this in everything as that seasoning

[5] Maier edition, pp. 103–184.

[*condimento*] without which all the other properties and good qualities would be of little worth."[6] The reply is given by Count Ludovico of Canossa, the main speaker at this point in the dialogue. He holds that if the courtier is to acquire grace. "he must begin early and learn the principles from the best of teachers. . . . But having thought many times already about how this grace is acquired (leaving aside those who have it from the stars), I have found quite a universal rule . . . and that is (to speak a new word perhaps) to practice in all things a certain *sprezzatura* [nonchalance], so as to conceal all art and make whatever is done or said appear to be without effort and almost without any thought about it."[7] A few lines farther on the count also joins grace to the quality of *sprezzata desinvoltura* (a cool frankness or ease).

These key words—grace, nonchalance, and ease—express the secret of the *cortegiano* or perfect gentleman. They isolate the "seasoning" in all his actions; they sum up his manner. They also denote the qualities that make for an enormous distance between him and the great mass of Italians, at the head of whom he stands, holding a place beside the prince. His exalted place in society draws him apart and in part isolates him. He shuns "the crowd, above all the ignoble crowd."[8] When in battle, "he should discreetly withdraw from the crowd and do the outstanding and daring things in as small a company as possible and in the sight of all the noblest and most respected men in the army, and especially in the presence of and, if possible, before the very eyes of his king or the prince he is serving."[9] He is warned against wrestling, running, or jumping with peasants because he may lose, and "it is too unseemly and too ugly a thing, and quite without dignity, to see a gentleman defeated by a peasant."[10] Again, certain dances, such as those entailing quick movements and double footsteps, he is not to do in public

---

[6] *Ibid.*, pp. 120–121.
[7] *Ibid.*, pp. 123–125; Singleton translation, pp. 42–43.
[8] Maier, p. 210.
[9] *Ibid.*, pp. 200–201; Singleton, p. 99.
[10] Maier, p. 204; Singleton, p. 101.

because they are incompatible with his dignity. And finally, it is also borne in upon him that "the true stimulus to great and daring deeds in war is glory, and whosoever is moved thereto for gain or any other motive, apart from the fact that he never does anything good, deserves to be called not a gentleman but a base merchant."[11] This gibe at trade comes in a passing remark, but the entire tenor of the work necessarily makes business enterprise a lowly activity.

The courtier's distance from most men—his isolation—is much greater than these quotations suggest. Thoroughly grounded in the classics, he has already been set off from other men by his education. But the differences go deeper. He combines his grasp of Greek and Latin letters, his knowledge of painting, music, and the principles of polite conversation, with a high excellence in arms and bodily exercises. And although he qualifies as a professional soldier, his achievements in a half-dozen other areas have the effect of turning him into a man without a profession. His first loyalty is to his prince. His life is converted into a ceremony of grace, nonchalance, and ease. These are not, however, qualities to be attained in a day. Their cultivation requires a lifetime, the lifetime of a man of leisure, and they can be pursued only at the court of a prince. No merchant or banker, no professional man, no one who has ever worked with his hands, can realistically aspire to be a perfect gentleman. This dignity belongs to the few who have been schooled in the ideal: those who frequent courts and live off large estates.

Cut off from the vast body of men, the courtier lost touch with everything that was dynamic and productive in Italian society: he lost touch with its economic infrastructure. He lived by a standard of courtly dreams. Therefore he also was condemned to live in exile; but it was the exile or, rather, the isolation of the political establishment itself, severed from the revitalizing forces of the larger human community. The brilliant ideal of the Renaissance gentleman thus concealed a kind of ghostly or unreal underpinning.

We learn in Book II of Castiglione's work that the courtier's

[11] Maier, p. 160; Singleton, p. 69.

raison d'être is service to a prince. When the question is raised for the first time, one of the interlocutors observes: "I would have the courtier devote all his thoughts and force of spirit to loving and almost adoring the prince he serves above all else, devoting his every desire and habit and manner to pleasing him." The objection that these are the doings of a "noble flatterer" is denied, "for flatterers love neither their prince nor their friends, which I wish our courtier to do above all else."[12] All his political responsibilities are to the prince. The prince is the measure of things; he alone can elevate the courtier. And the courtier has no relation to the larger human or political community save through the prince. Yet it is astonishing how isolated and wispy the figure of the prince is in Castiglione's pages: he is a man scaled off from the world by a band of wicked flatterers. His isolation is all but complete. Second only to his is the isolation of the perfect courtier, for it is this gentleman's mission to break through the circle of noble toadies, to win the favor and confidence of the prince, and to convey truth and good advice to him.

Baldasare Castiglione (1478–1529) was born near Mantua, the son of a nobleman.[13] His mother was a Gonzaga. Given a humanistic education and trained in the military arts, he frequented the courts of Milan, Mantua, Urbino, and Rome, and finally the imperial court in Spain. He was present at three or four major military engagements and conducted embassies to the kings of England and France, to popes, and to the emperor Charles V. His birth, talents, and rich preparation brought brilliant commissions and honors, which in turn provided him with a commanding view of Italian and European affairs. The view was to fill him with melancholy.

A French army marched into Italy when Castiglione was sixteen years old. The relative tranquillity of the peninsula was shattered almost overnight. Shattered too was the old system of

---

[12] Maier, p. 216; Singleton, p. 110.

[13] See A. Vicinelli, *Baldesar Castiglione, il cortigiano, il letterato, il politico* (Torino, 1931); J. Cartwright, *Baldassare Castiglione* (London, 1908); and the pieces by V. Cian, listed in Maier, pp. 57–58.

military and political balances among the different Italian states. For the next forty years Italy was to be the prey and the battleground of foreign armies—French, Spanish, German, and Swiss. It is an old story. Far from drawing together to resist the invaders, Milan, Venice, and the other Italian states formed alliances against one another, as often as not with the French or the Spanish. Italian armies were defeated in the field again and again. Capital from Italian banks was used to finance foreign princes with armies in Italy. Italian field commanders served in the armies of Spain and France. Governments were overturned and states were dismembered. Italy, a land of independent sovereign states, remained utterly divided in the face of persistent foreign invasion. There was no effective leadership, no vigorous direction, no farsighted policy.[14]

The Italian writers and thinkers who lived through some of these grievous decades expressed dismay and confusion. Some turned to the systematic study of history and politics, passionately seeking clarity or "laws" in the concise example or the sententious observation. Others, as indicated by the remarkable popularity of *Orlando Furioso*, yielded to "the desire to escape reality and to create a world which was all magic and fantasy."[15] But even the toughest of contemporaries, Machiavelli and Guicciardini, occasionally linked Italy's vast legacy of adversity to a sort of freewheeling, irrational force known as *fortuna* (fortune). Quite apart from all the astrological and occult baggage of the later Middle Ages, *fortuna*, already prominent in the vocabulary of the fourteenth and fifteenth centuries,[16] was now promoted and given an ever more dominant color in the spectrum of nonhuman or antihuman historical forces.

Castiglione did not escape the tide. *Il Libro del Cortegiano* shows that he was uncommonly attuned to his times. He refers to *fortuna* and its effects. At one point he makes "fortune" the

[14] Guicciardini's *Storia d'Italia* is still in some respects the best history of the period. There is a good account in J. R. Hale, *Machiavelli and Renaissance Italy* (London, 1961).

[15] Introduction to Maier edition, p. 10.

[16] See, e.g., C. Bec, *Les marchands écrivains: affaires et humanisme à Florence, 1375–1434* (Paris, 1967).

opponent of "virtue" and at another speaks of how often "in midcourse, and sometimes near the end, *fortuna* breaks our fragile and useless designs and sometimes sinks them before the port can even be seen from afar."[17] The ills of Italy thus seem to be transferred to the analysis of individuals. It is not, however, in his tribute to the power of *fortuna* that he best reveals the direction and disasters of the age, but rather in his whole conception of the courtier and in the structure of the work itself.

The Courtier pivots on a search for perfection which, as a mode of inquiry, was a common Renaissance approach. Political reality was grim and there was a taste for getting at ideal or perfect types. Also common was the use of the dialogue as a literary form, much favored by the humanists, in imitation of admired classical writers. Castiglione's nearest model was Cicero's *De oratore*. But it must also be pointed out, as is clear, for example, from Plato's dialogues, that the dialogue as a form and the pursuit of perfection as a mode of inquiry were not unduly restrictive. They were readily adaptable to the needs of authors and to the drift or the necessities of the age.

An adviser to princes, a man profoundly familiar with the ways of courts, Castiglione was writing about himself, about his ideal and the ideal of men like him. This identification has long been accepted by the scholarly tradition. When Castiglione died, the emperor Charles V reportedly declared: "Yo vos digo que es muerto uno de los mejores caballeros del mundo" ("I tell you that one of the most accomplished gentlemen in the world is dead"). Viewed in this biographical light, we can see that *Il Libro del Cortegiano* lays before us not only a search for perfection but a quest for identity. What is more, its fantasies, irresolutions, and structural looseness betray a crisis of identity. Because of the form of his principal question, framed in terms of an ideal perfection, Castiglione is necessarily striving to speak for his class, for noblemen at the forefront of public life. And he is asking: Who are we? Why are we here? How shall we carry out our mission?

---

[17] Maier, pp. 70, 445; Singleton, pp. 2, 285.

The interest of Castiglione's readers was immediate and keen. By the second and third decades of the sixteenth century, having lived through a flood of humiliations and stunning reversals, the more articulate and responsive members of the Italian governing classes were beginning to take stock. In posing his disarmingly simple question—How shall we define the perfect courtier?—the Mantuan nobleman was putting his finger, as Italians say, on the very sore: the question of leadership in Italy.

Castiglione's question is political through and through, but he does not take it up in a political way. He insists that the courtier's reason for being is to serve the prince, above all with good advice, but he does not organize the work around this perception. His grasp is uncertain, his vision unfocused and shifting. Again and again he forgets or abandons his theme. It is true that he has sought to catch the gay, relaxed atmosphere of the court of Urbino. In that he succeeds too well, for we often find ourselves wondering what his theme is. Not until Book II of the work, in the second day of the discussions, does he have one of the speakers get down to the question of the courtier's essential office. But the theme is soon pushed aside and we do not get back to it until the beginning of Book IV. For the rest, there are digressions on language, on the varieties of wit and humor, and on love and flirtation. Book III is devoted to a discussion of the ideal court lady, who turns out of course to be even less political than the courtier.

Castiglione's inability to hold on to his theme or to endow his courtier with more political substance is a gauge of the crisis in Italian political leadership. Italians of the upper classes were confused and disoriented. Castiglione is fully aware of the dangers posed by foreign armies; he is aware of the military weakness of the Italians and of a certain readiness to ape foreign manners and dress.[18] He sees the political ineptitude of Italian princes and recognizes that too often they are too easily led into irresponsibility. Yet these perceptions do not prevent him from making grace, nonchalance, and ease the capital attributes of the man who would embody Italian political leadership by

[18] E.g., Maier, pp. 161–162, 230–231.

serving as the chief aide to the prince. Whatever their corresponding inner virtues, the designated attributes are the courtier's outer marks or mask. Indeed, the mask *is* the man; he must never take it off. As we have noted, he is "to practice in all things a certain *sprezzatura*, so as to conceal all art. . . . Therefore, we may call that art true art which does not seem to be art; nor must one be more careful of anything than of concealing it, because if it is discovered, this robs a man of all credit and causes him to be held in slight esteem."[19]

The courtier is not a cheat but a performer and an artist. His His life is a work of hidden design and calculation, an effect achieved by means of *sprezzatura*. His overriding purpose is to use his noble talents and accomplishments to win the favor of the prince. So doing, he becomes the leading political counselor whose aim is not only to provide the prince with the truth but also to make an honest man of him.

It is here, in the relations between prince and courtier, that *Il Libro del Cortegiano* has its conceptual center. The courtier has no being outside the service of the prince. Yet Castiglione, who insists on this relationship, has no clear view of it. He touches on the problem in the second book, but only briefly, and does not return to it until the beginning of the fourth book. There, quite unexpectedly, we are rushed onto an almost pure moral plane; the entire section (IV, 6–48) has an insistent bookish flavor. The author praises virtue and condemns vice in princes; he draws heavily on Plutarch, Aristotle, Plato, and Cicero; and he emphasizes the importance to rulers of the virtues of justice, liberality, magnanimity, gentleness, continence, fortitude, and temperance. We are neither at the court of a prince nor in the train of an accomplished diplomatist but in the library or private study of a moralist. Castiglione seems unable to draw example, guidance, or instruction from his own rich political experience. The result is that his primary question, concerning the office of the courtier and hence touching the whole fabric of Italian political leadership, is consumed in moral and even aesthetic considerations.

[19] *Ibid.*, p. 124; Singleton, p. 43.

Castiglione has trouble holding onto his principal question because it requires him, will-nilly, to look coldly at the Italian ruling classes in their time of failure and disaster. Thus a man of the high establishment would either have to espouse cynicism (which is only another way of accepting things as they are) or turn into a revolutionary thinker. The latter is a rare solution and, in any event, much more in keeping with the development of the exile, the man in basic opposition to the establishment. But Castiglione takes a third route, the way of evasion and unreality. His constant tendency is to remove the primary question, which *is* political, onto another ground, leaving politics far behind. Partly, no doubt, this approach is a function of the dialectic of the dialogue. The interlocutors are, after all, striving to represent an ideal portrait of the courtier. But their eagerness to draw away from political questions and their facility in doing so are too remarkable not to require an explanation on other grounds. Grace, nonchalance, ease, and digressions, anecdotes, whim, and bookish rumination all come to Castiglione's rescue.

The images of the real world are often turned upside down in Castiglione's imaginary universe. Most noticeably, erotic love is turned into platonic friendship. But some of the images come through on occasion with an aura of haunting reality. The fact that his prince moves, as I have already pointed out, in a kind of supreme isolation is no accident. The typical Italian prince of the sixteenth century is a man cut off from the rest of the community; he is not, in constitutional terms, responsible to it; and the community is provided with no effective means of getting to him. Although surrounded by favorites, he is not hemmed in by a system of impartial courts and other bodies. He is an absolute prince, come forth in a world that once had seen intense civic energies and extensive participation of citizens in public affairs. This world is gone now, but the memory remains, making *a fortiori* for the image of a prince who is not vitally related to the community. Thus we see his insistent isolation in Castiglione's pages. The isolation of the perfect gentleman is different, for it stems from the fact that he is that rare good man who by his graces and talents cuts through a ring of toadies and flatterers to captivate the heart and the mind of his prince. The prince has been corrupted by flattery and lies; he is shut off from the world. Only the ideal courtier can break through to him and gradually nurse him back to moral health (the medical imagery is Castiglione's).[20]

In their isolation, which in a certain sense is their own exile, the prince and the courtier, at least as filtered through the mind of Castiglione, are emblematic of Italy's tragedy. The courtier is too mannered (he is a perfect work of art) and the prince is too corruptible. Having no essential contact with the vital forces in Italian society, neither is able to draw from them any support or vigor.

Castiglione knows that "countless considerations [may] force a gentleman not to leave a patron once he has begun to serve."[21] But he insists that when a prince is wicked or corrupt, the courtier has no choice but to leave his service. For the courtier—here again we see his estrangement—has no loyalties to a community, a land, or a people. His only practical human loyalties are to a prince, although he is guided, to be sure, by strong moral views. Finding himself in the service of a depraved man, he may work to effect a cure. But ultimately he withdraws and goes off to seek service in another court, whether Italian, French, Spanish, or German. In the context of an Italy overrun by French and Spanish armies and a Europe fast drifting toward the formation of national states, this cosmopolitan feature of the courtier is extremely significant. Castiglione does not see, as Machiavelli does, that Italy's place in the context of European politics has changed. He does not see that Italian diplomacy and military policy should also change. He therefore cannot see the precise ineptitudes of Italian political leadership, although he does not hesitate to make resounding moral indictments. As a working, committed member of the ruling establishment, he shares its myopia. The peninsula was kept divided and exposed to invasion by Italian princes and oligarchies, all mutually suspicious and keenly jealous. Castiglione, however, does not see

[20] E.g., Maier, pp. 457–458, 506.
[21] *Ibid.*, p. 224; Singleton, p. 116.

this fragmentation or cannot, in any event, accept its consequences. For him, as we have seen, serving the prince is the sole aim, the sole end, of the courtier's existence.

Recent studies indicate that in the fifteenth century Italian political society lost its capacity to grow.[22] Oligarchies drew in on themselves and became more castelike. In territories under princely rule, recruitment for regional administrative bodies depended increasingly on birth and blood. The miraculous age of the Italian economy had seen its end well before the middle of the fourteenth century. In the course of the sixteenth century the commercial and industrial initiative would pass to northern Europe. The Renaissance ideal of the courtier should be seen in this context of contraction and decline. Soon there would be a growing tide of talk about the "base merchant," and going into "trade" would seem less and less attractive socially. The courtier, as envisaged by Castiglione, is the product of a society in which all the salutary contacts between leaders and led have been lost.

One of the most able students of the period, Piero Pieri, has demonstrated that the startling military defeats suffered by Italians in the early sixteenth century resulted from the lack of an adequate infantry of pikemen. His analysis indicates that this deficiency was a function of nonmilitary factors.[23] The Italian nobility, unlike other nobilities, failed to evolve military practices that combined its own resources with those of the urban and country populace. It was a failure stemming from deep-seated suspicions; the nobility—and so, from another viewpoint, the state—shrank from the idea of arming the populace. Fear and distrust entered prominently into the nobility's relations with the populace, thus underscoring the distance that separated the broader communiy from its political leaders. The image of the isolated, aloof courtier fits perfectly into this setting.

[22] Cf. A. Ventura, *Nobiltà e popolo nella società veneta del '400 e '500* (Bari, 1964); M. Berengo, *Nobili e mercanti nella Lucca del Cinquecento* (Torino, 1965).

[23] Piero Pieri, *Il Rinascimento e la crisi militare italiana* (Torino, 1952), pp. 599–607.

For all its frivolities, charm, and high ideals, *The Courtier* gives off a melancholy cry. The Italian courtly literature that followed it is frankly and boldly apolitical; it is dominated by storytelling or by discussions of hunting, true love, beauty, honor, nobility, and so on. Typical concerns raised resonant questions: Which love is the greater and more ardent, that of a man for a woman or a woman for a man? Who suffers more, the courtier whose lady has died or the courtier who loves a lady who does not love him?[24]

In its quest for the ideal courtier, Castiglione's book is intensely political because it is a search for political identity. Castiglione senses a profound malaise but deals effectively only with its moral manifestations. He is bound by his place and background. He is not an exile, save in a psychological and metaphorical sense. He cannot, like Machiavelli, stand off and look at the high establishment from the outside. He therefore rises above it in idealization and fantasy, to a world where he can turn the corrupt into the pure, the humiliated into the elegant and triumphant. Escape and evasiveness win out and it is here, as well as in the courtier's isolation, that the book has its melancholy. Viewed in this light, the famous last speech by Bembo, one of the interlocutors, suddenly takes on a rather startling formal perfection. In this speech we learn that the old courtier, because of being old, may fall chastely in love with one of the beautiful young women of the court. The relationship is platonic, but the theme is brought in as a device to introduce a vision of divine beauty. At the height of his speech Bembo seems a man transported: the flesh, the senses, all temporal desires, and the world have been left behind. He stands in the holy light of divine beauty. The courtier has realized himself outside of time. And just as the whole book is both a quest for identity and an abdication, so it is absolutely fitting that it should end with a vision of the courtier's escape from the world, to a place where he has a higher, indeed a supreme, identity.

[24] For examples of these concerns, see T. F. Crane, *Italian Social Customs of the Sixteenth Century* (New Haven, 1920), chaps. 6–8.

IV

HERMETISM AS A
RENAISSANCE WORLD VIEW

John G. Burke

U NTIL THE twentieth century, Renaissance historians believed that the practice of Hermetism prevalent in the late
fifteenth and sixteenth centuries was merely a vestigial remnant
of the medieval tradition of magic and sorcery, a rather minor
aberration in that otherwise glorious era of humanism, art, architecture, and literature. Thus, for example, in the nineteenth
century, Jakob Burckhardt, in his magnificently written and
highly influential *Civilization of the Renaissance in Italy*,
praised Pico della Mirandola's *Oration on the Dignity of Man*
as expressing the loftiest conceptions on the subject of humanity, stating that "it may justly be called one of the noblest be-
quests of that great age." Burckhardt reserved for a footnote
the information that "a great part of the discourse is devoted to
the defence of the peculiar philosophy of Pico, and the praise of
the Jewish Kabbalah."[1] The "peculiar" philosophy was, in fact,
Hermetism, and Pico was only one of a galaxy of intellectuals
of the period who were sincere and fervent devotees of the
Hermetic tradition. Burckhardt and others, then, viewed Hermetism as idiosyncratic and uncharacteristic of the Renaissance,
an anomalous element soon to be swept away by the rising tide
of modern experimental science.

[1] Jakob Burckhardt, *The Civilization of the Renaissance in Italy*, 2
vols. (New York, 1958), II, 351–352.

This judgment now requires, if not complete revision, at least considerable modification. During the past two decades particularly, a number of scholars have engaged in painstaking research and thorough analysis of the pertinent Hermetic literature of the late fifteenth and sixteenth centuries.[2] Their work has, I believe, demonstrated conclusively that in scope, substance, and intent, Renaissance Hermetism differs sharply from the earlier tradition, and that it was by no means an unimportant philosophical trend. It is my purpose to present and synthesize some of their findings. I wish to concentrate on three separate but closely related problems concerning Renaissance Hermetism. First, why were so many educated and intelligent people of the Renaissance period attracted to and intrigued by this mass of esoteric and occult lore? Second, what was the relationship between the Hermetic tradition and contemporary religious attitudes, bearing in mind that the sixteenth century witnessed the great reforms of Luther and Calvin and the religious wars that followed in their wake? Third, what was the relationship between these astrological, magical, and Cabalistic practices and the rise of essentially modern experimental and theoretical science which occurred at the end of the sixteenth century and the beginning of the seventeenth? From the accumulated studies, it is now possible to suggest answers to these questions.

Hermetism may be defined as a body of philosophical and theological beliefs, speculations, and esoteric practices, possessing a large content of magic, astrology, and alchemy. There is no central unifying dogma; some Hermetists have stressed certain elements that others have rejected as fantasies. Nevertheless, from the Gnostics of the early centuries of the Christian era to the Rosicrucians and theosophists of the present time, numbers of men have believed that the Hermetic tradition incorporates deep insights into universal truths and possesses unquestioned validity.

[2] I depend particularly on the cited works of A. J. Festugière, Charles G. Nauert, D. P. Walker, and Frances A. Yates. Another comprehensive study appeared while this article was in the press: Wayne Shumaker, *The Occult Sciences in the Renaissance* (Berkeley and Los Angeles, 1972).

The strictly Hermetic literature, the kernel of these beliefs, although attributed to an ancient Egyptian sage or priest, Hermes Trismegistus, or Hermes the Thrice-Blessed, was actually composed between about A.D. 100 and 300.[3] Certain Hermetic treatises were known to at least some of the early church fathers. Lactantius, in *The Divine Institutes*, written about the beginning of the fourth century, mentions Hermes Trismegistus frequently, thus giving him the status of a historical personage. Lactantius states that Hermes gave the Egyptians their letters and their laws, that he founded a great city, that he was skilled in all the arts, that he wrote many books of wisdom, and that he was a monotheist. Further, he praises Hermes for his prophecy of the coming of the Son of God and for his prediction of the founding of the Christian religion.[4] A century after Lactantius, Saint Augustine, in *The City of God*, by repeated references to Hermes Trismegistus gave further credibility to the antiquity of the Hermetic writings and to the historical reality of their purported author. Augustine, however, was shocked by and strongly disapproved of Hermes' reported practice of drawing life into the statues of the Egyptian gods, a usage that Augustine

[3] A. J. Festugière, *La Révélation d'Hermès Trismégiste*, 4 vols. (Paris, 1950–1954), III, 1. Other related writings forming a part of the Hermetic tradition, broadly taken, are the Orphic hymns or poems, attributed to the ancient Greek mythological figure, Orpheus; and the Chaldean oracles, supposedly written by Zoroaster, the founder of the national religion of the Iranian peoples (Ivan M. Linforth, *The Arts of Orpheus* [Berkeley and Los Angeles, 1941], pp. 182–185; Willy Theiler, *Die Chaldäischen Orakel und die Hymnen des Synesios* [Halle, 1942], p. 1). The books of the Cabala, reputed to have been revealed by God to Moses and transmitted through centuries verbally by the Jewish high priests are also included (K. Seligmann, *The History of Magic* [New York, 1948], pp. 343–346; W. Westcott, *An Introduction to the Study of Kabalah* [New York, n.d.], pp. 2–3). The Cabalistic writings again date from the early centuries of the Christian era, but a somewhat later addition is the work of Pseudo-Dionysius, composed about A.D. 475. It was, however, attributed to one of Saint Paul's followers, mentioned in Acts 17: 34 (E. R. Dodds, ed. and trans., *Proclus:The Elements of Theology* [Oxford, 1933], pp. xxvi–xxvii).

[4] Lactantius, *The Divine Institutes*, trans. Sister Mary Frances McDonald (Washington, D.C., 1964), pp. 32, 155, 255–256, 262, 481, 520.

equated with the conjuring up of demons. Also, differing with Lactantius, Augustine believed that Hermes had prophesied the coming of Christianity with sorrow and anguish, rather than joyfully predicting the eventual arrival of the Redeemer.

Later, the Arabs became acquainted with and intrigued by the Hermetic writings, and through references to Hermes made by the church fathers and translations of the literature from the Arabic, portions of the Hermetic tradition passed to the Latin west. Another source for medieval students was the work of the eleventh-century Byzantine, Michael Psellus, who appears to have studied a major portion of the extant Hermetic literature.[5] Thus, many references to Hermetism occur in the scholastic writings of the Middle Ages. For example, the final words of the *Didascalicon*, written by the twelfth-century canon, Hugh of St. Victor—"to its pure and fleshless feast"—are also the final words of a well-known Hermetic treatise, *Asclepius*.[6] Another more esoteric and confused Hermetic text, *Picatrix*, translated from Arabic to Spanish in 1256 by order of Alphonso the Wise, was quoted extensively.[7] Hermes Trismegistus is cited in the works of Roger Bacon, Daniel of Morley, Albert the Great, and William of Auvergne.[8] Saint Thomas Aquinas, though condemning Hermes' demonic magic in the tradition of Saint Augustine, recognized Hermes Trismegistus as an ancient Egyptian sage, acquainted with the secrets and powers of the world of nature.[9]

Renaissance Hermetism had, if not its beginning, at least its inflorescence in 1460, when a monk employed by Cosimo de' Medici, the Elder, to collect Greek manuscripts brought to Florence an incomplete copy of the *Corpus Hermeticum*, a col-

[5] A. D. Nock and A. J. Festugière, eds. and trans., *Corpus Hermeticum*, 4 vols. (Paris, 1945–1954), I, xlvii–l.

[6] Jerome Taylor, ed. and trans., *The Didascalicon of Hugh of St. Victor* (New York, 1961), p. 20.

[7] Lynn Thorndike, *A History of Magic and Experimental Science*, 8 vols. (New York, 1923–1958), II, 813.

[8] *Ibid.*, II, 219.

[9] Frances A. Yates, *Giordano Bruno and the Hermetic Tradition* (Chicago, 1964), pp. 67–68.

lection of Hermetic treatises. Cosimo, the patron of Marsilio Ficino, ordered him to interrupt his studies of Plato's works to translate the new find immediately. Ficino's translation and commentary, entitled *Pimander*, actually the title of the first treatise of the *Corpus Hermeticum*, was published in 1471, and the fact that sixteen editions of this work appeared prior to 1500 attests to its tremendous popularity. Influenced by the authoritative assertions of Lactantius and Saint Augustine that Hermes Trismegistus was a historic personage of great antiquity and also by the fact that the content of the treatises incorporated many elements of the philosophy of Plato, Ficino mistakenly dated Hermes as having lived only two generations later than Moses and asserted that this author of Egyptian theology had passed on his wisdom to the Greek sage, Orpheus, from whom it had been transmitted successively to Pythagoras, Philolaus, and finally to Plato.[10] Those aspects of the treatises which Ficino recognized as Platonic were, in fact, the infusions of the Neoplatonists of the early Christian era.

We might pause here and review the mythological representation of Hermes. Hermes was the name given to the Egyptian god, Thoth, by the Greeks about the fifth century B.C. In the Egyptian pantheon, Thoth was considered to be the inventor of chronography; he computed the lengths of days, months, and years, and thus he also determined the length of a man's life. Thoth was also reputed to be the inventor of language and of writing and all branches of learning that depended upon writing: medicine, magic, astronomy, and astrology.[11] Somewhat later, some Egyptian priests elevated Hermes-Thoth to the rank of a creating god. In Greek mythology, Hermes was identified with Mercury. He was the messenger of the gods and carried the divine word from the gods to men. During the Hellenistic period, the Greek and Egyptian traditions fused; consequently, by the beginning of the Christian era, Hermes had become not only the bearer of the divine messages but also the creating god.

[10] *Ibid.*, pp. 12–17.

[11] C. H. Oldfather, ed. and trans., *Diodorus of Sicily*, I (Cambridge, Mass., 1946), 53–54.

Shorn of his divinity by monotheistic thought in the early centuries of Christianity, Hermes then became the thrice-blessed prophet, and having been the inventor of writing, he also became the author of the most sacred texts.[12] Clement of Alexandria, writing at the beginning of the third century, speaks of forty-two books written by Hermes on such varied subjects as law, medicine, astronomy, and theology, which, Clement asserted, were "indispensable" for the acquisition of knowledge.[13] The actual authors were probably Greeks, perhaps living in Egypt, who in their writings reflect elements of the Platonic and Stoic philosophies as well as the magical, astrological, and alchemical lore of that era.[14]

Taken as a body, the Hermetic literature is noticeably inconsistent. Some tracts are distinctly pantheistic, representing divinity embodied in all aspects of nature, not only in the celestial bodies but also in the leaves of grass, in flowers, plants, and trees. In contrast, others are highly mystical, describing God as ineffable, unapproachable, and far removed from all earthly affairs. Some are optimistic, portraying a joyous natural order, while others are pessimistic, emphasizing the fatal influence of the stars on an evil material world and stressing that the only possible escape is through a rigid asceticism. All, however, are heavily impregnated with astrological cosmography, teaching that the sun, moon, stars, planets, and signs of the zodiac directly influence the lives and fortunes of men.[15] There is the attempt to make the celestial bodies serve as a kind of vinculum between God and mankind. Further, the writings incorporate the doctrine of sympathy and antipathy, wherein the celestial bodies are capable of imparting or infusing their respective powers into every kind of terrestrial matter: herbs, stones, flowers, liquids. Because of the influx of these celestial essences into terrestrial things, the earthly materials themselves acquire the same occult virtues passed on to them by the heavenly bodies and thus come

---

[12] Festugière, *Révélation*, I, 67–75.
[13] Thorndike, *History of Magic*, I, 289.
[14] Festugière, *Révélation*, I, 81–82.
[15] Yates, *Bruno*, pp. 22 ff.

to possess divine efficacy. Having a sympathetic conjunction with a particular planet or zodiacal sign, an herb or a stone, then, might be used to influence the stars, either to neutralize hostile celestial combinations or to augment the beneficial effects of a favorable heavenly configuration. These influences, some Hermetists believed, were transmitted through the medium of a cosmic spirit that pervades the entire material universe.[16]

Let us turn to the place of man in this scheme. Paralleling Genesis, the Hermetic writings state that man is made in the image of God and has been given dominion over all creatures. Significantly, however, the Hermetic texts declare that man was created as a divine being with divine creative power, and man is characterized as being a "brother" of the creating demiurge, who is the divine Word and the Son of God. Here one detects the influence of the mythological tradition of the god, Hermes-Thoth. In contrast with the Hebrew account, however, man takes on a mortal body of his own volition, and in so doing he voluntarily submits to the domination of the stars and other celestial bodies. Becoming human, then, is not a fall from grace as in the Hebrew tradition, because, despite his humanity, man's immortal component remains divine and creative. Also, according to the Hermetic teachings, man can recover his divinity through a regenerative experience, by casting away material preoccupations and purifying the soul. Thus regenerated, the individual again becomes a son of God. The true sage, the magus, cleansed of evil, has knowledge of God and of the truth; and, in regaining his original divinity, he reacquires an intimate knowledge of nature and an ability to employ the powers of nature for beneficial purposes.[17] This ability to control nature was the goal of the serious Renaissance magus.

The principal ingredients of Renaissance Hermetism, then, were a mystical religiousness, a conviction that man was essentially divine, and a belief that an enlightened and purified man

[16] *Ibid.*, pp. 45 ff.; D. P. Walker, *Spiritual and Demonic Magic from Ficino to Campanella* (London, 1958), pp. 12–15; Giovanni Battista Porta, *Natural Magick* (New York, 1957), pp. 1–14.

[17] Yates, *Bruno*, pp. 25–31.

could manipulate and direct the powers of nature. It was thought that one method by which the magus could control nature was through language. Hermes or Thoth, we recall, was the messenger of the gods, the bearer of the divine Word, and the inventor of language. Words, then, according to this magical theory of language, are not just verbal symbols attached to things by conventional usage; they have a very real connection with things; there is direct correspondence between a word and the divine idea it expresses.[18] Properly applied by a magus, words could produce extraordinary effects. This notion had particular force among Renaissance Hermetists, first, because of the Catholic emphasis on the doctrine of the divine Word imparted in the Gospel according to Saint John, and second, because in such Catholic sacramental rites as transsubstantiation, the words uttered by the priest are considered to give effect to the miraculous change that occurs, the transformation of bread and wine into the body and blood of Christ. The priest in this situation may be considered as an enlightened magus.[19] If the power of words could be efficacious in one situation, the Hermetist reasoned, there seemed to be no ground for doubting that this power could not be used to produce extraordinary effects in another. Martin Luther addressed himself to this very problem and inveighed against the extension of priestly power by the Hermetists. Speaking about the sacrament of baptism, he declared:

> For there is a great difference between this baptism and all others invented by men and then considered to be something that counts with God. For example, the magicians, witches, and weather prophets also employ a sign or creature, such as a root or herb, and speak over it the Lord's prayer or some other holy word and the name of God. This, they say, is not an evil thing but rather both a creature of God and precious words and holy names; therefore it should possess power and accomplish what it is used for. . . . When such words are not commanded [by God], then it is nothing and counts for

[18] Walker, *Spiritual and Demonic Magic*, pp. 67 ff.
[19] *Ibid.*, p. 78; Yates, *Bruno*, pp. 26, 31, 85.

nothing, no matter what sign or word is used. Even baptism would not be a sacrament without [God's] command.[20]

Words, then, in Luther's view, have no power to produce a real effect in any nonreligious rite, nor even in a Christian ritual unless expressly sanctioned by God. It was on the basis of this criterion that Luther believed that extreme unction, the final rite performed for the dying, was not a sacrament, not having been decreed by God.[21] In this whole matter, of course, Luther and the Renaissance Hermetists were at opposite poles.

The powers acquired by the magus might be employed to enhance his own knowledge, goodness, and virtue or to influence the lives and fortunes of others. Prospero, the wise magus in Shakespeare's *The Tempest*, employs his powers in both ways. His long hours and years of contemplation on a lonely island give him wisdom and peace of mind. But he uses his powers also to raise the tempest, to bring his enemies to reason, and eventually to establish justice and harmony in the duchy of Milan and the kingdom of Naples. In the Middle Ages, it was the use of the magician's powers to control external events which was stressed, and this attitude accounts for the popular appeal of the Hermetic work, *Picatrix*, in medieval times. This treatise describes the images and talismans that could be employed to get rid of rats and mice, free prisoners, cause a siege to be successful, prevent the erection of buildings, make two persons enamored of each other, cause one to fall into disfavor with the king, cure bites, and prevent rainfall.[22]

According to Saint Thomas Aquinas, however, such powerful effects could not result from incantations over images engraved on talismans; any consequences were the work of evil demons who produced the effects because the operator had entered into a pact with the devil. Saint Thomas, therefore, considered such practices to be heretical. Marsilio Ficino and other Renaissance Hermetists were well aware of Saint Thomas's

[20] *D. Martin Luthers Werke*, XLIX (Weimar, 1913), 128–129.

[21] Margaret A. Currie, trans., *The Letters of Martin Luther* (London, 1908), pp. 377–378.

[22] Thorndike, *History of Magic*, II, 821.

stricture, and hence Ficino employed the Hermetic lore only subjectively in order to increase his wisdom and to aid in making his spirit divine.[23] To accomplish these ends, one eats food and drinks beverages containing celestial effluvia, such as wine, pure white sugar, gold, and attar of roses or cinnamon. Further, particular planetary influences might be attracted by the use of images, by playing music and singing lyrics in keeping with the musical harmony of the planetary sphere, and by employing scents and entertaining friends whose horoscopes showed them to be subject to that planet's domination.[24] We can imagine Ficino playing a lute while singing an Orphic hymn, occasionally drinking wine and contemplating a talisman, with burning frankincense scenting the air.[25] How strikingly similar is this scene to a modern "turn-on-" party: the music, poetry, wine, and images remain, as does the frankincense in order to mask the odor of marijuana! The purpose is the same: to understand the universe and to experience heaven on earth.

To ensure the efficacy of such rituals, the magus had to possess an exhaustive and tremendously complex store of information concerning the sympathetic powers of terrestrial materials as related to the planets, stars, constellations, and signs of the zodiac, as well as the propitious times at which these powers might be employed. He had to know the proper materials from which the talismans should be made and what images should be engraved on them. In gathering such data, he relied almost exclusively on the Hermetic literature. For example, *Picatrix* describes an image of Mars as "the form of a man, crowned, holding a raised sword in his right hand," and an image of Venus as "the form of a woman with her hair unbound, riding on a stag, having in her right hand an apple, and in her left, flowers, and dressed in white garments.'[26] Also, the magus had to determine what type of terrestrial musical harmony might effectively attract the planetary powers, a difficulty that Ficino over-

[23] Walker, *Spiritual and Demonic Magic*, pp. 43–45.
[24] *Ibid.*, pp. 13–14.
[25] *Ibid.*, p. 30.
[26] Yates, *Bruno*, pp. 52–53.

came by imitating in music the characteristics of the gods for whom the planets were named. Thus, the proper music to attract the powers of Jupiter should be "grave, earnest, sweet, and joyful with stability," whereas for Venus the music should be "voluptuous with wantonness and softness."[27]

How extensively such rites were practiced will, of course, never be known. But one notable example illustrates the profundity of the Renaissance belief in astrological influences as well as the conviction that the terrestrial magus possessed the knowledge and the powers to overcome maleficent omens. In 1628 the pro-French pope, Urban VIII, was deeply apprehensive of an approaching eclipse which his Spanish enemies had loudly predicted was a prophecy of the pope's death. Aided by the Dominican Hermetist, Tommaso Campanella, the pope performed a magical ritual to neutralize the evil. They sealed the doors and windows of a Vatican apartment to prevent the infiltration of outside air and hung white silken cloths on the walls. They sprinkled the room with rose vinegar and other aromatics and then lit two candles and five torches representing the seven planets. All the other persons present had horoscopes immune to the evils of the eclipse. They played music attuned to the harmony of the planets, Jupiter and Venus, employed appropriate stones, plants, and odors, and drank astrologically distilled liquids.[28] The ceremony was evidently efficacious, since the pope not only survived the eclipse but lived for another sixteen years, during which time he pressed the prosecution of Galileo for heresy.

The Church had, of course, for centuries inveighed against and anathematized astrological determinism. The belief that the destiny of human beings is irrevocably governed by the position or pattern of stars and planets either at conception or birth precluded chiefly the doctrine of free will but also had implications for the belief in the efficacy of prayer. If all events in a man's life, if all traits of his character and personality, if his intellect and bodily appearance marking his individuality,

[27] Walker, *Spiritual and Demonic Magic*, p. 18.
[28] *Ibid.*, p. 205.

were inexorably determined at birth, the Church would be left with no basis in logic for teaching moral responsibility or for promising eternal rewards or threatening eternal punishments for deeds beyond human power to influence or change. The Christian magicians of the Renaissance had to avoid such determinism in order to keep within the bounds of theological prescription. Therefore they taught that their magic, although based on astrological patterns or influences, was, in fact, a method of avoiding astrological determinism, because the magician, through his talismans, music, and knowledge of sympathies, gained control over the stars and channeled their influences in beneficial directions.

This was the approach of Giovanni Pico della Mirandola. While condemning judicial astrology or astrological determinism, Pico contributed to the development of Renaissance Hermetism in two distinct ways: first, by aiding Ficino in redefining the roles of the nine angelic hierarchies, and second, by merging the Cabala into the Hermetic tradition. These contributions are mentioned in sequence.

The writings of Dionysius the Areopagite were first brought to light at the Council of Constantinople in 533; they were considered to be the authentic work of a Greek disciple of Saint Paul; thereafter they were swiftly integrated into the body of Christian theology. During the Renaissance both Lorenzo Valla and Erasmus challenged their authenticity as first-century treatises, but it was not until the nineteenth century that scholars proved indisputably that the writings had been composed in the fifth century. Though masked in Christian phraseology, the works are unquestionably based on a book entitled *Elements of Theology*, written by the pagan Neoplatonist, Proclus.[29] The pseudo-Dionysian treatise entitled *Concerning the Celestial Hierarchy* bears directly on our subject. In it the author describes a transcendent and triune God who is reflected by three triads of the celestial hierarchy. Seraphim, cherubim, and thrones compose the first triad, which contemplates the divine emanations and reflects them to the second. The second triad,

[29] Dodds, *Proclus*, pp. xxvi–xxvii.

consisting of dominations, virtues, and powers, in turn reflects the divine radiation to the third triad, principalities, archangels, and angels, which ministers to man. Collectively, the celestial hierarchies elevate mankind to God through purification, illumination, and perfection. It is apparent that this scheme has much in common with the original Hermetic literature; the resemblance is not surprising because the common source is the Gnosticism of the early Christian era. The angelic hierarchies, however, can be a ready substitute for the celestial influences of the stars and planets. In the medieval period Dante and Saint Thomas, particularly, outlined the duties and functions of the nine choirs of angels in more descriptive detail. Dante linked the hierarchies with the planetary and stellar spheres, and Saint Thomas taught, for example, that the virtues moved the heavens and as God's instruments worked miracles, that the principalities watched over the affairs of kingdoms or their princes, while the lowest rank of angels superintended minor affairs and took charge of individuals as their guardian angels. All hierarchies, Saint Thomas wrote, were still located in the empyrean heaven beyond the sphere of the fixed stars.

Pico sharply modified the locations of the angelic hosts. He placed only the first triad above the sphere of the fixed stars; the second occupied the celestial region between the moon and fixed stars, while the third operated in the terrestrial realm extending to the moon.[30] Also, Pico revealed his ambitions in his *Oration on the Dignity of Man* when he stated:

> Let us put in last place whatever is of the world; and let us fly beyond the chambers of the world to the chamber nearest the most lofty divinity. There, as the sacred mysteries reveal, the seraphim, cherubim, and thrones occupy the first places. Ignorant of how to yield to them and unable to endure the second places, let us compete with the angels in dignity and glory. When we have willed it, we shall be not at all below them.[31]

[30] Yates, *Bruno*, pp. 117–129.
[31] Pico della Mirandola, *On the Dignity of Man*, trans. Charles Glenn Wallis (Indianapolis, 1965), p. 7.

Note that Pico wishes to displace the first triad of angels; he does not even mention the second or third angelic orders. The reason behind this audacious undertaking is that Pico is confident that he can not only contact but also utilize the powers of the terrestrial and celestial triads. His tool was the Jewish Cabala.

The two major books of Cabala are the *Sephir Yetzirah*, or *Book of Formation*, and the *Zohar*, or *Book of Light*. The former describes a scheme of creation, drawing an analogy between the origins of the universe—the sun, the stars, the planets, the four elements, the seasons, and mankind—and the twenty-two letters fo the Hebrew alphabet. It was compiled about A.D. 200. The latter, a collection of treatises about God, the angels, souls, and cosmogony, is ascribed to Rabbi Simon ben Jochai, who lived about A.D. 160.

From another point of view, Cabala may be divided into two parts: the first is doctrinal, relating to ideas about God, the angels, the human soul, preexistence, reincarnation, and the several levels of existence; the second is practical, involving the mystical or allegorical interpretation of the Old Testament. Doctrinal Cabala resembles Neoplatonism; a central idea is that the universe is produced from God through ten successive divine emanations or agencies, called the Sephiroth. The basis of practical Cabala was the belief that since God had spoken to Moses in Hebrew, it was a sacred language. Practical Cabalists, therefore, studied the phrases, words, and letters of the writings of the Prophets and derived the connection and interrelation between letters and numbers, from which basis information was obtained as to the proper design, manufacture, and use of talismans with such images as magic squares for calling the divine and angelic names and for implementing their powers.

In one method of Cabalistic interpretation, the letters of words are transposed according to certain rules or replaced by other letters according to a definite pattern. One half of the alphabet may be written over the other half in reverse order; an original phrase thus modified by the replacement of the new letters supposedly becomes a meaningful message. Also, each letter of the Hebrew alphabet was assigned a number, so that, in another mode of interpretation, a word or phrase having a certain total numerical value was considered to have a definite correspondence with another word or phrase having the same total. Thus, "Messiah," spelled *M SH I CH* totals 358 as does the phrase *IBA SHILH*. This phrase, meaning "Shiloh shall come," appearing in Genesis 49:10, was therefore deemed to be a prophecy of the coming of a Messiah. Again, a word can be formed from the initial and/or final words of a sentence. For example, in Deuteronomy 30:12 Moses asks: "Who shall go up for us to heaven?" The initial letters of the Hebrew words of this question form the word meaning "circumcision," and the final letters spell the name of Jehovah. Hence, Moses' question is interpreted as indicating that circumcision is a feature of the path to God in heaven. Further, each planet had a number and a letter assigned to it. For Jupiter the number was 4 and the letter was Daleth, also allotted the number 4. A talisman designed for Jupiter, therefore, had engraved on it a magic square having within it sixteen smaller squares. The squares were numbered from 1 to 16 in such a way that each column totaled thirty-four. The most auspicious symbol was the Tetragrammaton, the divine four-letter name, IHVH, which totaled twenty-six.[32]

Practical Cabala, then, incorporated the magical theory not only of language but also of number. Its adepts insisted that numbers have, in themselves, real significance, and they believed that nature could be controlled by the manipulation of numbers which corresponded to the names of angels. One disciple of Pico's Cabalist teachings, Johannes Trithemius, the abbot of Sponheim, through elaborate and intricate calculations assigned numbers to the names of the superior and inferior angels. For example, the name of the angel Samael corresponded to the number 4,440, which was also the sum of the numbers of his eight inferior angels. Knowing these numbers, Trithemius believed himself able to send messages to distant friends via the angelic network. He read the message aloud over the image of

[32] Seligmann, *History of Magic*, pp. 338–365; Westcott, *Study of Kabalah*, pp. 23–27.

a planetary angel at time determined by astrological calculation and then buried the image together with an image of the intended recipient under a threshold. The friend might expect to receive the message within twenty-four hours.[33] Failure in such enterprises could be attributed to erroneous calculations. Further, there were inconsistencies in Cabalist interpretations and practices, a major one being the assignment of different numbers to the various letters of the Hebrew alphabet.

The main features of Hermetism did not change when the tradition penetrated France, but certain elements in sixteenth-century French Hermetic writings are worth remarking. First, French Hermetists were much more cautious than their Italian or German counterparts about the magical ingredient in Hermetism. Although most believed in the magical power of words, numbers, and symbols, they appeared genuinely worried that there was no clear distinction between good and bad magic, in other words, whether the produced effects were owing to the manipulation of words or talismans or were the work of evil demons. By and large, the French were content to speculate theoretically about the power of good magic rather than to attempt its practice. Second, while the predominant French view of ancient Hermetism was that Moses had taught the truths of religion to Egyptian priests who passed on his revelations imperfectly to Orpheus, Pythagoras, and Plato, all of whom journeyed to Egypt for this purpose, such Frenchmen as Symphorien Champier and Guy Lefèvere de la Boderie took a more chauvinistic approach. Both believed that Hermetism was French to start with, that the Druids of ancient Gaul had a place in the tradition. Champier asserted that the Greeks had purloined their religious and philosophical ideas from the Druids, while de la Boderie insisted that civilization in ancient Gaul commenced immediately after the deluge and that the Druids had transmitted the secret knowledge not only to the Greeks but also to the Egyptians and to Moses. There were several

[33] Walker, *Spiritual and Demonic Magic*, p. 87; Yates, *Bruno*, p. 145; Charles G. Nauert, *Agrippa and the Crisis of Renaissance Thought* (Urbana, Ill., 1965), p. 276.

difficulties to be ignored or explained away in order to maintain this view: first, the Druids almost certainly practiced human sacrifice; second, they were polytheistic; third, they left no written records. Only the latter was handled satisfactorily in the explanation that the Druids wished to conceal the sacred mysteries from the multitude and hence passed on the tradition orally.[34]

This discussion of Renaissance Hermetism and the examples given of its practical aspects indicate, first, that it was not only an important but also a central element in Renaissance culture, and second, that it was most popular among the more learned and prominent members of society. Of the great humanists, only Erasmus held reservations about magic and failed to share the world view of his contemporaries. The impact and acceptance of Hermetism can first of all be attributed to the supposed vast antiquity of the tradition, an idea that gained support from the writings of Clement of Alexandria, Lactantius, and Saint Augustine. The Hermetic texts, purporting as they did to represent the most ancient knowledge and revelation, were avidly sought and read by humanist scholars who longed to possess and revel in the wisdom of the ancients. Supported by the newly translated literature, the Renaissance humanists saw little or no continuity between the sordid magical practices of the medieval period, which Saint Thomas had decried, and the reestablished Hermetic world view, which they espoused. Indeed, Renaissance Hermetism *was* novel, having been invested not with ancient Egyptian wisdom as the humanists supposed, but rather with the Gnostic and Neoplatonic ideas of the early Christian era. Hermetic religious and philosophical beliefs, along with the associated magic, astrology, and Cabala, became not only respectable during the Renaissance, but dignified. Hermetism was a worthy pursuit for the serious scholar, intent on learning about his world and his God.[35]

Yet, if Hermetism flowered in the Renaissance because of

[34] D. P. Walker, "The Prisca Theologia in France," *Journal of the Warburg and Courtauld Institutes*, XVII (1954), 204–259.

[35] Yates, *Bruno*, pp. 6, 21, 41, 156; Nauert, *Agrippa*, pp. 231–232.

the awe and respect shown by humanists for the ancient wisdom, still this magical world view required roots in contemporary culture. Here one notes a similarity between the emotional attitudes of the early centuries of the Christian era and those of the fifteenth and sixteenth centuries. In the former there had been a rejection of Greek rationalism, while in the latter there was a general suspicion of the complex, rational arguments of scholastic philosophy, which was, by and large, despised by the humanists. Again, both periods witnessed a significant religious reorientation: the peoples of the first overthrew the pantheon of gods and established a monotheism based on faith within the confines of the Roman Empire, while those of the second attacked a decadent ecclesiastical structure whose hierarchy was largely interested only in the preservation of its own pomp and power. Large numbers of people in both eras were convinced of a general cultural decline because of the political and social upheavals and were certain that civilization was doomed. And, in both periods, men resorted to a belief in the magical and the marvelous, for if the world could not be understood through logic and reason, it might be apprehended or approached through faith or trust (*fiducia*) in a divinely ordained sympathetic relationship of all aspects of nature.[36]

Thus, prior to the Reformation, Hermetists pointed to the miraculous works of the apostles as evidence of their spiritual knowledge and contrasted the powers of those saints with the corruption of contemporary theologians, who lacked the power to perform miracles. Hermetism appeared as a way to infuse morality, piety, faith, and awe into a worldly religion that had become decadent through the centuries. For example, Cornelius Agrippa of Nettesheim, the possible prototype of Marlowe's Dr. Faustus and of Goethe's Faust, was severely anticlerical, castigating and condemning many of the actions of the Papacy. Yet Agrippa did not wish to see the Church rent asunder and its universality destroyed, and he refused to join the Lutheran movement. Rather, Agrippa pictured a renovated Catholic

---

[36] Festugière, *Révélation*, I, 82; Yates, *Bruno*, pp. 81, 448; Nauert, *Agrippa*, pp. 141, 201–203, 225–226.

church, one whose teachings would be more attuned to the
Hermetic philosophy and whose priests, steeped in the Her-
metic lore, would act as the intermediaries and arbiters between
God and mankind.[37]

Although individuals among the Catholic clergy, including
at least two popes, Alexander VI and Urban VIII, were intrigued by Hermetism, it failed to penetrate into the body of
Catholic theology. Further, this approach to religious reform
which called for the introduction of more esoterism into the
rituals and theology of Christianity was, of course, in sharp
contrast with the path taken by the great Reformers who simplified the rites, stripping their churches of images, and eliminated
the agency of the angels as intermediaries between man and his
God. Luther and Calvin, to whom the Bible was a unique source
of revelation, paid little attention to or rejected classical non-
Christian literature. Calvin anathematized Agrippa for believing
in and using such sources and labeled astrology as "nothing but
a divelish superstition."[38] He pointed to the danger that through
such belief the Christian religion would be made subject to the
stars, and he asserted that it was against God's commandment to
call upon the angels to perform any task.[39] Similarly, Johann
Wier wished religion to be divested of all magical rites such as
exorcism, the wearing of amulets, and the consecration of bells
and images, since he considered these practices rank superstition.[40] The Reformers, of course, believed in the reality of
angels and demons. Luther, we recall, had many bouts with the
devil himself. Calvin admitted that the planets and stars im-
printed certain qualities on men, but he denied any causal efficacy in the stars. The Reformers rejected the practice of magic
because they believed any result must be the work of demons.
Rather than a new approach, this attitude was actually a return

[37] Nauert, *Agrippa*, p. 82; Yates, *Bruno*, pp. 137–143.

[38] John Calvin, *Commentaries on the Catholic Epistles*, trans. John
Owen, XLVI (Edinburgh, 1855), 59–60; Jean Calvin, *An Admonicion
against Astrology Iudiciall*, trans. Th. G. G[ylby] (London, 1561),
p. 10.

[39] Calvin, *An Admonicion*, pp. 24, 105.

[40] Walker, *Spiritual and Demonic Magic*, p. 146.

to the position of Saint Augustine; in fact, it was based partly upon his arguments.

In general, the approach of the Hermetists of the latter half of the sixteenth century and of the early seventeenth century was to employ Hermetism either to promote toleration between Catholics and Protestants, to put an end to the terrible religious wars that were devastating western Europe, or to reconcile and reunite Christianity. The Protestant Hermetist, Phillipe du Plessis Mornay, believed that religious tolerance would be attained by a return to a Hermetic religion of the world on the part of both antagonists.[41] Francesco Patrizi, thinking that the Hermetic tradition would be the most effective means of restoring a united Christendom, published the Hermetic corpus in his *Nova de universis philosophia* (Ferrara, 1591). In his dedication to Pope Gregory XIV, Patrizi urged the pontiff to implement his views. Patrizi's work, however, was condemned and placed on the Index, although Patrizi escaped personal punishment.[42] Tommaso Campanella, the Hermetist who worked magic with Urban VIII, went further, pleading for not only a religiously but also a politically united Europe. At first Campanella thought that the Spanish monarchy was capable of achieving his goals and thus supported its ambitions. Later, disgruntled at the Spanish, Campanella hoped that the French might succeed in creating a universal empire, and he greeted the birth of the future Louis XIV in 1638 with the prediction that the infant was destined to rule a united world together with a reformed papacy.[43]

The position of Giordano Bruno was, if not unique, highly unusual. Bruno shared the beliefs neither of the pre-Reformation Hermetists that Christianity should be renovated by introducing more magical rituals, nor of those of the post-Reformation era who thought that religious tolerance, reunion, or reconciliation might be effected by a general acceptance of the Hermetic tradition. Rather, Bruno believed that the ancient

[41] Yates, *Bruno*, pp. 176–178.
[42] *Ibid.*, pp. 181–185.
[43] *Ibid.*, pp. 385–390.

Egyptian religion as revealed in the Hermetic writings was the true religion, which had been corrupted both by Judaism and by Christianity. He deplored the fact that Christianity had destroyed this ancient worship; he praised the Egyptian hieroglyphs as holy inscriptions; and he viewed the cross as a sacred Egyptian symbol which the Christians had appropriated. Bruno shared the feelings of contemporary Hermetists that there should be one universal religion, but it was not a reformed Christendom that he desired. Instead, it was a return to the worship of ancient Egypt as described in the Hermetic literature. To Bruno, Christ was a good magus, well schooled in the ancient lore, a Son of God in the Hermetic sense of those words. He abandoned the idea of the angelic network or hierarchy stressed by Pico; Bruno's infinite universe was again populated with stars and planets that, as powerful animated beings, moved through space of their own volition. Bruno, then, was not and should not be considered a prophet or a philosopher of the new science. Rather, he was a radical representative of an irrational, magical world view that threatened the very foundations of Christianity; and it was this attitude that brought him to the stake in Rome in 1600.[44]

At first glance it would appear that there can be no relationship between Hermetism and modern theoretical and experimental science, except that it would be necessary to discredit and extirpate the entire tradition and belief structure before a rational science might progress. Indeed, destruction of the tradition began in 1614 when Isaac Causabon dated the principal Hermetic treatises and demonstrated that their supposed antiquity had no basis in fact.[45] Though Causabon destroyed the major foundation upon which the belief in Hermetism rested, there were many who ignored or refused to credit his findings. But Father Marin Mersenne, the informal link between Descartes and other prominent European scientists of the early seventeenth century, used Causabon's conclusions to attack the magical thinking of Robert Fludd and other Hermetists, on

[44] *Ibid.*, pp. 11, 214–215, 257 ff., 355.
[45] *Ibid.*, pp. 398–403.

the one hand to vindicate the true religion with its revelation, miracles, and mysteries, and on the other to advance a true science of nature.[46]

Still, there is an ill-defined area where practical magical manipulation meets scientific experimentation and where Hermetic archetypal symbolism approaches scientific theory. For example, Giovanni Battista Porta's book, *Magiae naturalis*, first published in 1558, is a veritable handbook for the practical Hermetist. Using the doctrine of sympathy and antipathy, Porta warns the reader that if one puts on the clothes of a harlot or looks in her mirror, one becomes impudent and lecherous; that if a pregnant woman fixes the image of a picture or a statue in her mind, her child will resemble the image. But simultaneously, Porta investigated magnetism, the reason for the attraction of iron to lodestone, and he made the suggestion, which proved to be erroneous, that longitude was correlated with the variation of the compass. Nevertheless, such activity constitutes genuine scientific inquiry and hypothesis. Further, Porta suggested drugs to induce sleep, to cure headaches or colic, to cause conception, and to combat syphilis.[47] Similarly, Johann Kepler labored long hours to find the true musical harmony produced by the planets as they moved in their orbits and to determine precisely how the regular solids of Euclidean geometry were incorporated into the framework of the heavens. Simultaneously, however, he worked out his famous laws of planetary motion, which form one of the principal bases of modern astronomy. The realm of magical thinking dwindled and that of science increased when causality came to be defined in mechanistic rather than in psychic terms. Herein was the essential irrationality of Hermetism.

Finally, there is one other important correspondence between Hermetic beliefs and those of the adherents of the new science. Inherent in both Hermetism and science is the idea that man can obtain power over nature and thus control it. The

[46] R. Le Noble, *Mersenne ou la Naissance du Mécanisme* (Paris, 1948), pp. 93–95, 133.

[47] Porta, *Natural Magick*, pp. 19, 54.

differing methods are not in question here; what is important is that the mental outlook and the desire are exactly the same. Johannes Trithemius desperately wished to send messages to his distant friends through space; the power of science fulfilled his dreams in the nineteenth century. Porta longed to be able to make antidotes for poison, to prevent plagues, and to discover drugs that would give restful sleep; medical science has accomplished these goals. With a maturing natural science, the deeply ingrained faith of the Hermetists in the ability of man to acquire power over nature has been realized, at least in part. But it was accomplished not by magical but by rational thought.

V

STRUCTURES OF RENAISSANCE MYSTICISM

Kees W. Bolle

IN MANY ways Renaissance mysticism cannot very well be
called irrational. Paradoxically to a modern at least, the great
mystical writings of the Renaissance force us to look for irrational and obscure features in other places than we might have
expected them. The trouble with great mystics is that they are
great people. Trying to understand them, we find obscurity not
so much in them as in ourselves.

Let me first set down what I am not going to do. I am not
going to speak about a man like Dionysius the Carthusian, a
prolific writer, who seems to have spent just about as much
time having nightmares as writing theological treatises. I admit
that I am fascinated by his nightmares, especially since they
seemed to be as real to him as the theological subjects of which
he treated. Neither shall I attempt to elaborate on the influences
of the Hermetic tradition, which Professor Burke has outlined
for us, although Nicholas of Cusa or Cusanus, whom I mention
a number of times, relied on Hermes Trismegistus. What appealed to Cusanus was the universal propensity in those strange
texts. For the same reason Cusanus relied on many ancient
philosophers whom no historian would dare call obscure.

Instead, I single out certain "structures" of religious experience and expression which take on special significance in the

119

Renaissance. I make no special scholarly pretentions in using the term "structure." I use it to group together certain facts that in the documents present themselves as belonging together. The existence of such structures is quite evident, although an effort is needed to understand their significance, for that time and for ourselves. Needless to add, the following list of structures is not meant to be exhaustive: liturgy, love, concern for a livable life, authority, purification, and deprovincialization.

Liturgy

It is best to examine "liturgy" first. It is the most obvious element and at the same time the most frequently overlooked one.

Huizinga, in his famous *Waning of the Middle Ages*, approvingly quotes William James's *Varieties of Religious Experience*: "There is about mystical utterances an eternal unanimity which ought to make a critic stop and think, and which brings it about that the mystical classics have, as has been said, neither birthday nor native land."[1] And Huizinga goes on to explain that concrete embodiments of ideas and traditional symbols fade for the mystic, and that in Eckhart's mysticism, for instance, Christ is scarcely named, and neither are the Church and the sacraments. With all admiration for the great historian, one wonders whether his explanation is entirely accurate. After all, the majority of mystics were still members of religious congregations. Eckhart was a Dominican and an ordained priest who not only preached, but must have administered the sacraments innumerable times. And we remember that Nicholas of Cusa, in many ways the most "modern" thinker, was bishop and cardinal.

Huizinga may have felt that he overstated the popular opinion about mysticism, for a few pages later, dealing with the same subject, he speaks of the "lonely heights of individual mysticism without forms and images," but he adds: "Those heights are obtained only via the taste of the liturgical-sacra-

[1] J. Huizinga, *Herfsttij der Middeleeuwen* (Haarlem: Tjeenk Willink, 1952), p. 270.

mental mystery."[2] I suggest that these two statements are not one man's contradiction of himself but part of a much more general state of mind. We are so imbued with the idea that in the later Middle Ages and especially the Renaissance there was a slackening of the forms that we ourselves, in our conscious thought, have lost altogether, that we easily pass over the significance of such things as liturgy reflected in the documents.

It is of course true that one cannot read mystical accounts without being impressed by their universal intention. But it must be said that all religious imagery has such intent, wherever it occurs and however unmystical it may be. The universality of mystical experience is not so certain as to permit us, as outside observers, to lump all mystics together. No one can speak of universal validities by ignoring the language he learned to speak. The Renaissance mystic is no exception, and the liturgy of the Church is an integral part of that language.

Pointing to the function of the liturgy is of special value in avoiding the confusion mentioned above. Mysticism at the time was a much discussed issue in theological circles, the principal area of intellectual discourse. A contemporary took the trouble to point out that John Gerson (1363–1429), famous theologian and sometime chancellor of the University of Paris, was not a genuine mystic because he regarded the clear vision of God as an eschatological experience.[3] Gerson and many others denied the possibility of gaining perfect insight into the wisdom of God in this life. It is significant, however, that the restrained theologians who were skeptical of or even inimical to the "perfect" mysticism of an Eckhart allowed for mystical experience, admittedly of a less perfect nature, in one area: that of the Eucharist. That they did so is not at all surprising. The celebration of the Sacrament was not only the traditional form of the Church

<hr/>

[2] *Ibid.*, p. 275.

[3] See Heiko A. Oberman, "Gabriel Biel and Late Medieval Mysticism," *Church History*, XXX (1961), 267, where reference is made to E. Vansteenberghen,, "Autour de la 'Docte Ignorance': Une controverse sur la théologie mystique au XV siècle," *Beiträge zur Geschichte der Philosophie des Mittelalters*, XIV (1915), 2–4.

to manifest the communion of the Lord and the faithful, but it had always provided a concrete way to practice humility, the virtue that is stressed in all mystical texts of the time, whatever their theological leanings. We know that many disputations took place about the meaning of the Lord's Supper. The doctrine of transubstantiation, although it had had its preludes for centuries, was not accepted until 1215 (Fourth Lateran Council) and did not put an end to the discussions. Well known are the controversies about the Lord's Supper among the Reformers. For our purposes the precise doctrinal differences need not be discussed. The ongoing debates do not single out one intellectual problem among many on the fringes, but they do reveal the vital importance of the Sacrament. Many of those who pleaded for an inner reform of the Church as well as those who came to be known as the Reformers advocated a more frequent celebration of Communion than was customary. The infrequency of the celebration was regarded as a symptom of spiritual decay. The same council that established transubstantiation found it necessary to make annual celebration of the Sacrament mandatory.[4]

Language and topics of discussion in Renaissance mystical writings speak volumes. The preparation for the Communion, humbling oneself before God, and the receiving of the Lord in the Sacrament are crucial points, especially for those who sing praises of God's love. It may be least surprising that we hear about them in that spiritual sphere in which the *Devotio Moderna* was born. A towering figure in the early period was the Flemish mystic Hadewych (13th century), who describes a vision in these words:

> Once, on a Sunday after Pentecost, our Lord was secretly brought to my bed. For I felt so strongly drawn by my spirit within myself, that I knew I would not have been able to control myself outside among the people if I had gone to them. And this demanding urge I had within me was to be one with

[4] J. N. Bakhuizen van den Brink and J. Lindeboom, *Handboek der Kerkgeschiedenis* (The Hague: Daamen, 1946), I, 260 (Mirbt 329).

God in enjoyment. I was too much of a child for it and not grown up enough; I had not labored enough for it or lived long enough to attain the level of so high a dignity as belonged to it; that was clear to me then and it still is.

When I had received the Lord, he received me to himself. He lifted me up, with all my senses no longer occupied by anything else, to commune with him in oneness.[5]

These few lines illustrate a typical concentration on humility, and especially the spectrum of meaning given with the receiving of the Sacrament. The most widely distributed mystical text from the Low Countries, Thomas a Kempis's *Imitation of Christ*, may also be mentioned. The last of its four parts deals explicitly with the devout meditation required to receive the Sacrament properly. The fact is of special significance since all later Renaissance mystics seemed to be quite familiar with the *Imitation*.

The life of Saint Catherine of Genoa (1447–1510) narrates how at a certain moment—the precise date was March 25, 1474—"her Lord gave her the desire of Holy Communion, a desire which never again failed her throughout the whole course of her remaining life. And He so disposed things that Communion was given her, without any care on her part; she was often summoned to receive it, without any asking, by priests inspired by God to give it to her."[6] The example is interesting because it stresses the desire for communion. At the same time, there is no reason to call Saint Catherine's mysticism "eucharistic."[7] It is the sort of desire that strikes the reader by its ordinariness, its

[5] Text in J. van Mierlo, *Hadewych, een bloemlezing uit hare werken* (Amsterdam: Elsevier, 1950), p. 47. Complete text of the visions is in J. van Mierlo, *Visioenen* (Antwerp: Standard-Boekhandel, 1924–1925). A German translation is given in J. O. Plassmann, *Die Werke der Hadewych* (Hannover: Lafaire, 1923); a modern Dutch translation by Albert Verwey is entitled *De vizioenen van Hadewych* (Antwerp: "De Sikkel," 1922).

[6] Quoted and discussed in Friedrich von Hügel, *The Mystical Element of Religion as Studied in Saint Catherine of Genoa and Her Friends*, 4th impr. (London: Dent, 1961), I, 113–114.

[7] *Ibid.*, p. 116.

self-evidentness. Catherine made no special effort to link the desire to her ideas on meditation or doctrine. According to one story, a "holy Friar," apparently in order to test her, uttered the suspicion that there might be an imperfection in so frequent a taking of Communion. Catherine then suspended her custom for awhile, but it caused her a great deal of distress, which did not come to an end until the friar urged her to resume her daily communions.[8] The diary of Ignatius of Loyola (1491–1556) is filled with references to the tears he shed during the masses in which he was the officiant. He tells how long he had had this reaction and how often he lost his power of speech. We must keep in mind that his experience was not an idiosyncrasy, but that is was part of a spirituality shared by many.[9]

A special and related liturgical form, sometimes overlooked but abundantly documented, is prayer. It is the focal point in the writings of Saint Teresa of Avila (1515–1582), who says in her autobiography:

> I can say what I know by experience—namely, that no one who has begun this practice [of prayer], however many sins he may commit, should ever forsake it. For it is the means by which we may amend our lives again, and without it amendment will be very much harder. So let him not be tempted by the devil, as I was, to give it up for reasons of humility, but let him believe that the words cannot fail of Him Who says that, if we truly repent and determine not to offend Him, He will resume his former friendship with us and grant us the favours which He granted aforetime, and sometimes many more, if our repentance merits it.[10]

In her inimitable style, sublime and down to earth at the same time, Saint Teresa wrote a booklet, *The Way of Perfection*, for

[8] *Ibid.*

[9] See Jean J. Navatel, *La dévotion sensible: les larmes et les exercices de Saint Ignace*, Bibliothèque des Exercices, no. 64 (Enghien, 1920); selections from Ignatius' diary are given in Elmer O'Brien, *Varieties of Mystic Experience* (New York: Holt, 1964), pp. 255–264.

[10] E. Allison Peers, trans., *The Autobiography of St. Teresa of Avila* Garden City: Image Books, 1960), p. 110.

the edification of nuns. A good part of it is devoted to the Lord's Prayer; the author herself referred to the book as *Paternoster*.[11] Presumably by an early editor, one chapter is deemed "very suitable for reading after the reception of the Most Holy Sacrament." It is a fitting description. In this chapter Teresa writes:

> *We have now reached the conclusion that the good Jesus, beings ours, asks His Father to let us have Him daily*—which appears to mean "for ever." *While writing this* I have been wondering why, after saying "our 'daily' bread," the Lord repeated the idea in the words "Give us this day, Lord." *I will tell you my own foolish idea: if it really is foolish, well and good—in any case, it is quite bad enough that I should interfere in such a matter at all. Still, as we are trying to understand what we are praying for, let us think carefully what this means, so that we may pray rightly, and thank Him Who is taking such care about teaching us. This bread, then* is ours daily, it seems to me, because we have Him here on earth, *since He has remained with us here and we receive Him;* and if we profit by His company, we shall also have Him in Heaven, for the only reason He remains with us is to help and encourage and sustain us so that we shall do that will, which, as we have said, is to be fulfilled in us.[12]

The question may be raised whether the evidence of liturgical moments I present here is not somewhat slanted. I do not think one could look upon these quotations as examples of mere devotionalism. Certainly that would not be true of Teresa, whose mysticism was built on prayer. Granted that the line between mysticism and devotion is often fluid, the emphasis in typical devotional literature of the period is different. Running the risk of oversimplification, one might say that in mystical literature the liturgical forms are unmistakable, given forms of life, whereas in devotional literature an active participation in those

[11] *Ibid.*, p. 17.

[12] *Ibid.*, pp. 222–223. The italics indicate the text of the so-called Escorial autograph, which is homier in style but also shows more freshness.

forms is presented rather as a goal. A notable instance is the work of the bishop and saint Francis of Sales (1567–1622) (especially in his *Introduction á la vie dévote*), which, for all its fame, is still rather "sweet" in comparison with classical mystical writings.

Huizinga, in speaking of the fading importance of the traditional forms of the sacraments and even of Christ himself, specifically mentions Eckhart. Can we apply this generalization at least to one mystic, this master of stirring, almost shockingly simple, expressions? It is not enough to reply that almost every single one of Eckhart's sermons ends with a prayer, in spite of the unspeakable essence of God. One can also sample texts by him which seem to belittle traditional forms like penance, fasting, and so on. One would have to be very selective, however, or lift parts of sentences, to see in Eckhart someone who disqualifies tradition altogether. A characteristic statement says: "What is truth? Truth is something so noble that if God could turn aside from it, I could keep to the truth and let God go."[13] It seems hardly the thought of a submissive sacramental spirit, but it would be wrong to jump to the conclusion that all tradition was abandoned by Eckhart. Not only did he urge people to partake of the Lord's body in the Sacrament; not only did he insist that man, if properly prepared, could nowhere find grace so evident as there;[14] not only did he defend himself at length against accusations of heresy[15]—but many of the most unliturgical-sounding mystical expositions have an important reservation that is supported by tradition.

In one of his sermons Eckhart speaks about traditional religious activities. He sounds completely traditional when he says: "Praying, reading, singing, watching, fasting, and doing penance—all these virtuous practices were contrived to catch us and keep us away from strange, ungodly things."[16] Then he seems

[13] Trans. by R. B. Blakney, *Meister Eckhart* (New York: Harper & Row, 1941), p. 240.
[14] For example, see *ibid.*, p. 27.
[15] *Ibid.*, pp. 258–305.
[16] *Ibid.*, p. 115.

to go a step farther: " ... if a person who has vowed many things such as prayer, fasting, or pilgrimages, should enter an order, he is then set free from the vow, for once in the order, his bond is to all virtue and to God himself."[17] But in fact such a statement is in perfect harmony with traditional distinctions: the religious life is higher than secular life; mystical theology is by nature theology of a higher sort. Elsewhere Eckhart says, "To seek God by rituals is to get the ritual and lose God in the process,"[18] but he adds, "for he hides behind it."

It is temptingly easy to misunderstand Eckhart's insistence on the worthlessness of vows and rituals and on the necessity of emptying oneself completely in order to arrive at a true mystical union as a kind of "revolt." But we can make this mistake only by superimposing a historical scheme of our own making. The emphasis is not on the discarding of forms, but on the meaning of God behind those forms. Eckhart argues that the very purpose of fasting, praying, and performing good works, of baptism and of the Incarnation itself, is to make the birth of God in the soul possible or, perhaps more accurately, to make it manifest. This is what is meant by such words from the Psalms (82:6) as, "Ye are gods." Thus the mystic engages in an allegorization of such force that a new symbolism emerges.

The temptation is strong to see only the novelty and explain it as a revolt against what we understand to be the tradition. It is the temptation to schematize, which we must resist. It occurs in many intellectual endeavors to account for mystical tendencies. All handbooks of Indian history mention the Vedas, the ancient writings, and the ritual life reflected therein, as well as the historically later texts, known as the Upanishads, which were added to the sacred scriptures. Virtually all popular expositions present the materials as if these later writings constituted a rejection of the earlier traditions. At one time it even became fashionable among scholars to see the Upanishadic philosophy as akin to German idealistic philosophy. To say the least, this

17 *Ibid.*, p. 116.
18 *Ibid.*, p. 127.

interpretation is one-sided. The principal problem is that the earlier ritualistic customs have never really been understood by modern intellectuals as observances that could have had a meaning in the first place. What is one to think of a horse sacrifice with all its subsidiary ceremonies which could keep many people active for a long period? A later text elaborating on the hidden, mystical intention of such an event seemed a tremendous step forward in the evolution of human consciousness. It must be reiterated that the new emphasis on inner experience did not put an end to the externals of the tradition. To see it otherwise (in spite of the lack of evidence) is to give in to the temptation to schematize. It is certainly not by coincidence that the temptation always happens to be in harmony with one's own intellectual self-esteem.

Similarly, the novelty and the widening spiritual horizon of the Renaissance mystics must not be seen merely as a prelude to modern enlightenment and to the urge for public education. Renaissance mysticism is a great deal more fascinating than that; witness its adherence to traditional forms. I venture to say that in its light our own age, with its craving for intellectual self-justification, looks like an age of hopelessly superficial generalizations, or even superstitions. Among the latter is the evolutionistic schematization of human consciousness, a false attempt at objectivity.

Reflection on the function of liturgy for Renaissance mystics may be useful for understanding one point. It indicates my theme: obscurity lies in us rather than in them. The fundamental mysteries of human orientation—in which mystics are experts—do not occur outside the ingredients of human existence, that is, history. It is difficult because our views of history, often in spite of our conscious ideals, are codetermined by a naïve concept of science. We like to think that certain stages of the historical process made short work of forms that we think of as meaningless survivals. The liturgical forms functioning in the mystical texts of the Renaissance show that this does not have to happen at all. The new thoughts are built on those forms. And above all, the new ideas, of wider scope than those of an earlier period, do not have to resemble our own ideas just because they are new.

It was the work of theologians, to be sure, which led to the condemnation of Eckhart. Today every account of a juridical process against a heretic reads like something from a dim and gruesome past. Still it seems to me that accusing a classical mystic of heresy is not much worse than reducing him to a precursor of our own meager rational age.

The historian of theology is less given to simple schemes of progress than is the general historian. He can point to the doctrinal dangers inherent in many mystics, but particularly evident in Eckhart. The Church's teachings concerning the fall of man and the reconciliation are no doubt shortchanged in Eckhart. His constant theme is God's birth in the soul. The creation is, as it were, re-presented in his mysticism and made timeless. In religiohistorical terms one could say that the mythology of creation and the mythology about the final purpose of the world coincide. It is a radical mysticism indeed, but no interpretation should lose sight of the fact that this mysticism understands itself as revealing the inner sense of the tradition.

Love and Concern for a Livable Life
Compared with the element of liturgy, the other structures seem simple. Love was as mysterious and had as many facets then as it does now. People were as little aware of the traditional forms of their love experience as we are. The distance that separates us from them is actually an advantage, for it helps us to recognize certain forms of which the mystics who used them did not make a special issue.

Even before the Renaissance there were tendencies to humanize the figure of Christ. His love, as depicted in his life and suffering, could be spoken of in terms bordering on sentimentality. There were also tendencies to depict the wisdom of undisguised worldly love. Then, as always, divine love and worldly love were not utterly separated. The nuptial imagery of a Ruysbroeck had its model in Bernard's mysticism.

Speaking of medieval mystics like William of Saint Thierry

and Bernard of Clairvaux, Etienne Gilson neatly summarizes their leanings: "Secular schools teach profane love according to the *Ars amatoria* of Ovid; the cloisters should be religious schools where divine love is taught."[19] It is obvious, however, that worldly love was not just a matter of reading classical texts. A powerful influence came from the poetry of courtly love; the form of poetry used by minnesingers was employed even before the Renaissance by such mystical authors as the thirteenth-century Saint Mechtilde of Magdeburg and Hadewych. In the next century Heinrich Suso (1296–1366), one of the famous disciples of Eckhart but more restrained in his expressions than his master, wrote verses in the language of the minnesingers. Evidently this style was accepted. Of course, the continuation of this style does not sum up the mystery of love in Renaissance mysticism. But it is an eloquent sign that divine love could be spoken of in words that did not coincide with official doctrines. It might be called a sign of an "expanding consciousness," if that phrase had not become suspect.

This expanding consciousness is not due to one simple cause, such as the poetry of the minnesingers. Long before their time mystics (like Plotinus) had spoken of the beauty of the divine. But now it was as if the style of secular love songs, the human features of the Lord, and many other factors cooperated to produce this phenomenon. Saint John of the Cross (1542–1591) sang of God's beauty with a rapture like no one's before him. Eckhart and others spoke with fondness of the child Jesus. Love has many sides, but in all these aspects one senses that man is addressed in his human experiences. It is a new, total experience, not an anxious attempt to preserve a particular religious community. Saint John of the Cross was one of those who suffered persecution; his life shows that the established community was not always eager to own this new expansiveness of the inner life.

Love is a dynamic element of tremendous scope. One should not think of it as a mere metaphor used to adorn theological propositions. With it the peculiarly mystical imaginative power

[19] Etienne Gilson, *History of Christian Philosophy in the Middle Ages* (New York: Random House, 1955), p. 167.

to understand common things anew and to transform them into forceful symbolisms reaches its peak. The movement of love encompasses doctrines concerning both God and the enigmatic world. Everything vibrates through its dynamic.

Not all mystics are poets, but in the theme of love all Renaissance mystics become poets. Striking is the transformation, or even a subordination of dogma through the new propelling force. Catherine of Siena exclaims that "nails would not have held God-and-Man fast to the Cross, had love not held Him there."[20] The English woman mystic Julian of Norwich (1343–1416) repeats that love is the ground of our beseeching and that love is our Lord's meaning. Her revelations show her a correspondence between the nature of the Trinity and the human soul, a correspondence not in terms of a static image, but in terms of movement. The "higher part" of the soul is rooted in God and the birth of Christ must be understood as a happening in the soul, whereby the higher part and the lower part, one's sensual nature, are united:

> And thus in Christ our two kinds are oned; for Christ is comprehended in the Trinity, in whom our higher part is grounded and rooted; and our lower part the second Person hath taken—which kind was first prepared for him. For I saw full truly that all the works that God hath done, or ever shall, were full known to him and before-seen, from without-beginning. And for love he made mankind; and for the same love himself would become man.[21]

And with the liberal application of the notion of motherhood—strange to us, but not unusual then—she writes:

> For in that same time that God knit himself to our body in the maiden's womb, he took our sensual soul. . . . Thus our Lady is our Mother in whom we are all enclosed and of her,

[20] Vida D. Scudder, trans. and ed., *Saint Catherine of Siena, as Seen in Her Letters* (London: Dent, 1906), p. 8.

[21] James Walsh, trans., *The Revelations of Divine Love of Julian of Norwich* (London: Burns, 1961), pp. 156–157 (chap. 57).

born in Christ. For she that is Mother of our Saviour is our
true Mother, in whom we are endlessly borne; and we shall
never come out of him.[22]

Elsewhere, with the imagery of motherly love, Julian reiter-
ates: "Jesus Christ, who doeth good against evil, is our very
Mother. We have our being of him, there where the ground of
Motherhood beginneth; with all the sweet keeping of love that
endlessly followeth. As truly as God is our Father, so truly is
God our Mother."[23]

From a dogmatic point of view much of the foregoing seems
a watering down of orthodox propositions. Nevertheless, the
theme of love is sung by all mystics of the time in many modu-
lations and with great force. And it always creates a new opening in the traditional frame of certainties, not to destroy those
certainties, but rather to let them flow forth anew. We are very
far away from an escapism or a reveling in individual experiences alone. In the final analysis, the love the mystics speak
about is the secret ingredient that makes new thoughts possible.
Cusanus, that most difficult mystical intellect, exclaims: "O
Jesu my Love, Thou hast sowed the seed of life in the field of
the faithful, and hast watered it by the witness of Thy blood,
and hast shown by bodily death that truth is the life of the rational spirit."[24] The outward discoveries of the Renaissance
period no doubt made much of traditional religion irrelevant.
But after new continents and scientific achievements—and often
before them—mystics experimented in the inner universe and
discovered a dynamic that is no less, although it is more difficult
to tabulate.

The inner dynamic of the Trinity as discussed by the greatest
intellects—like Cusanus—might lead one to speculate on relationships between experiences of love and the stimuli to form

[22] *Ibid.*, p. 157 (Chap. 57).
[23] *Ibid.*, p. 161 (chap. 59).
[24] *De Visione Dei*, XXIV, in E. G. Salter, trans., with introd. by E.
Underhill, *Nicholas of Cusa: The Vision of God* (New York: Ungar,
1960), p. 120.

new rational views of the universe. One might think of Spinoza's philosophy, his insistence on an *amor Dei intellectualis* and his treatment of ethics following a mathematical model. One might think also of Calvin, who tried, with all the forms of thought available in his time, to probe into the inner workings of God's dispensation of Providence. In all instances there was a concern for the inner movement in God and, connected with it, a new tempo of life.

It would be foolish to suggest that all these expositions are the same, or to declare one the cause of the others. It is certain, however, that the mystical raptures in love were part of the Renaissance fabric and could be understood by many contemporaries, even those whose ideas did not focus in mystical experiences.

One source of mystical love is quite evident. It stems from a new feeling of life, rather than an organization, in the Low Countries. It does not have the intellectual flamboyance of a Cusanus nor the ecstatic flamboyance of Saint John of the Cross. Its best-known exponent was Geert Groote of Deventer (1340–1384), the central figure of the so-called *Devotio Moderna*. He was a great preacher and was quite familiar with monastic life, but he never entered an order. His zeal was for an ascetic life lived in the world, rather than in a monastery. This new "feeling of life" is reflected somewhat earlier in the great mystic Ruysbroeck (1294–1381), who belonged to a spiritual order (Augustinian). In *The Spiritual Espousals* he speaks at length about "the active life" which is "needful to all men who wish to be saved."[25] He knows that "the supernatural life of the contemplation of God" is attainable only by the few—he so states in his prologue—but he emphasizes that they can attain it "by way of their exalted and excellent way of living."[26] In the same context we should think also of the devout men, and perhaps even more so of the devout women, living together without taking a monastic vow, for whom a life of prayer is integrated with

[25] Jan van Ruysbroeck, *The Spiritual Espousals*, trans. Eric Colledge (New York: Harper. n.d.), p. 44.
[26] *Ibid.*

something we would call "social work." Geert Groote established many such groups. Especially in Thomas a Kempis's *Imitation of Christ* did the mystical devotion of the Low Countries find its ideal expression, and it reached a worldwide audience. Nicholas of Cusa spent some years as a student in the school Geert Groote founded in Deventer.

The nature of this "modest" mysticism makes it difficult to measure its influence on Renaissance mysticism elsewhere. But one point is important: its down-to-earth character, in comparison with other forms of mysticism, is as much a sign of the expanding consciousness as the love structures in the great speculative systems. Nicholas of Cusa is an illustration that the two can be interwoven.

Naturally, the practical side of the *Devotio Moderna* appeals to moderns, but it did not amount to a total embrace of the world or a radical revolution. Neither Geert Groote nor any of his pupils would have thought of their movement in that way. Finally, his movement gave rise to the establishment of monastic institutions. Although the pressure of church authorities may have had something to do with this development—shortly before his death Geert Groote was deprived of his license to preach—traditional ways of leading a spiritual life were not abandoned. There was no turning against tradition in these circles, but I think we may speak of a new "concern for a livable life." Clearly visible in the *Devotio Moderna*, this concern is part of Renaissance mysticism and adds a special stamp to its glorification of love.

The modern inclination to think highly of a mystical devotion with down-to-earth tendencies is, it must be remembered, a rather recent phenomenon. The difficulty of assessing the value of the concern for a livable life, this practical component, becomes evident when we see alongside our own reaction the reaction of a great historian less than a century ago. In 1882 C. Busken Huet wrote a classical work on the civilization of the Netherlands. In it we find something very different from a positive appreciation for the *Devotio Moderna*, along with a rather romantic reveling in the greatness of the Italian Renaissance. Huet tells how a famous follower of Geert Groote, Wessel Gansfort (1419–1489), once visited the pope (Sixtus IV). Before Wessel left Rome, the pope urged him to choose a gift from the Vatican library. The author marvels at the possible choices Wessel could have made but, alas, did not make: "... a manuscript with a text of Virgil, Plato or Homer or any of the texts whose discovery had so thoroughly occupied the minds of Petrarch and Boccaccio." But, the author reports disdainfully, Wessel chose none of these. Instead, he selected a New Testament in Greek and an Old Testament in Hebrew. "For Wessel religious matters superseded everything else. He did not know of anything higher than unadulterated Jewish-Christian edification."[27] To be sure, Wessel Gansfort was no mystic. Nevertheless his choice from the Vatican library could hardly have been what it was had it not been for the impact of the mystical devotion of his circles. In my opinion, few modern historians would fully share Busken Huet's disdain for Wessel's choice. The concern for a livable life included a preoccupation with elementary matters.

Authority

Closely related to the experience of love in all its manifestations and to the concern for a livable life is authority, which to us might seem not to be related at all. The exercise in love on the mystical path is first and foremost humility. But humility is always humility before someone. As Saint Teresa of Avila writes, in describing the life of a nun, "the whole point of *true* humility is that she should consider herself happy in serving the servants of the Lord and in praising Him. For she deserves to be a slave of the devils in hell."[28]

The notion of authority often has a vehemence that we can hardly imagine. For us, ideas of love are usually associated with self-fulfillment or with feelings of gratification which are not

[27] C. Busken Huet, *Het Land van Rembrand* (Haarlem: Tjeenk Willink, 1946), p. 132.

[28] E. Allison Peers, trans., *"The Way of Perfection" by St. Teresa of Avila* (Garden City: Image Books, 1964), p. 124.

always of a very high order. Most of us are able to understand Nietzsche's disgust with the Christian idea of love as an unworthy self-effacement, an appalling submissiveness, hypocritical at that. I am not suggesting that the Renaissance knew nothing of self-centered fulfillments or of unworthy, cringing humility. But in the Renaissance mystics the notions of humility and of its complement, authority, are rather different. For us, the notion of love may seem difficult to relate to the notion of authority, but a largely feudal society yields images constitutive of love experience, and many mystics speak of "submission" to the lover.

Strong notions of authority were available, just as available as the liturgical forms of the Church, to serve mystical apperception. The function of authority is difficult to understand if one thinks of the Renaissance as a period of liberation or even as a prelude to a modern form of egalitarianism. Indeed, "feudalism" is a derogatory word for us, but the existence of authorities was a fact of life then. It was a fact of life even for so typical a Renaissance spirit as Benvenuto Cellini (1500–1571), who was autobiographer, sculptor, craftsman, and a marvelous gold-and silversmith. He worked for various patrons, many of whom were noble and among whom were popes and cardinals. On various occasions, when Cellini was in trouble, often as a result of duels or fights, these patrons had to come to his rescue. Even Cellini, who led a Renaissance life to the hilt and had little respect for the societal hierarchy, demonstrates that life could not be lived without the authority of lords. They were not only external social facts, but facts that determined his inner experience in his artistic work. When he was at work on a large bronze sculpture and all odds were against successful completion of the piece, he cried out to God for help; when he did succeed—miraculously, it seemed to him—he fell on his knees and with all his heart gave thanks to God.[29]

The Renaissance still knew what it was to bow and to serve. The exuberance of feeling did not diminish the image of God,

[29] J. A. Symonds, trans., *The Autobiography of Benevenuto Cellini* (New York: Washington Square Press, 1963), pp. 372–374.

but, if anything, exalted it even more. Teresa of Avila's insistence on humility is seen in all the mystics of the time. Acceptance of the authority of God had its realistic complement in
other authorities. Again, Teresa of Avila gives the most empha-
tic expression to the idea. She wrote her autobiography in obedience to spiritual authorities, and we are bound to take her
literally when she says: "Your Reverence must take the responsibility for everything beyond the simple story of my life . . . ,
if it be in accordance with the truths of our holy Catholic Faith;
and if it be not, Your Reverence must burn it at once—I am
quite willing for you to do that."[30]

Since life includes the structure of authority, what I have
called "the concern for a livable life" also includes authority;
this concern is a far cry from a sense for rebellion, either in
social or in intellectual life. Thomas a Kempis takes up biblical
words of God saying: "My judgments are to be feared, not to
be discussed; for they are incomprehensible to human understanding."[31] C. Busken Huet deplored the fostering of ignorance
in the *Devotio Moderna* (see pp. 134–135, above). But the awareness of authority should not be confused with intellectual
servility. No Renaissance mystic would have contradicted
Thomas a Kempis's words concerning the authoritative judgments of God.

In the last resort authority is linked with, even identical with,
God's unity. In an interesting way the significance of authority
comes out in Nicholas of Cusa. He says, in *De Pace Fidei* ("The
Peace of Religion"), that there was once a man who was so
distressed by religious controversies—especially as a result of
rumors about gruesome events in the conquests by the Turks—
that he began to meditate on the problem of the plurality of
sects and religions. He arrived at a vision, the vision of a meeting
at which authoritative spokesmen of all religions were present.
An account of a discussion in the court of heaven ensues. It is
perhaps the most fascinating text a general historian of religions

[30] Peers, *Autobiography of St. Teresa*, p. 123.
[31] Thomas à Kempis, *Of The Imitation of Christ*, trans. Abbot Jus-
tin McCann (New York: Mentor Books, 1957), Bk. III, chap. 58, 1.

can read. All groups, Arabs and Indians included, have their spokesmen. It is demonstrated that no unity can be arrived at by sacrificing the individual character of any group. On the contrary, the nature of unity, the unity that can establish peace, is such that it is attainable only when each searches for it through a proper understanding of his individuality. The paradox is a perfect illustration of Cusanus's thought. What I want to emphasize is the manner in which the whole treatise is pervaded by the acceptance of authority.

The authority of God is, of course, basic. The scene of the disputation—heaven—makes that perfectly clear. Further, Cusanus assumes without question that each religion can be adequately represented by some authority. Most revealing seems the manner in which Cusanus broaches the subject and states the purpose of the treatise. For example, he tells how the man who had the vision introduces the heavenly discourse: "He presented his vision as follows, simple and clear, as well as his memory enabled him, in order somehow to bring it to the attention of those who decide in these weighty matters [*eorum qui his maximis praesunt*]."[32] Thus, on the most practical level, it is not felt necessary to prove that some are "in charge"; it is assumed that there are such authorities.

Purification

By whatever name it is called, all mystics know a process of purification. Although it occurs everywhere, there is a special reason to stress its significance in the Renaissance.

Earlier in this volume Lynn White presents a frightening picture of demonic powers and mass hysteria. It is natural to think of purification first against this background. Physical and mental torture, immoral atrocities, all cried out for remedy. And it is true that all mystics know of the necessity to cleanse one's life of evil desires, of evil behavior, of deceit. But their goal

---

[32] *De pace fidei*, I., translation, author's own. The texts cited here and in footnotes 35 and 36 can be most conveniently found in vols. 1 and III of Nikolaus von Kues, *Philosophisch-theologische Schriften*, ed. Leo Gabriel (Vienna: Herder, 1964/67).

is more than the cure of moral and social ills. All these ills are merely symptoms of an evil that is radical, far below the surface. If social reform, an idea to which all present-day academicians must pay service, occurs, it is almost like a by-product of their quest. Their quest concerns the supreme Good, the lover, the essence of God. Cusanus's heavenly disputation gives us some idea of how the quest for the supreme Good and the overcoming of the evils of the world are related. Since the nature of the mystic's quest concerns the supreme Good, his is the task to see the manifold evils in their real, devilish shape.

The artist can give a picture of this quest as vivid as our worst nightmares or, for that matter, our clearest reasonings. In one painting Hieronymus Bosch portrays a saint with scenes that are the opposite of holy. The artist, who can see more clearly than others, causes not only incidental desires, but also cardinal sins, to become manifest before the saint. Such art portrays visibly what is experienced by mystics and what is difficult to transpose into the world of sensations.

It is always easier to say of a mystical structure what it is not than what it is, and in this instance a negative statement will be useful to clarify understanding. When the mystics speak of evil, they do not have in mind any sort of pathology. They do not merely think of evil deviations of small or large crowds of people. The purification they speak of deserves attention because it is purification from evil itself. This fundamental evil is not the deviations of a few, but it is part of man's existence. No wonder then that the mystics turn to the classical notions that deal with it. They do so with renewed force. In the *Dark Night of the Soul* Saint John of the Cross systematically discusses the difficulties of the mystical path. He begins with the imperfections of beginners and then treats in detail pride, avarice, luxury, wrath, gluttony, envy, and sloth. The point is that all these sins are to be understood in their spiritual sense, for it is in their grasp on spiritual life that they stand in the way of a union with God. That is their true devilish nature.

It would be pleasing for a modern reader if Renaissance mystics had risen as one man to cry out against the burning of witches and similar atrocities. It has been suggested—rightly, no doubt—that religious and philosophical arguments failed to reverse the incredibly cruel trends of the time. Nevertheless, if we should study the obscurities of the Renaissance in order to learn how to control mass insanity, we would discover that Renaissance mystics played a crucial role. They knew what the mass insanities of our own time have perhaps not yet taught us, in spite of the horror they may have inspired: that evil is not a deviation from normalcy, but a part of the abnormalcy that is our life. Scientific analyses are not enough to rectify wrongs.

Mystic purification has many forms, but it is always radical; it concerns the root of human imperfection just as it deals with the foundation of goodness. A quest to cleanse human will and knowledge goes against the stream of common ideas at any time. It is especially at odds with the modern concern to find psychological gimmicks to make life more "balanced" or better "adjusted." At every stage, with every new conquest, the mystic is aware of the dangers that lurk along his way: the radically evil one never rests, and he too takes many forms. A common form is that of knowledge and the pride that comes with it. The necessary purification of knowledge is not merely a reaction against scholastic tradition, the reaction that found such vociferous spokesmen in the Italian Renaissance. Especially in the discussion of knowledge, the great mystics are not inventors of new ideas. They are concerned with what might be called with due respect, a process of unlearning. Long ago, Dionysius the Areopagite was concerned with this subject. Man must become fully aware of the inadequacy of his knowledge. His ignorance, if only it were properly realized, relates somehow to the fundamental incomprehensibility of God. The awareness of his ignorance is, so to speak, the condition for his supreme union. The most famous renewal of this theme of purification—an intellectual purification—is presented in Nicholas of Cusa's great work, *De Docta Ignorantia* ("About Learned Ignorance").

Perhaps the new knowledge brought by the Renaissance in many areas can explain in part the renewed pre-occupation with a proper process of unlearning. At the same time we must admit that we do not know any simple causes that can explain the process fully. Fourteenth-century England had already produced a mystical text that, significantly, is entitled *The Cloud of Unknowing*. At any rate, the mystical quest for purification runs counter to all ordinary assumptions, then as well as now. On the one hand it is akin to the almost rebellious thoughts rejecting scholastic certitudes; in this respect it seems to foreshadow modern thinking. On the other hand, it went much deeper than the rejection of accepted ideas. In doing so it related itself to classical notions; and in this respect the Renaissance mystical quest is separated by an unbridgeable gulf from the modern fashion of asking more and more questions about more and more things with the belief that finally the accumulation of information will somehow be unified.

Deprovincialization

One would search mystical texts in vain for the term "deprovincialization." Nevertheless, the term may indicate a structure of mysticism to which all the other structures point. In them we have seen the significance of earlier traditions; we have also seen that the earlier traditions—of liturgy, of love, of authority, of purification—do not exhaust the subject of Renaissance mysticism. There is a new quality; a new and wider world opens up, the very world we like to think of, rightly or wrongly, as our own. There are specific elements in the Renaissance mystics which reveal a new, universal vision and indeed break through the limits of a closed world. These elements may justify the use of the term "deprovincialization" and may suggest that our own world, in comparison, is rather narrower than we like to think.

We have seen some democratic tendencies in those who spoke of mystical experience. We have also noted that not all mystics of the period were to be found in monasteries and convents. But these facts are rather more superficial than the meaning I have in mind for "deprovincialization."

Let us recall Cusanus's vision of the heavenly debate among religions that were searching for unity. It is inconsequential that no one listened to this fifteenth-century thinker and that no one universal peace was effected by his treatise. The crucial point is that true unity can be attained only through the specificity of each given tradition, and this truth is offered as being universally valid. No one can reach the goal by donning the spiritual garments of another; one's own garments are always sufficient.

This vision was indeed new. Its universalism implies the end of every kind of provincialism, and one would do wrong to think that it is merely a matter of common sense. It has nothing to do with the modern assumption that every view is relative. On the contrary, the potentiality of each tradition is as complete as anything in the created world can be, and precisely in this respect is it related to God. Thus Cusanus is fully conscious of the endless complexity of man's world, but any relativism or atomism is foreign to him.

Sometimes the deprovincialization process takes place as if it were a movement from concreteness to abstraction. This too can be seen in Cusanus's treatise on peace. In the most literal sense of the word a power of abstracting is needed to present the points of view of Muslims, Christians, Persians, Jews, and Indians on the same high philosophical level. The process of increasing abstraction seems natural enough to us, since we see such problems as "unity" and "infinity" not so much as indications of the divine, but as problems of mathematics. To see in Renaissance mysticism only a link in this developmental scheme leading to ourselves would be but half of the truth. The problem for our understanding is rather that the power of abstraction does not manifest itself at the expense of concreteness. In Cusanus's treatise, God is a concrete reality whose *Verbum* ("Word") participates in the discussion.

It is unlikely that anyone would think that Teresa of Avila had anything to do with the rise of modern mathematics, or that she stimulated a new science-oriented feeling of life. One cannot doubt her concrete reliance on a concretely present God. Yet it seems to me that the experience of divine reality becomes a problem in many places in her writings and that it is consciously spoken of as a problem. I fully realize that the crux of understanding mysticism is always located in some inscrutable experience, especially so in our own day and age. Few mystics have presented experience itself—and it is the only channel through which the concreteness of God can come to people—as a problem. As Saint Teresa emphasizes, "However clearly I may wish to describe these matters which concern prayer, they will be very obscure to anyone who has no experience of it."[33]

Specifically because of this kind of statement, Teresa of Avila appeals to a modern reader as remarkably honest. Her straightforwardness is indeed a sign of something new. It could not have been quite like that in an age of undisturbed traditions. The new question one senses is whether such a concrete divine experience is indeed possible and, if possible, whether it would make any sense or be of any importance. This type of question is new; it leads to a new age—our own.

The issue of experience as a problem is also related to the democratic tendencies mentioned earlier. In a more balanced religious setting and a steadier society most people accepted the notion that the highest mysteries of experience were within the grasp of exceptional individuals. It is not quite like that today. Teresa finds it necessary to say in her spiritual counsel that one should not indulge in the comparison of experiences or of the spiritual achievements resulting therefrom: "Close the eyes of your thought and do not wonder: 'Why is He [the Lord] giving devotion to that person of so few days' experience, and none to me after so many years?' "[34] Such is the problem of experience. In this manner the concreteness of God's reality becomes a problem. One cannot gloss over these problems by saying that mystical experiences are always mysterious. Of course they are, but this emphasis is new in the Western world. It suggests a turning point in spiritual orientation.

One might see decay in this shifting to a new direction. After all, there is decreasing self-evidentness of the presence of God.

[33] Peers, *Autobiography of St. Teresa*, p. 124.
[34] *Ibid.*, p. 130.

One might also hail the change and point to the correlate of increasing power of abstraction. Neither of these judgments is quite right. The deprovincialization in Renaissance mysticism is the simultaneity of posing the problem of experience (without belittling it) and of showing the courage to pursue the highest goal with all powers of the intellect.

The importance of concrete experience is beyond dispute. The central function of love and authority is witness to that fact in Nicholas of Cusa. Yet at the same time, in the same mystic, we find surprising examples of abstract reasoning, particularly in his presentation of the so-called negative theology. It must be borne in mind that negative theology is intended as the clearest expression of the mystical way. Also, it is not meant as a rebuttal of affirmative theology, but rather as its complement. The latter speaks of God in positive statements as the One and the Triune; it attributes to him positive qualities (supreme wisdom and goodness, etc.). Negative theology is a necessary comlopement in that it prevents a worship of God as if he were a creature, for all positive pronouncements are by nature finite, whereas God is infinite. Thus we have the paradox that negations must be made for the sake of the truth concerning God. Then, making an explicit reference to Dionysius the Areopagite and to "Rabbi Solomon and all the wise men," Cusanus says "there is neither Father nor Son nor Holy Spirit according to this negative theology, since according to it God is the Infinite.."[35] It follows from the ineffability of God that "He is known only to Himself."[36]

The opposite poles of concrete experience and the courage to reason until the end are related. The statement that God is known only to himself is obviously not based on skepticism. Scholars are undoubtedly correct when they speak of the stimulus Cusanus gave to the development of modern scientific ideas. Mathematics has a prominent place in his expositions. Yet it also seems obvious that the development of a scientific world view via Kepler and Leibnitz to the present day is a continua-

[35] *De Docta Ignorantia*, I, 26.
[36] *Ibid.*

tion of only one side of Cusanus. The other side—its necessary counterpart, the concreteness of experience and of the presence of God—has passed out of our awareness. The question may be raised whether this new world of ideas of ours is not somewhat unbalanced. At any rate, there is reason to doubt that our science-ridden existence means progress vis-à-vis those strange mystical authors. Chances are that Cusanus would have similar doubts if he could look down from his present location. He might even find reason to see in our one-sided development a massive submission to black magic.

VI

THE HIDDEN GOD: REFORMATION AWE IN RENAISSANCE ENGLISH LITERATURE

Paul R. Sellin

I

A BOUT 1485, when Henry VII, the first Tudor monarch of England, ascended the throne, or about the time of birth of that courageous victim of hallucinations, Martin Luther, one of the finest surviving products of medieval literary artistry made its appearance on the Pan-European scene: the Flemish morality play *Den spieghel der salicheit van Elckerlijc*.[1] We know it in translation as *Everyman* or, as the text itself prefers, *The Summoning of Everyman*.[2]

---

[1] Usually attributed to Pieter van Doorlandt (1454–1507), a vicar of the Carthusian cloister at Zeelhem, Belgium, though this attribution is denied by R. Vos, ed., *Elckerlijc*, Bibliotheek van Nederlandse letterkunde, no. 4 (Groningen, 1967), who dates the play much earlier than is usual.

[2] Whether *Everyman* or *Elckerlijc* is the original has been much debated. For a summary of assertions and refutations, see R. W. Zandvoort, "*Everyman: A Comparative Study of Texts and Sources.* By Henry de Vocht," *RES*, XXV (1949), 66–68. The preponderance of argument and evidence plainly favors the priority of *Elckerlijc*. R. Vos ("*Elckerlijc—Everyman—Homulus—Der Sünden Loin ist der Toid,*" *Tijdschrift voor Nederlandse tàál-en letterkunde*, LXXXII [1966], 129–143) thinks that at least five recensions of the play intrude between the known Flemish, Low German, English, and Latin versions of the play and the original. His grounds for attributing the English translation to Caxton are most appealing, but cf. A. C. Cawley, ed., *Everyman* (Manchester, 1961), pp. x–xiii.

As one might expect, *Everyman* exhibits a number of features that in northern literature are usually considered "medieval." Such, for example, is its allegorical method—that is, the use of dramatis personae representing abstract concepts like Good Deeds, Beauty, Everyman—or its reliance on the macabre figure of Death for effects to which preceding chapters have pointed. These, however, are not the matters of prime interest here, but rather the theological content of the work. Precisely because of *Everyman*'s belated appearance on the threshold of the Reformation—it survives in one manuscript and several printed versions, the earliest dating from about 1490[3]—and the irony of its popularity in the very lands—Germany, the Low Countries, and England—to be most permanently affected by the Reformation, its views of the Deity and human life afford remarkable contrast with the thought and attitudes expressed by the Reformers, who were even then furiously constructing systems based on a dynamism entirely different in principle. Chronologically, the play is but a hundred years away from Shakespeare, yet emotionally *Everyman* seems to lie centuries, if not ages, distant. To my mind, the contrast between *Everyman* and the utterances of the Reformers illustrates something of what happened to the psyche of northern Europe at the end of the fifteenth century. By starting with the play, perhaps some of the effects that immersion in Renaissance "irrationality"—or "suprarationality"—produced in the transalpine heart and mind can be readily isolated.

The Summoning of Everyman is a didactic play designed to heighten the spectator's awareness that man is mortal, that he ultimately faces the judgment of his Maker, and that it behooves him in this life to take measures to ensure that after the experience of the grave he may stand before God in righteousness. "Man," says the prologue,

> in the begynnynge
> Loke well, & take good hede to the endynge
> Be you neuer so gaye

[3] The four surviving exemplars in English were printed sometime between 1508 and 1537.

Ye thynke synne in the begynnynge full swete
Whiche in the ende causeth thy soule to wepe
Whan the body lyeth in claye
Here shall you se how felawshyp and iollyte
Bothe strengthe pleasure and beaute
Wyll vade from the as floure in maye
For ye shall here how our heuen kenge
Calleth eueryman to a generall reckenyngc.[4]   (vv. 10–20)

Accordingly the drama presents God's charge to Death that he warn unsuspecting Everyman of the impending summons. When Everyman comes to realize his predicament, he turns to the comforts of this world for help, but in vain. Though of avail, his own good deeds are so encumbered with his avarice that they cannot stir to help him. Everyman has certain resources on which he can rely, however. With the aid of knowledge and the powers of mind, he is brought to confession and performs penance, freeing his good deeds. Donning the garment of contrition, he proceeds with his faculties and merits to Priesthood and there receives redemptive grace through the Eucharist and the last rite (Extreme Unction). With true satisfaction now made, Everyman approaches his final moment, a difficult encounter nonetheless, since it entails the loss of the very faculties—beauty, strength, mind, and senses—that elemented his acquisition of righteousness, including even the steadfast Knowledge. With only Good Deeds to plead for him, Everyman commends his spirit to God, steps into the grave, and to the joy of heaven mounts up to his reward.

Now I do not for the moment wish to suggest that there is something particularly rational in the beliefs reflected in *Everyman* regarding the mystery of God and his ways with men which is not to be found in the Reformers, or that by comparison the thought of the Reformers is irrational. Obviously, though we may not wish to call them "mad," the bases of

[4] *Everyman Reprinted by W. W. Greg from the Edition of John Skot in the Possession of Mr. A. H. Huth*, Materialen zur Kunde des älteren Englischen Dramas, vol. 28 (Louvain, 1909). References are to this edition.

Christian or any other religious belief are scarcely to be termed "rational." Yet so far as implications for art are concerned, there is a significant difference between the attitudes toward the Deity which one finds in the Reformers and what is to be found in *Everyman*, and one is not wholly certain that it is merely a difference in degree. What I have in mind is simply that unlike much art following the advent of the Reformation, *Everyman* exhibits a great deal of sureness about how God relates to man. The benevolence of divine concern for all humankind is assumed, and the means by which man can ensure the certainty of enjoying grace are relatively precise, systematic, and reliable.

First, the matter of divine benevolence. Consider, for example, the figure of Death. Following traditional patterns, such as the Dance of Death in graphic arts, the play makes him thrillingly horrid and relentless. Props, costuming, and makeup hold infinite possibilities for exploiting the *Beinhaus* potentialities in the role, and the actor is given speeches portraying spectral gloating and mindless, sadistic cruelty. Even so, the play makes it quite clear that Death is the direct instrument of the Deity and one instituted as an act of mercy to boot. God looks down from his majesty on his creatures in disappointment. Unmindful of him, they live

> without drede in worldely prosperytye
> Of ghostly syght the people be so blynde
> Drowned in synne, they know me not for ther god
> In worldely ryches is all theyr mynde
> They fere not my ryghtwysenes that sharpe rod
> My lawe that I shewed whan I for them dyed
> They forgot clene & sheddynge of my blod redde.
>   (vv. 24–30)

It is with sorrow rather than anger that God reacts to man's heedless viciousness so deep as to make the seven sins "in the world commendable." At issue is not the disobedience in Eden. Rather, God sees that the more he forbears mankind,

The worse they are from yere to yere
All that lyueth apperyth fasre
Therfore I wyll in all the haste
Haue a reckenynge of euery mannes persone
For and I leue the people thus alone
In theyr lyfe and wycked tempestes
Verely they wyll be cume moche worse than beastes. (vv. 43–49)

Knowing the sentence that must ultimately be passed on sin, God chooses to preserve man from plunging deeper into depravity. Though the means employed to spare him are horrible, the rationale underlying even Death's most repugnant characteristics is sufficient to justify them, and there is no doubt whatever that the intention of the Father is as kindly as possible. From the standpoint of the play, God is anthropocentric. He has the good of each of his creatures in view, and the benevolence behind his measures shines readily through them.

Consider next Everyman's nature. From the beginning, the aim of creation was to benefit the creature: "I hoped well that euery man," God says,

> In my glorye shulde make his mansyon
> And therto I had them *all* elect.[5] (vv. 52–54)

The issue is not that all deserve to perish, but that though man is intended to eternal life and his justification is already effected by the shedding of Christ's blood, people "forgot clene" the "lawe" that God showed "whan I for them dyed . . . & shed-

---

[5] Italics mine. The Dutch text omits the "all" (it takes for granted that all are chosen) and emphasizes the intensity of God's benevolence instead (vv. 35–39):

> ic hoepte, dat si bi desen [the Passion]
> Mijnder eeuwiger glorien ghebrukick souden wesen,
> Daar ic se seer toe hadde vercoren.
> Nu vinde ic datt et al is verloren
> Dat ic se so costelic hadde ghemeent.

dynge of my blod redde." Man is not incipiently evil, not fallen, but redeemed. The problem is that he continues to fall and through wicked acts forfeits "the heavenly company" of angels to which by right he belongs. Thus, when the final judgment is to be passed, his evil works are liabilities; his good deeds, merits. In face of his redemption *accomplie*, man is here obliged to stand or fall by his works.

Such a position, of course, assumes that man is so constituted as to be capable of righteous action. And so it is in the play. Though Everyman's good deeds are negated by his sins, the implication is that right action would have been possible had he paid conscientious heed to the Lord's intention. Furthermore, as he is constituted of certain faculties—strength, beauty, senses, and the powers of mind—it is possible for him to know what he must do and to act accordingly. If we are not convinced, that is exactly what happens in the play. Once Everyman realizes his plight, Knowledge leads him to the proper forms of atonement, and through atonement he qualifies for grace. Last, Everyman has effective volition. Through his faculties he can choose between alternatives and suit his actions to his will. Indeed, the function of death is to frighten him into facing his predicament and to influence his will so that the right option will be selected. For unless Everyman can reject as well as elect the way to grace, no merit can accrue to his acts, and mortification, accomplished through flagellation in the play, would have no point.

In addition to constituting man sufficient to have stood in the grace of his Redeemer, had he so willed, and endowing him with powers to repair his lapses, God has also provided an abundance of means by which grace can be secured. If the play is anything, it is a testimonial to the efficacy of the sacraments as literal vehicles for bestowing grace, and it reflects the central position of the Church as their keeper and dispenser. In the play, Baptism has in effect removed the guilt of original sin. Confession and Penance are indispensable, for through them Everyman becomes fit to receive mercy. And in the Eucharist and Extreme Unction, actual grace is bestowed.

The main elements in the world of Everyman, then, are ultimately secure and benevolent. One has the certainty of knowing that however horrible, capricious, or painful temporal life may be, salvation is assured to all who will, and that the minimal conditions of qualifying for grace are simple and sure. Such comfort is bound to affect the mentality of those who accept it fully, particular if it is endemic to the culture surrounding them. And so it was in the Middle Ages. One may fear, one may be wayward, but one never forgets whether this or the next world is to be heeded. As the late C. S. Lewis put it, so very beautifully, when the "children" of the Middle Ages hear the bell clang, "suddenly hushed and grave, and a little frightened, [they] troop back to their master." [6] The point here is that one can be sure that the bell is going to sound. This is perhaps why *Everyman*, though a serious and moving play, is ultimately joyous rather than tragic in effect.[7] As many others have pointed out, it is questionable whether Christian schemes entailing systems of just reward or punishment can be reconciled with tragedy.[8] The constant possibility of ultimate grace undermines the illusion of regrettable and irremediable loss of happiness from which come the sympathetic affections that we describe as tragic.

II

How different is the tide of feeling expressed by the Reformation in the very decades of *Everyman's* greatest currency! In sharp contrast with the anthropocentric benevolence exhibited in the play, the "new" irrationality places the main emphasis on the absolute majesty and sovereignty of God, and for most of the great figures of the Reformation, those attributes were the cornerstone of their theology. Let us begin with Luther, who

[6] *The Allegory of Love* (New York, 1958), p. 43.

[7] In this respect, the title of the Flemish play is much more appropriate than that of the English rendering, in that it stresses Everyman's "salicheit" (bliss).

[8] E.g., Clifford Leech, *Shakespeare's Tragedies and Other Studies in Seventeenth Century Drama* (London, 1950), pp. 18–19.

pioneered in expressing the strong impulses animating the change.

To the heretic of Wittenberg, God is a terrible and glorious, though to be sure an infinitely loving and bountiful, mystery whose omnipotence is eternal, incomprehensible, inscrutable, infallible, immense, awesome, and above all hidden—*verè a Deus absconditus* (Isa. 45:15). Just as but a portion of the moon's superficies is ever visible to us, and that in varying degrees, so even in Revelation only a modicum of God's nature is disclosed, and we do not apprehend even that from a constant angle. And just as it is not the moon's surface—but its mass and constituency—which accounts for lunar operations, such as the influence over tides, the distortion of our globe, and the mysterious habit of presenting one side only, so the real being of God—that in which the dynamics of his operations are rooted—is cloaked to our view. Indeed, the undisclosed immensity itself refuses to revolve. "God," as Luther puts it,

> in His own nature and majesty is to be left alone; in this regard, we have nothing to do with Him, nor does He wish us to deal with Him. We have to do with Him [only] as clothed and displayed in His Word, by which He presents Himself to us. That is His glory and beauty, in which the Psalmist proclaims Him to be clothed.[9]

Our proper business is the beams and the beauty they cast, not the dark body animating the light. Indeed, even at the moment of fullest disclosure in Scripture, God remains paradoxically arcane. His very sacrifice on Calvary is itself a gift hidden in mystery.[10] Man never experiences *Gotteserkenntnis* directly, for even on the cross, where God is most accessible, He remains a hidden god, one who to reveal Himself stays obscure, who to

[9] *Martin Luther: Selections from His Writings*, ed. John Dillenberger (New York, 1961), p. 191. All subsequent references to Luther are from this source.

[10] John Dillenberger, *God Hidden and Revealed: The Interpretation of Luther's Deus Absconditus and Its Significance for Religious Thought* (Philadelphia, 1953), p. xiv.

be an object of belief viels Himself in the ignominy and suffering of the cross.[11]

There is nothing about the Deity or his purposes or his operations, then, which permits man to treat them like more familiar things or to take them for granted. Not only God's being is hidden to us, but also the rationale underlying the processes by which his purposes are fulfilled. To Luther, it is fundamentally "necessary and wholesome for Christians to know" that God "foresees, purposes, and does all things according to His own immutable, eternal, and infallible will" (p. 181), yet these qualities are hard to see even in things amenable to our faculties. "Behold," Luther says,

> God governs the external affairs of the world in such a way that, if you regard and follow the judgment of human reason, you are forced to say, either that there is no God, or that God is unjust. . . . See the great prosperity of the wicked, and by contrast the great adversity of the good. Proverbs, and experience, the parent of proverbs, bear record that the more abandoned men are, the more successful they are. . . . Is it not, pray, universally held to be most unjust that bad men should prosper, and good men be afflicted? Yet that is the way of the world. (p. 201)

This, of course, is an old problem, and the standard solution is the one in *Everyman*: the Gospels answer that there is life after this life in which justice will be done. To Luther, however, that answer, though correct, is but one "which shines only in the Word and to faith." The full and true answer must await the moment "when the light of the Word and faith shall cease, and the real facts, and the Majesty of God shall be revealed as they are" (p. 202).

If, then, God cannot be grasped either through his works, through what we experience in this world, or even in the cross, how can the human mind possibly dare to speculate about matters not revealed or about things deliberately withheld from

[11] See Walter von Loewenich, *Luthers Theologie crucis*, 4th ed. (Munich, 1954), pp. 16–17, 22, 30–38.

human ken? Although faith may tell us that man is one of the immediate objects of God's mercy, what mortal is to say that the salvation of fallen man is the central event, rather than one of several means to far grander ends, or to spell out the principles of divine operation? One fact that is clear, however, is that God's activity cannot be commanded. Indeed, Luther goes so far as to say that God's own promises are not binding upon Him: being "all in all," He has set no "bounds to Himself by His Word, but has kept Himself free over all things." In short, God "does many things which He does not show us in His Word, and He wills many things which He does not in His Word show us that He wills" (p. 191). Plainly, grace derives solely from God's pleasure, and it is imputed ultimately for the sake of his unknown purposes.

Even when it is hardest to defend divine mercy and equity, as when ungodly persons can by no means "avoid being ungodly, and staying so, and being damned, but are compelled by natural necessity to sin and perish," Luther says that

> God must be reverenced and held in awe, as being most merciful to those whom He justifies and saves in their own utter unworthiness; and we must show some measure of deference to His Divine wisdom by believing Him just when to us He seems unjust. If His justice were such as could be adjudged just by human reckoning, it clearly would not be Divine; it would in no way differ from human justice. But inasmuch as He is the one true God, wholly incomprehensible and inaccessible to man's understanding, it is reasonable, indeed inevitable, that His justice also should be incomprehensible: as Paul cries, saying: "O the depth of the riches both of the wisdom and knowledge of God! How unsearchable are His judgments, and His ways past finding out!" [Rom. 11:33]. They would not, however, be "unsearchable" if we could at every point grasp the grounds on which they are just. . . . If, now, even nature teaches us to acknowledge that human power, strength, wisdom, knowledge and substance, and all that is ours, are as nothing compared with Divine power, strength, wisdom, knowledge and substance, what perversity is it on

our part to worry at the justice and the judgment of the only God, and to arrogate so much to our own judgment as to presume to comprehend. . . . Ask reason whether force of conviction does not compel her to acknowledge herself foolish and rash for not allowing God's judgment to be incomprehensible, when she confesses that all the other things of God are incomprehensible! (pp. 200–201)

God is doubtless great and good and just, but from a subjective point of view it is impossible to fathom his ways. Gone forever is the psychological comfort of being able to discern with certainty the Lord's intentions, especially in particular instances. Divine goodness is now a matter of belief, not of experience.

Naturally, this affects Luther's view of how God relates to His creatures. In the medieval scheme, two things appear to have troubled him. Though the fundamental condition for qualifying for grace in *Everyman* was Confession, Luther seems to have doubted that this course was possible. Could *all* sins be confessed? Could one even remember them, much less grasp and repent for them in full? (One thinks here of Luther's own exaggerated attempts at penance during his monastic career.) Even if full confession were possible, is man capable of willing an adequate relationship with the Creator? Even granting the realities of the sacraments, is it possible for even the best acts of men to satisfy the demands by God's infinite righteousness, or for the best men to reciprocate his immeasurable love?[12] The solution was Luther's famous doctrine that history does ill to proclaim "justification by faith." The formula is far better described as "justification by grace through (or expressed in) faith," the main point being that it entails a notion of mercy so totally gratuitous as to be incomprehensible. Luther's aim, of course, was to comfort the recipients of mercy with maximum assurance of salvation; yet he raised issues of explosive implications from which, characteristically, he did not shrink.

One of the most crucial implications is the degree to which

[12] Dillenberger, pp. xvi-xvii.

God controls the actions of men. In opposition to determinist teachings, Erasmus's attack on Luther, *On the Freedom of the Will*, divided the opponents of Pelagianism—that is, the denial that the fall of Adam had permanently corrupted human nature—into three classes. The first supposedly held that without the grace of God, men can do nothing good; the second, that free will commands the power to sin while grace only works the good; and the third, that God moves both evil and good in us, that everything that happens, happens with absolute necessity.[13] As the preceding discussion has undoubtedly suggested, there is absolutely no question as to which group Luther belongs in. For him the will of God is sovereign. It governs all things, and everything depends on it, including the sinful deeds of men. It covers even the original fall of man through Adam's disobedience in the Garden of Eden. Luther is perfectly aware of the difficulties his position entails, but he specifically ascribes everything, including our own, Adam's, or Satan's sin, directly to the eternal, infallible, and immutable will of God.

First, the question of our sin. "Do you suppose," he asks scornfully, that God

> does not will what He foreknows, or that He does not foreknow what He wills? If He wills what He foreknows, His will is eternal and changeless, because His nature is so. From which it follows, by resistless logic, that all we do, however it may appear to us to be done mutably and contingently, is in reality done necessarily and immutably in respect of God's will. For the will of God is effective and cannot be impeded, since power belongs to God's nature; and His wisdom is such that He cannot be deceived. Since, then, His will is not impeded, what is done cannot but be done where, when, how, as far as, and by whom, He foresees and wills. (p. 181)

[13]Ernst F. Winter, trans., *Erasmus-Luther: Discourse on Free Will* (New York, 1961), pp. 30–31. For a sensitive summary that preserves the subtlety of Luther's controversy with Erasmus, see Heinrich Bornkamm, "Faith and Reason in the Thought of Erasmus and Luther," in *Religion and Culture: Essays in Honor of Paul Tillich*, ed. Walter Leibrecht (New York, 1959), pp. 133–139.

We men know future things only because they are certain to occur. For example, the moon does not suffer eclipse because we have previous knowledge of the phenomenon. On the contrary, precisely because an eclipse is certain to occur, we are able to know beforehand that it will. With God, things are just the other way around. Things happen because he knew they would, for he wills what he foreknows and cannot be mistaken. Therefore, because God had previous knowledge of sin, sin was necessary; because he foresaw the fall of Adam, Adam was bound to fall.

Now the consequence of such a stand is the doctrine of double predestination. That is, the eternal will of God not only elects some to salvation, but effects as well the reprobation of others who are thereby doomed to everlasting destruction. To Luther, the point is readily verifiable: but look about you, and it is obvious that some people scorn the offer of grace (p. 190). So far as the elect are concerned, there is no problem. Grace is freely given to the undeserving, thereby redounding to the donor's glory, and the doctrine of predestination affords "unspeakable comfort" to the recipient of grace, assuring him that as God's love is given without regard to the unworthiness of its object, and as it is extended by the pleasure of the "all-changing changeless Ancient Days," [14] it stands absolutely fast.

But when it comes to the matter of God "damning the undeserving"—that is, those "who, being born in ungodliness, can by no means avoid being ungodly, and staying so, and being damned, but are compelled by natural necessity to sin and perish; . . . created such by God Himself from a seed that had been corrupted by the sin of one man, Adam" (p. 200)— when it comes to these, then men balk. In so doing, of course, they err, for unless one is willing to say—an unthinkable idea to Luther—that the deity desires our death, "it must be laid to the charge of our own will if we perish" (p. 191).

God is not to be defended as in *Everyman*, however, by at-

[14] John Donne, "La Corona 1: 'Deign at my hands this crown of prayer and praise,'" v. 4.

tributing efficacy to human will. To Luther, the "published offer of God's mercy" in revelation is one thing, his "dreadful
hidden will" another (p. 190), and there is a vast difference
between them. It is indeed right to lay our destruction to the
charge of human will if one speaks only of "God preached."
According to Luther, the Deity indeed

> desires that all men should be saved in that He comes to all by
> the word of salvation; and the fault is in the will which does
> not receive Him: as He says in Matt. 23 [v. 37]: "How often
> would I have gathered thy children together, and thou
> wouldst not."

But,

> why the Majesty does not remove or change this fault of will
> in every man (for it is not in the power of man to do it), or
> why He lays this fault to the charge of the will, when man
> cannot avoid it, it is not lawful to ask; and though you should
> ask much, you would never find out; as Paul says in Rom. 11
> [actually Rom. 9:20]: "Who art thou that repliest against
> God?" (pp. 191–192)

Indeed, although the polity of God's hidden will, as opposed
to his revealed will, remains thus inscrutable, the process by
which the human will accumulates blame is readily discerned.
The Lord galls the ungodly by hardening and embittering them
and by capitalizing on their self-seeking:

> The ungodly man, like Satan his prince, is wholly turned to
> self and to his own. He does not seek God, nor care for the
> things of God: He seeks his own riches, and glory, and works,
> and wisdom, and power, and sovereignty in everything, and
> wants to enjoy it in peace. If anyone stands in his way or
> wants to detract from any of these things, he is moved with
> the same perverted desire that leads him to seek them, and is
> outraged and furious with his opponent. He can no more re-
> strain his fury than he can stop his self-seeking, and he can no

morc stop his self-seeking than he can stop existing—for he is still a creature of God; though a spoiled one.

When God hardens the hearts of such people, this is the effect:

> As of themselves they are turned away from God by the very corruption of their nature, so their antipathy greatly increases and they grow far worse as their course away from God meets with opposition or reversal. Thus, when God purposed to deprive ungodly Pharaoh of his kingdom, he galled and hardened him, and brought bitterness to his heart, by falling upon him through the word of Moses, who seemed about to take away his kingdom and deliver the people from under his dominion. He did not give Pharaoh the Spirit within, but allowed his own ungodly corruption, under Satan's sway, to blaze with anger, to swell with pride, to boil with rage and to advance along the path of scornful recklessness.

Yet in attributing this process to God, one must take care, for to say that God hardens us or works evil in us is not the same as to say that by doing so, as it were, he creates "fresh evil in us":

> When men hear us say that God works both good and evil in us, and that we are subject to God's working by mere passive necessity, they seem to imagine a man who is in himself good, and not evil, having an evil work wrought in him by God; for they do not sufficiently bear in mind how incessantly active God is in all his creatures, allowing none of them to keep holiday. He who would understand these matters, however, should think thus: God works evil in us (that is, by means of us) not through God's own fault, but by reason of our own defect....
>
> Thus God, finding Satan's will evil, not creating it so (it became so by Satan's sinning and God's withdrawing), carries it along by His own operation and moves it where He wills; although Satan's will does not cease to be evil in virtue of this movement of God. (p. 193)

Obviously, all this avoids the question of how evil began in the first place—is not Satan's evil chargeable to God? Luther knows that it is, but the question is irrelevant to his purposes. He is trying to describe what he thinks God reveals of himself in the Scriptures, particularly in the New Testament and the Epistles of Saint Paul, not to explain why God baffles our desire that he conform to human criteria. If, then, someone asks why God does not "cease from that movement of omnipotence by which the will of the ungodly is moved to go on being evil and grow worse," the answer is that "this is to desire that for the sake of the ungodly God should cease to be God; for you are desiring that His power and activity should cease—that is, that He should cease to be good, lest the ungodly should grow worse!" This is the very concern that motivated the Deity to institute Death in *Everyman!*

If one proceeds further to ask why God does not "alter those evil wills which he moves," Luther's reply is that

> this question touches on the secrets of His Majesty, where "His judgments are past finding out" [cf. Rom. 11:33]. It is not for us to inquire into these mysteries, but to adore them. If flesh and blood take offence here, and grumble, well, let them grumble; they will achieve nothing; grumbling will not change God! And however many of the ungodly stumble and depart, the elect will remain.

So to those who murmur at original sin and ask, "why did God let Adam fall and why did He create us all tainted with the same sin, when He might have kept Adam safe, and might have created us of other material, or of seed that had first been cleansed?" this reply should be given:

> God is He for Whose will no cause or ground may be laid down as its rule and standard; for nothing is on a level with it or above it, but it is itself the rule for all things. If any rule or standard, or cause or ground, existed for it, it could no longer be the will of God. What God wills is not right because He ought, or was bound, so to will; on the contrary, what takes place must be right, because He so wills it. (pp. 195–196)

Despite the overt proclamation in Revelation that God "preached works to the end that sin and death may be taken away and we may be saved," the fact remains that God "hidden in Majesty neither deplores nor takes away death, but works life, and death, and all in all" (p. 191). For mere human kind, it is enough to

> keep in view His Word and leave alone His inscrutable will; for it is by His Word, and not by His inscrutable will, that we must be guided. In any case, who can direct himself according to a will that is inscrutable and incomprehensible? It is enough simply to know that there is in God an inscrutable will; what, why, and within what limits it wills, it is wholly unlawful to inquire, or wish to know, or be concerned about, or touch upon; we may only fear and adore! (p. 191)

Election and reprobation, thus, depend neither on us nor on our deserts. Acceptability is imputed: righteousness accrues by divine grace alone. Indeed, faith—far from being a condition of attaining righteousness, as much contemporary Protestantism would have it—becomes a manifestation of grace, a mode of existence animating all else.[15] Similarly, works point no longer to the qualifications of self for salvation but to the irresistible power and mercy of God; they stem from faith as faith stems from grace. On the medieval church establishment (upheld as the figure Priesthood in *Everyman*), the effect of this approach was truly revolutionary, for it utterly destroyed the idea of the Church as a sacramental agent obtaining in the morality play. The Church becomes instead but a community of believers where the Word is preached, its sacraments, the seals of a grace already working. And within the visible church lies hidden, perhaps even to themselves, the body of God's elect, the true church itself.

What, finally, about the object of God's predestination? What is the predicament of the human being who, so to speak,

---

[15] One should be aware at this point that Luther (p. 187) defines anything that the grace of God does not do as "not good."

is at the mercy of God? While the notion of God in Luther is grand, mysterious, and austere, the situation of man if taken from a human standpoint is tragic. He not only inherits a proclivity toward sin, as Everyman did, but he partakes in the actual curse of Adam's sin, a virulent form of depravity that Baptism does not wash away. Furthermore, the earth, too, was cursed through Adam, and a little comfort, particularly for the just, is to be had in this world. As for the faculties, Luther's man is not quite so blessed as Everyman. Although doctrines of predestination are popularly believed to deny the existence of free will this is a grave distortion, for the plight of man is far more dramatic. In respect "not of what is above him, but [of] what is below him," man definitely has will. He can use his money and his possessions, can "do or leave undone" according to his own wishes, though God's pleasure can of course overrule them at any time. But when it is a question of human will opposed to divine will, then the very power of will becomes a deadly liability. Far from being nonexistent, the will is ineffective, of itself can do nothing but evil, and thus compounds offenses in the eyes of God. If we simply meant by the phrase "power of free will," the power that makes human beings "fit subjects to be caught up by the Spirit and touched by God's grace," says Luther, "we should have a proper definition," for "I certainly acknowledge the existence of *this* power, this fitness, or 'dispositional quality' and 'passive aptitude' . . . which, as everyone knows, is not given to plants and animals." But people wrongly think the expression means

> a power of freely turning in any direction, yielding to none and subject to none. If they knew that this was not so, and that the term signifies only a tiny spark of power, and that utterly ineffective in itself, . . . it would be a wonder if they did not stone [us theologians who insist on improperly applying the term to man].

Taken in this sense, free will is too fulsome an appellation for humankind; it is applicable solely "to the Divine Majesty; for only He can do, and does ... 'whatever he wills in heaven and earth.' " The limited power in man is but the

> permanent prisoner and bondslave of evil, since it cannot turn itself to good. This being so, I give you full permission to enlarge the power of "free-will" as much as you like; make it angelic, make it divine, if you can!—but when once you add this doleful postscript, that it is ineffective apart from God's grace, straightway you rob it of all its power. [And] what is *ineffective* power but (in plain language) no power? (pp. 187–188)

Luther's homunculus thus lacks not the power of choice but the options available to Everyman in matters of faith and salvation.

Men, then, have little notion of God's plans either for this world or for the next; they exercise little control over the one, none over the other; their faculties are useless toward salvation, though plunging them ever deeper into guilt. There is no recourse but to trust in God and to hope for regeneration in his totally gratuitous mercy. Perhaps the most awesome, though also one of the most dramatic, aspects of Luther's emphasis on the dark and hidden in divinity is not merely that the great man of faith must be ready to accept the possibility of damnation if God so wills.[16] It is rather that he who believes must also accept damnation not only as an act of justice redounding to the luster of the Ancient of Days, but as the absolutely unsurpassable expression of a love exceeding all comprehension.

Although the doctrine of double predestination is popularly associated with John Calvin, it is fair, I think, to say that in these matters he rather followed Luther, and there is little fundamental difference between their positions. Calvin too begins with reverent awe for the mysterious sovereignty of God,

[16] See Dillenberger, *God Hidden and Revealed*, p. 20, quoting Karl Holl.

transcendent in majesty and unsearchable wisdom.[17] In Calvin's mind, God "to keep us sober" speaks but "sparingly of his essence." Yet

> by those two titles [of immeasurable and spiritual] I have used he both banishes stupid imaginings and restrains the boldness of the human mind. Surely his infinity ought to make us afraid to try to measure him by our own senses. Indeed, his spiritual nature forbids our imagining anything earthly and carnal of him. For the same reason, he quite often assigns to himself a dwelling place in heaven. And yet as he is incomprehensible he also fills the earth itself.

Like Luther, Calvin holds that we apprehend only the superficies of God revealed through Scripture and the Spirit, though he lays great stress on how the beauty of the earth and all creation testify to the divine qualities too (*Institutes*, I.v. 1-2). Nevertheless, God's true essence and the processes of his will remain closed to us, and it is blasphemous presumption to seek to lay these matters bare (e.g., I.v.8-9; III.xxiii.2-7).

Calvin likewise agrees that all things occur through the deliberate operation of the divine will. Not fate, or chance, or a God who merely permits happenings, governs creation and its processes, but an omnificent being. Calvin's word for God's direct activity is "Providence." But "since the order, reason, end, and necessity of those things which happen for the most part lie hidden in God's purpose, and are not apprehended by human opinion," those things that certainly take place by God's will often seem fortuitous, whether considered "in their own nature, or weighed according to our knowledge and judgment" (I.xvi.9). Suppose a man accidently strays from his companions and is slain unexpectedly by thieves. To Calvin his death was not only forseen by God's eye, but also determined by God's decree. So, while even a Christian may consider such a hap fortuitous by nature,

[17] E.g., *Calvin: Institutes of the Christian Religion*, ed. John T. McNeill and trans. F. T. Battles, Library of Christian Classics, Vols. XX and XXI (London, 1961), I.i.1–3, I.xiii.1. All subsequent references to Calvin are from this translation.

yet he will not doubt that God's providence exercised authority over fortune in directing its end. The same reckoning applies to the contingency of future events. As all future events are uncertain to us, so we hold them in suspense, as if they might incline to one side or the other. Yet in our hearts it nonetheless remains fixed that nothing will take place that the Lord has not previously foreseen. (I.xvi.9)

As in Luther, all that God does is assumed to be good and all his actions redound to his glory, but the principles informing them are closed to the human mind.

Much like Luther, Calvin treats sin and the fall of man as events also determined by the will of God, though his standpoint varies slightly. Calvin, too, will have nothing to do with a God who merely foresaw the lapse of Adam and his descendants, and he disagrees utterly with the teaching that evil occurs only with the permission but not by the active will of God. To him, as to Luther, Scripture demonstrates clearly that men effect nothing, including their evil, except "through the secret will of God." Indeed,

If God only foresaw human events, and did not also dispose and determine them by his decision, then there would be some point in [asking whether] his foreseeing had anything to do with their necessity. But since he foresees future events only by reason of the fact that he decreed that they take place, [people] vainly raise a quarrel over foreknowledge, when it is clear that all things take place rather by his determination and bidding. (III.xxiii.6)

God could have prevented evil had he so willed, but as the Lord chose not so to will, the exercise of his will involves the operation of evil as well as good. One must only remember that God is a great and wise architect who "out of the pure light of his justice and wisdom tempers and directs these very movements in the best-conceived order to a right end." Since we, however, are entrammeled in the means and cannot see the ends of the design, it is up to us to avoid the "sheer folly" of those who dare "to call God's work to account, and to examine his secret plans, and to pass as rash a sentence on matters unknown as they would on the deeds of mortal men" (I.xvii.1).

This stand constrains Calvin also to embrace the doctrine of double predestination, for which he is so famous—or infamous, depending on one's upbringing. Just as Luther does, Calvin notes that "in actual fact, the convenant of life is not preached equally among all men" the world over. Moreover, "among those to whom it is preached, it does not gain the same acceptance either constantly or in equal degree." In just such diversity, however, the "wonderful depth of God's judgment is made known," for "there is no doubt that this variety also serves the decision of God's eternal election" (III.xxi.1).

In itself, Calvin's notion of predestination is practically identical with Luther's. When we attribute foreknowledge to God, Calvin says,

> we mean that all things always were, and perpetually remain, under his eyes, so that to his knowledge there is nothing future or past, but all things are present. And they are present in such a way that he not only conceives them through ideas, . . . but . . . truly looks upon them and discerns them as things placed before him. And this foreknowledge is extended throughout the universe to every creature.

Therefore,

> we call predestination God's eternal decree, by which he determined with himself what he wills to become of each man. For all are not created in equal condition; rather, eternal life is foreordained for some, eternal damnation for others. Therefore, as any man has been created to one or the other of these ends, we speak of him as predestined to life or death. (III.xxi.7)

What perhaps differentiates Calvin from Luther is Calvin's emphasis on the idea that before creation God in eternity formulated a master plan and issued certain decrees affecting the means by which his blueprint was to be given realization. Hence all the earth and all God's creatures, including the reprobate, take on their being through the divine decrees, and conversely, all, including the elect and the reprobate, are organic and necessary to the grand design. If God in fact "once established by his eternal and unchangeable plan those whom he long before determined once for all to receive into salvation, and those . . . whom he would devote to destruction," then it is quite clear that in some sense men do evil expressly through the will of God. Indeed, he spurs the reprobate to ill. One of the ways he does so is simply to withdraw the light of his spirit, which hardens their hearts and warps them into "obliquity." In this sense he can be said to blind, harden, and incline "those whom he has deprived of the power of seeing, obeying, and rightly following." Another is when in order "to carry out his judgments," God through Satan destines "men's purposes as he pleases, arouses their wills, and strengthens their endeavors" (II.iv.3). Like Luther, Calvin sees God moving the reprobate to compound their guilt actively as well as passively.

All this calls God's equity in dealing with men into question, of course. Does it not make God the author of sin and evil? Basically, Calvin's stand is like Luther's though it exhibits a somewhat different rationale. In the first place, as Adam's sin corrupted all his seed, all men deserve to die. It is therefore in no sense unjust to select some men for a salvation they do not merit and leave the rest to their proper deserts. As for attributing responsibility to God for specific evil perpetuated by the reprobate, Calvin is not so quick as Luther to seek refuge in exalting the Godhead above standards of human justice. In dealing with individual acts, he prefers to draw distinctions between the aims and manner of God's working and those of the evildoers themselves. In allowing the Chaldeans to kill Job's shepherds and ravage his flocks, for example, God's aim was good: to exercise the patience of his servant. But Satan's purpose was to drive the righteous man of Uz to despair; the purpose of the Chaldeans was the unlawful acquisition of gain. As the ends differed according to the various parties to the crime, so too did the particular ways the act was done.

The Lord permits Satan to afflict His servants; He hands the Chaldeans over to be impelled by Satan, having chosen them as His ministers for this task. Satan with his poison darts arouses the wicked mind of the Chaldeans to execute that evil deed. They dash madly into injustice, and they render all their members guilty and befoul them by the crime.

In this way there is no inconsistency in assigning the same particular deed at once to God, Satan, and man. The distinction in "purpose and manner causes God's righteousness to shine forth blameless there, while the wickedness of Satan and of man betrays itself by its own disgrace" (II.iv.2).

But the moment one raises the question of why Adam's sin irremediably carried with it the death of so many seemingly innocent people, or whence Satan's power derives, Calvin's kinship with Luther becomes instantly apparent. Candidly admitting ignorance, he simply attributes the "dread decree" (*decretum horrible*) to the mystery of divine, hidden will (III.xxiii.7). Indeed, if foolish persons ask "by what right the Lord becomes angry at his creatures who have not provoked him by any previous offense; for to devote to destruction whomever he pleases is more like the caprice of a tyrant than the lawful sentence of a judge," the answer seems to echo Luther's own words:

it is very wicked merely to investigate the causes of God's will. For his will is, and rightly ought to be, the cause of all things that are. . . . For God's will is so much the highest rule of righteousness that whatever he wills, by the very fact that he wills it, must be considered righteous. When, therefore, one asks why God has so done, we must reply: because he has willed it. But if you proceed further to ask why he so willed, you are seeking something greater and higher than God's will, which cannot be found. (III.xxiii.2)

God, thus, is "irrational." That is, he lies beyond the scope of human reason, and ours is but to recognize that "by free adoption God makes those whom he wills to be his sons; the intrinsic cause of this is in himself, for he is content with his own secret good pleasure" (III.xxii.7). In so harnessing the working of sin and evil to the execution of the divine decrees, Calvin goes further perhaps than Luther in unfolding the paradoxical teaching that the reprobate "are raised up to the end that through them God's glory may be revealed" (III.xxiii.11). We do not know why; we are only to rest assured that both the reprobate and the elect serve to magnify the holy name.

There remains, finally, the object of God's predestination, man and his predicament. As in Luther, he is mortally tainted by original sin, incapable of establishing himself before God, and—unless visited by grace—burdened with faculties that but plunge him deeper into evil. For some of the scant few blessed with election, Calvin arranges a great happiness; through "knowledge of God's name" and assurance of special sanctification through the Lord's spirit manifested in a distinct call and "justification," the "sort of judgment" awaiting them is revealed (III.xxi.7). But from the psychological standpoint, their destiny is not quite so secure as it at first seems. Election itself is not manifest to the chosen in the same degree; it is neither immediately apparent from birth nor is it made manifest at one and the same time in their lives to the faithful who, until the moment of their summons, differ in no wise from the others and wander "scattered in the wilderness common to all" (III. xxiv.10). Much more unsettling is the notion that momentary awareness of God's grace which afterward vanishes is also possible. For the reprobate too are "sometimes affected by almost the same feeling as the elect, so that *even in their own judgment* [italics mine] they do not in any way differ from the elect." They too are granted faith for a time, "not because they firmly grasp the force of spiritual grace and the sure light of faith, but because the Lord, to render them more convicted and inexcusable, steals into their minds to the extent that his goodness may be tasted without the Spirit of Adoption" (III.ii.11). Nothing, it seems to me, could be better calculated to instill humility and compassion for a fellow creature than such expressions, for at this point nearly all human certainty fades before the myserious terror of God's ways. No room here for pride, or self-righteousness, or supercilious grudging of the reprobate, or discrimination against the infidel. Instead, the soul even of the self-centered should thrill with empathy and commiseration, for all thoughtful persons must say not only "there, except for the grace of God, go I," but likewise *quo vado*: "whither do I go?"

Much as Luther's great man of faith, then, Calvin's too must be ready to accept human reprobation if that is God's will, and to accept damnation as an act of both perfect justice and of surpassing love and compassion. To this Calvin adds that he must also be prepared to accept it as indispensible to God's plan and therefore a necessary instrument in magnifying a divine glory of which the sinner nevertheless remains the complete negation.

Such, then, is the path defined by Luther and Calvin which nearly all Protestant orthodoxy in western Europe was to take; the views of the Reformers therefore afford a convenient profile of the venture into Augustinian "irrationality" which in one form or another captured the mind of northern Europe during the sixteenth and seventeenth centuries. In view of the pressures of the world, the flesh, and the devil, which shattered hopes of a united Protestant front and pitted Lutheran against Calvinist in a furious display of shameful pettiness, the fundamental agreement on these issues which actually prevailed is rather astonishing. Though everything militated against it, the hold that notions of the hiddenness of God and his free election maintained over the Lutheran movement is evident in Articles II, IV-VI, XVIII-XX of the Augsburg Confession (1530), despite the political considerations that tempered its language. It is likewise manifest in the third article on the creed in Luther's Large Catechism (1529) and (despite the great anxiety on the part of Lutherans later to avoid the label "Calvinist") in the Formula of Concord (1580), especially Articles II-IV and XI.[18]

[18] Texts of the Lutheran confessions may be found in *The Book of Concord*, trans. and ed. Theodore G. Tappert (Philadelphia, 1959).

We are particularly familiar with the power of Calvin's teachings over the traditions of the Reformed churches as evinced, for example, in the Second Helvetic (1566), Gallican (1559), and Belgic Confessions (1561), the Heidelberg Catechism (1563), the Scottish National Covenant (1580), and the Canons of the Netherlands Synod of Dort (1619).[19]

As for the Church of England, doctrinal acceptance was assured from the very beginning of the Anglican reformation. Indeed, in Articles VIII-XIII and particularly Article XVII of the Edwardine formulary of 1553, one finds an English enunciation of Calvinist doctrines which in fact antedates nearly all of the authoritative confessions of the Reformed churches on the continent. Much more Genevan in their expression than, say, the Augsburg Confession or the Formula of Concord, the Forty-Two Articles provided the basis of Queen Elizabeth's religious settlement, and accordingly the Thirty-Nine Articles (1563 and 1571) still remain an admirable expression of moderate Calvinist orthodoxy touching matters of grace, sin, and predestination. With the Lambeth Articles (1595), designed to make Anglican endorsement of Augustinian doctrines of free will, election, and perseverance of the saints as explicit as possible for those who thought the Elizabethan creed too weak, the Calvinist temper of the Church of England at the end of the sixteenth century is unmistakably clear. By 1615 the Anglican establishment in Ireland had gone almost completely Calvinist, adopting a confession that, as fascicles XI-XXVIII and XXXI-XLV of the Irish Articles make plain, accorded fully with the spirit of Lambeth in matters of election, reprobation, and justification by grace through faith, to say nothing of positions taken on the sacraments or on church government. And three years later, at the Synod of Dort, representatives of the Church of England, under the express command of King James to prevent any innovations in doctrine and discipline among the Reformed churches of

[19] The Reformed and Anglican creeds are conveniently accessible in Philip Schaff, *The Creeds of Christendom*, Bibliotheca Symbolica Ecclesiae Universalis, III (New York, 1877), 233–704.

Holland,[20] joined with Genevan orthodoxy abroad to stamp out the last major effort to preserve teachings in support of free will in the Netherlands establishment. The rise of the Laudian party after 1620, of course, provided a temporary setback. But with the promulgation of the Westminster Confession by the victorious Puritans in 1647, the last official resistance to these views in Britain was swept away until the Restoration. In fact, to the surge of popular feeling that brought about the Westminister Assembly and the judicious restatement in the confession of doctrines long at home in the English breast,

[20] The royal instructions may be found in Thomas Fuller, *The Church History of Britain*, ed. J. S. Brewer, V (Oxford, 1845), 461–465. The articles pertinent here are nos. iii (that if unexpected items should arise in debate at the synod, the English were to agree privately before the debate in a fashion "agreeable to the scriptures and the doctrine of the Church of England"), v (that the Dutch "use no innovation in doctrine, but teach the same things which were taught twenty or thirty years past, in their own churches, and especially that which contradicteth not their own confessions so long since published and known unto the world"), and vi (that "they conform themselves to the public confessions of the neighbour-reformed churches, with whom to hold good correspondence shall be no dishonour to them"). In the 145th session, the Belgic Confession was brought into the synod, reports Fuller, containing "matter both of doctrine and discipline, and the public consent thereto was required" (pp. 470–471). The head of the English delegation approved *all* [italics mine] the points of doctrine" but entered a protest on the matter of discipline "that his mother church and his own order might not suffer therein." His analysis of the *presbyteros-episcopos* problem was designed tactfully to avoid the horns of dilemma; the synod refrained from any quarrel on church discipline; and so little offense was taken that "to this interpellation of the British divines nothing at all was answered"—these points Fuller used to refute the charge that the Synod of Dort condemned the discipline of the Anglican church. Von Ranke and others misconstrue, it seems to me, the silence of the continental Calvinists as giving the British no hearing. On the contrary, they *were* heard courteously and their views on *adiaphora* were allowed to stand unrefuted. So far as the Church of England is concerned, Dutch and continental Calvinism at Dort clearly exhibited a much more latitudinarian attitude toward worship than either Archbishop Laud or his precisionist opposition in England in the next generation.

Calvinism owes one of its most graceful *symbola* in any tongue.

Nor ought one, finally, to think of the sentiment described in these pages as exclusively Protestant. As has been suggested, what Luther and Calvin represent is a kind of triumph for Saint Augustine and Saint Paul, on whose writings each had drawn for inspiration and confirmation of his thought. Instead of viewing the Reformers as causes of the revolution in mentality which I have treated, it is perhaps better to think of them as symptomatic of impulses within the Renaissance Church. The Reformers' line of descent can be traced through Saint Anselm, Thomas Bradwardine, or William of Occam, and Erasmus was by no means comfortable in refuting Luther's determinism. Even during the Council of Trent itself, strain between Augustinian and Thomist views of grace broke out between Michel Baius and his colleagues at Louvain University, and the strife was silenced only with the greatest difficulty. Allied issues underlay the friction between the Jesuits and the Dominican opponents of the doctrines of Luis de Molina in the post-Tridentine years of the sixteenth century, and the struggle under Louis XIV between Jansenist and Jesuit, which grew out of the earlier strife over grace in Belgium, persisted into eighteenth-century France. Certainly, two of the finest monuments to the hold of such irrationality over the northern mind and imagination are not Protestant, but Catholic: the gentle skepticism of Michel Eyquem de Montaigne and the affecting insights of Blaise Pascal.

III

It would be hard to believe that a change of such magnitude as the Reformation could permanently transform the material, social, political, and intellectual life of Europe without leaving some impression on the arts, the artists, and the mental and emotional conditions on which their existence depends. For that reason, let us now turn to the question of what some of the artistic ramifications of the sixteenth-century excursion into the Augustinian "irrational" might be. Could it have affected literature, and if it did, in what ways? Although its implications for writers such as Racine are obvious, the topic is too large for attempting more here than to offer a few suggestions, and those only in connection with English literature of the late sixteenth and the seventeenth centuries. It should be borne in mind, however, that the aim of my attempt is not to credit the Reformation with the glories of Elizabethan stage art or anything of the kind. It is rather to muse on what impress such change as underlay the Reformation itself may have had on certain of the art forms of the time.

At least two kinds of English poetry are particularly suitable for discussion in this context. The first is Elizabethan tragedy. Everyone who turns to it is immediately struck by what an enormous change took place between the decades of *Everyman* and the year 1600. Shakespeare, Marlowe, Webster —all make the point obvious. The shift has been attributed to many causes: the conditions surrounding the stage; the optimism and ebullience of a Renaissance rich in physical and intellectual discoveries; the flowering of medieval traditions long nascent in England; change in tastes occasioned by humanistic learning, and especially the recovery of the classical tradition. Certainly, the particular truths in all these approaches cannot be denied, and none can be ignored without peril. But, in addition, is it not possible that when the "new" Augustinianism seized the English heart and mind, a new mentality also emerged, one with a set of special proclivities and sensibilities that opened fresh possibilities for poets? Perhaps Renaissance irrationality as I have described it stimulated a number of changes in attitudes toward human life, values, happiness, Providence, and the hereafter. These changed attitudes, in turn, were peculiarly conducive to those feelings for the plight of others which we consider tragic. As the public changed, of course, so did the assumptions on which artists built their works. A new range of emotions lay readily open for exploitation, and once dramatists learned to appeal to these emotions they were led to mold the kinds of objects—that is, deeds, characters, and feelings—which one finds in the best tragedies of the age.

For example, in one of the earliest of the great tragedies in English literature, Christopher Marlowe's *Doctor Faustus*,[21] Marlowe places before our eyes a doctor of divinity who, having attained the summit in every kind of learning, chafes at the limitations of each and turns to necromancy to achieve "a world of profit and delight, / Of power, of honour, of omnipotence" (I.i.51–52). To this end, he fearlessly abjures the Trinity and binds soul and body over to Lucifer in return for the powers he seeks. After twenty-four years, and now certain of the damnation he once dismissed, he would gladly repent but cannot. When his last moment comes, he is given to see a vision of the redemptive blood of Christ in the firmament but is not empowered to reach it. He cries out for the mercy of Christ, but his eyes fall instead "where God/Stretcheth out his arm and

---

[21] References are to W. W. Greg, *The Tragical History of the Life and Death of Doctor Faustus: A Conjectural Reconstruction* (Oxford, 1950). I have deliberately refrained from textual versions that specially lend themselves to my readings, and I have endeavored to avoid slanted appeals to special features such as the Latin epigraph at the close, which perhaps suggests Calvin's notion of the Great Artificer rather than the hour of Marlowe's completing the play. For kindred views of the theology in *Dr. Faustus*, see Clifford Davidson, "Doctor Faustus at Rome," *SP*, IX (1969), 231–239; Joseph Westlund, "The Orthodox Framework of Marlowe's *Faustus*," *SEL*, III (1963), 190–205; Ariel Sachs, "The Religious Despair of Doctor Faustus," *JEGP*, LXIII (1964), 625–647; and (to a lesser extent) Robert Ornstein, "Marlowe and God: The Tragic Theology of *Dr. Faustus*," *PMLA*, LXXXIII (1968), 1378–1385. For opposed "free-will" interpretations, see for example F. P. Wilson, *Marlowe and the Early Shakespeare* (Oxford, 1958), pp. 78–85 (drawing on W. W. Greg, "The Damnation of Faustus," *MLR*, XLI [1946], 97–107); Leo Kirschbaum, "Marlowe's Faustus: A Reconsideration," *RES*, XIX (1943), 236; Paul Kocher, *Christopher Marlowe* (Chapel Hill, 1946), p. 108; G. I. Duthie, "Some Observations on Marlowe's *Doctor Faustus*," *Archiv für das Studium der neueren Sprachen und Literaturen*, CCIII (1966), 88–90; Frank Manley, "The Nature of Faustus," *MP*, LXVI (1968–69), 219; and Kristian Smidt, "Two Aspects of Ambition in Elizabethan Tragedy: *Doctor Faustus* and *Macbeth*," *English Studies*, L (1969), 240–241. For charming iconoclasm, which offers much to ponder if Faustus is to be viewed in the traditional fashion, see A. L. French, "The Philosophy of *Dr. Faustus*," *Essays in Criticism*, XX (1970), 123–142.

bends his ireful brows" (V.ii.148–149). Seeking to hide, finding no harbor, pleading for respite, he wishes himself a creature
"wanting soul." Then, cursing his parents, himself, and Lucifer,
who has cost him the joys of heaven, the unfortunate Faustus is
dismembered by Mephostophilis (so W. W. Greg would have
us read it: *mephosto* = "anti-Faust") under the "fierce" look
of God and his soul is carried off in a final shriek of pain.

The impact of Reformed doctrine on this play seems obvious,
if one reflects a bit. Indeed, overly simplistic readers can—and
do—take it as a Protestant morality or even a miracle play,
though few dare to link the ideas in it directly with Reformation
Augustinianism, preferring to emphasize the freedom of Faustus's will to the point of attributing uncongenial passages to
hands other than Marlowe's. But even though most modern
critics assume the freedom of Faustus's will vis-a-vis salvation,
a reading of Calvin and Luther leads one to question whether
the drama really does make Faustus's powers of choice as unmistakable as some insist. Surely the play in either of the forms in
which we know it can just as readily be viewed as a consistent
attempt to present a vivid exemplum of the plight of the reprobate envisioned in orthodox Protestant theology. Certainly it
was Marlowe himself who elected to keep Faustus a theologian,
for example. Like the *Faustbuch*, Marlowe also conceived of
him as a Protestant divine—and that at Wittenberg, known
especially during the 1580s and 1590s for its crypto-Calvinist
faculty. The crucial thing in the plot common to all versions,
however, is that the fundamental error into which Faustus is
made to stumble is not one of just abandoning theology, the
field of specialization he esteems above all others, for necromancy, but one of forsaking it under conditions that seem to
afford nothing less than a classic instance of what Calvin himself describes as the Lord's sending "his Word to many whose
blindness he intends to increase" (*Institutes*, III.xxiv.13), that
is, to "instruments"of divine wrath whom God at times "blinds
and stuns" by the preaching of his Word (III.xxiv.12). What
most readers seem to overlook is the possibility that Faustus is
deliberately portrayed as a person who does not "obey God's

Word when it is made known" to him (III.xxiv.14), as one of those to whom God transmits his doctrine so "wrapped in enigmas" that "they may not profit by it except to be cast into greater stupidity" (III.xxiv.13). Indeed, when dissatisfaction with the humane sciences leads him to turn to the queen of disciplines, Faustus naturally goes to the well spring of divinity in search of its utility. Endeavoring to "view it well" in his moment of need (*Faustus*, I.i.38), what passages in the Bible do his eyes "chance" to light upon? Romans 6:23 (". . . the wages of sin is death") and 1 John 1:8 ("If we say that we have no sin, we deceive ourselves, and the truth is not in us"), both of which are key texts in Augustinian schemes of original sin and predestination. In each instance, as many have noticed, Faustus ignores the contexts of the passage, the first exhorting men newly freed from sin by grace to be mindful of their priceless gift, "eternal life through Jesus Christ our Lord"; the other, to think on the joy of fellowship with the Eternal Father and on the blood of Christ which "cleanseth us from all sin" (1 John 1:2–7). The point is that to the schooled Protestant, as Professor Battenhouse has observed, both are to be viewed as declaring the love of God manifested to the recipients of his grace. But instead of accepting them (as Luther and Calvin insist one should) with a spirit of submissive trust in divine Providence and with faith in the ultimate justice of God, the irony is that Faustus reacts by terming the one passage "hard"—the pejorative adjective commonly thrown up to Calvin's teachings on election—and by concluding from the other

> Why, then belike we must sin, and so consequently die,
> Ay, we must die an everlasting death.

The consequence is a fatal misinterpretation of Scripture, of course. But it is not a matter simply of Faustus's overreaching. Rather, his reaction to the Word of God—his muttering at the logic of the scriptural message—classes him among the "impious" who complain "that God with unbridled power abuses his miserable creatures for his cruel amusement" (*Institutes*, III.

xxiv.14). In human terms, of course, Faustus does not seem wholly at fault for his error, as the response of most readers to his situation implies. For even if in reading or seeing the play, neither text nor extant stage directions make exaggeratedly explicit the notion that at the moment of his decision to abandon theology, Faustus was tempted without knowing it, so things went nonetheless. One does not need to have Mephostophilis's later revelations about his tampering with Faustus's reading of Scripture to reach the conclusion that at the moment when the Wittenberg divine took "Jerome's Bible"—surely the first misstep?—in his hands "to view the scriptures," the powers of evil and not the Holy Spirit turned "the leaves / And led" his eye, thereby damming up his "passage" just as he entered "'i' the way to heaven" (*Faustus*, V.ii. 91–94). What Mephostophilis's taunts toward the end of the play do, of course, is to confirm what the opening leads us to suspect anyway, and whether they are the work of Marlowe or of a collaborator, they seem quite in keeping with the main events of the play.

Thus, even though Faustus may not have intended to distort Scripture, the hard fact remains that, in terms of God's hidden will, he did not "obey God's word" when it was "made known" to him, and while in one sense he could not keep from it, such error as his will inexorably be, as Calvin says, "justly charged against the malice and depravity of [his heart]" regardless. Just as all the reprobate whom the Geneva reformer describes as having been "given over to this depravity" (*Institutes*, III.xxiv.14), Faustus too seems to have been "raised up by the just but inscrutable judgment of God to show forth his glory in their condemnation." The great sin to which the learned doctor is constrained, therefore, is not just pride or despair or uncertainty regarding self or intellectual Prometheanism or plain stupidity and egotism, but a very Protestant kind of self-will, the exercise of which (as Luther warned) can lead only to further evil. For Faustus takes scriptural doctrine like an "impenitent" sinner, as the *Lutheran Formula of Concord* (pp. 497, 631–632) puts it: not "according to the Word and will of God, but in accord with his reason and under the direction of the devil." So, instead of viewing the Word as designed for instruction to the end that by steadfastness and biblical encouragement men should have hope, Faustus turns his back on the entire testimony of Saint Paul which, since the reading of it is not illumined by the Spirit, seems to lack true savor and remains tasteless. Therefore, plunging witlessly into error, he cries in accusation,

> What doctrine call you this? *Che serà, serà*
> What will be, shall be! (*Faustus*, I.i.45–46),

and bids theology adieu for magic. To Faustus as to the reprobate, the audience is asked to conclude, God has directed his voice

> but in order that they may become even more deaf; he kindles a light but that they may be made even more blind; he sets forth doctrine but that they may grow even more stupid; he employs a remedy but so they may not be healed. (*Institutes*, III.xxiv.13)

Like the Jews in Calvin's eyes, Faustus cannot believe the teaching of Christ because the curse of God hangs over him.[22]

So too for the operations of the good and bad angels in the play. These I take to represent nothing less than the offers of grace God extends to the wicked in order that, as beings denied the illumination of the Spirit, they will, according to Calvin (III.xxiv.17), spurn mercy and thereby forfeit any claim that "they lack a sanctuary to which they may hie themselves from the bondage of sin, inasmuch as they, out of their own ungratefulness, reject it when offered." Though in his initial encounter with the angels Faustus (I.i.68–75) inclined toward the course of action suggested by the evil messenger, God's warning fell chiefly on a deaf ear. But thereafter (II.i.15–23; ii.12–15, 80–86;

---

[22] Cf. *Dr. Faustus*, V.i.118–119: "Accursèd Faustus, miserable man / That from thy soul excludst the grace of heaven / And fliest the throne of his tribunal seat!"

IV.v.21–26; V.i.37–88) he responds to the visitations as one would expect. In the first place, either he heeds the wrong voice, or if he begins to obey the right one, the devils are empowered to circumvent him. More important, his temporary yielding shows that each urging to repentance has force sufficient to start him on the right path. But as with the reprobate, not only is he unable to persevere, but the net effect each time is to increase the intensity of his despondency rather than allay it and to make his need for escape into the distractions (and hence the power) of Mephostophilis ever greater. Indeed, the calling induced by the succession of divine promptings reaches its peak of exacerbation in his reaction to the "kind rebuke" the Old Man offered expressly to mend his soul (V.i.52), and it is remarkably similar to the response to Moses which Luther envisioned in Pharaoh.

Since the admonitions oppose Faustus's "course away from God," one would expect them to make him worse, to make him hold all the faster to his wrongful path. Sure enough, Faustus now dashes "madly into injustice," as Calvin would say, and prepetuates the one unforgivable, base crime he commits against an innocent and helpless person. Moved by good intentions, the Old Man urges Faustus to repent of his offenses. Pierced by remorse—much like Spenser's Knight of the Red Crosse (*Faerie Queene*, I.ix.48–54)—Faustus despairs to the point of self-violence, but desists when comfort is brought by further words of hope of grace. His pain is only aggravated, however, for when he (quite unlike the Red Crosse Knight) perceives that mercy does not crown his impulse to repent, that his was but false hope, he repents his repentance; reaffirms his vow with the devil; in rage and fear, spitefully bids Mephostophilis to repay the kindness that "durst dissuade me from thy Lucifer" with "greatest torments our hell affords"; and as the fiends lay cruel hands on his once "sweet friend," loses himself in the sensual ecstasies of Helen's lips (*Faustus*, V.i.37–126). Though he began in unbelief unthinkable even to Mephostophilis (I.iii.55–85; II.i. 119–140), Faustus has come not only to dread divine retribution but to suffer under the knowledge that he is, as the Old Man seems to fear (V.i.67–68), not elect and never will be, that his heart is so

> hardened, I cannot repent.
> Scarce can I name salvation, faith or heaven,
> But fearful echoes thunder in mine ears
> "Faustus, thou art damned!" (II.ii. 17–19 in Greg's numbering)

And well he should fear divine retribution. His own assessment is correct; damnation is to be his fate. Covet heaven as he may, bewail his transgressions as he will,

> the devil draws in my tears.
> Gush forth blood instead of tears, yea life and soul!
> O, he stays my tongue:
> I would lift up my hands, but see, they hold 'em, they hold 'em.
> (V.ii.56–58 in Greg's numbering)

Faustus is right in thinking that he has been given over to Satan's power, and even though "the serpent that tempted Eve may be saved," he knows that his offense can indeed "ne'er be pardoned" (V.ii.41–42).

Faustus's estimate of his plight seems plainly confirmed by the ending of the play. When damnation is sure, he does not resort (as modern undergraduates would sometimes prefer) to hurling recriminations at heaven. Though he knows full well that God hardened him so that he cannot repent, he readily acknowledges his own guilt instead of impugning the justice of God or his ways, and even in the moment of extremity curses rather himself and Lucifer in full concurrence with the rightness of his fate. As for the climax of the play, grace is, as one would naturally expect, withheld in spite of the convincing intensity of Faustus's pleas, and there are almost no grounds for the denial to make it dramatically acceptable to the audience in terms of either the play or common charity. The contrast between Faustus and the Old Man or Spenser's Red Crosse parallels that between the pious and the impious in Calvin. Both are offered mercy through the Gospel. But the first are elect through the gift of faith and empowered to feel the working of the evangel; the latter are denied divine illumination and therefore derive no profit from the Word. The play seems to assume with Calvin that "illumination itself also has God's eternal election as its rule" (*Institutes*, III.xxiv.17), a sentiment with which *The Faerie Queene* (I.x.1) thoroughly agrees.

But however interesting the incorporation of the doctrine of the hidden God in the play may be, it is in itself not the main issue here, for it is not what makes *Dr. Faustus* a tragedy. Faustus stirs the tragic emotions because he has been given a winning dimension on the human level. However wrong he may be in abstract terms of God's arcane will, he generally does not, and cannot, seem to human eyes wholly responsible for his errors. He was led astray, for reasons that in our terms are not readily accepted as utterly reprehensible. His impatience with the limitations of human science, for instance, captures most readers. We share it and would fain transcend them, too. His employment of the black arts manifests what to generations of readers has been an admirably Promethean dimension, not simply because it defies divine injunctions but because his concern is not merely that of self. He seeks a world of profit and delight. He will put schoolboys in silk, fly to India for gold, bridge the ocean, wall Germany with brass, enfoss Wittenberg, and—patent appeals to the sympathies of anti-Spanish patriots—capture "old" Philip's gold and drive the Habsburg invader from the Low Countries. Even in the most flamboyant episodes, Faustus is designed to play on audience prejudices. He uses his power to confound what any good Elizabethan Protestant would have known to be a wicked pope and an evil retinue, and he places his magic, albeit for reward, at the service of the great as befits dutiful subjects. Even his sensuality surpasses ordinary grossness, for it springs from a capacity for longing, sorrow, and despair exceeding ours, and his passion for sensual beauty is too intense to be easily dismissed.

Above all, in showing how Faustus "doth demean himself"

as he goes to his fate, the close of the play ennobles him. He leaves his servant a generous and undeserved bequest, to which Wagner responds with professions of faith and duty. Similarly the love and respect of Faustus's scholars are carefully displayed, and their affection is made so deep as to prompt them wittingly to face even the powers of hell to aid their master. But instead of grasping at any and every vain hope, Faustus has the courage to face reality and (as his bidding his friends "Talk not of me, but save yourselves and depart" makes clear) to transcend thought of self despite the imminence of his doom (*Faustus*, V.ii.74). Far from eliciting contempt, or satisfaction at seeing a malefactor receive his deserts, the spiritual sufferings implied by Faustus's closing soliloquies are pathetic because of his full awareness of the issues, his acceptance of what is happening to him, the sincerity and intensity of his longing for what he has forfeited, and the mental, not material, agony he feels. His danger is so real, the torments racking him so terrible, that they bestow on him a final aura of grandeur, for what he suffers is that which we readily imagine to be felt by good men who would undo the past and cannot. His end, in brief, is one that every heart indeed "laments to think on," for, like his scholars (V.iii.13–19), we too "once admired" his "wondrous knowledge," and his "heavy funeral" is something that we should also like to "wait upon."

It is here—that is, in the affecting discrepancy between Faustus's deserts as a man and his actual fate—that the artistically significant mark of the Reformation on the play can be recognized. For in shaping his drama, what Marlowe seems to have assumed was an audience prepared to yield to the notion of an undecipherable Providence whose processes are hidden both to the onlooker and to the protagonist on whom they work. He also expected it to accept a heaven that refuses to conform to human standards of punishment or reward on the one hand, and yet not to react, on the other hand, with feelings of shock and outrage so strong as to obliterate the requisite emotions or to elevate the defiance of Providence into a kind of alternate salvation for the tragic hero. (The importance of Marlowe's attitude becomes clearer if we recall that two generations later John Dryden felt obliged to assume that Restoration audiences should not be exposed to spectacles involving principles of injustice even in this life, and to juggle plots accordingly.)[23] Furthermore, Marlowe assumed his audience to be capable of getting beyond itself and its self-interests, for he asked it to sympathize with, not just look askance at, one reprobate and specifically to identify with such a character. Or at least he postulated spectators who could accept such a person in human terms as one like themselves, esteem his virtues despite his faults, and vividly entertain his sufferings. Accordingly the poet sought to present a spectacle of an excellent man placed in a situation where the obligatory exercise of virtue brought with it permanent destruction of life and happiness, for he was certain that to such an object his audience would respond with and take delight in the feelings evoked by regrettable loss. In short, the introspective humility, empathy, understanding, capacity for rue and pity, and all else that one would expect in personalities attuned to the predicament of man in Reformed doctrine seem to have been what Marlowe relied on, and it is this expected response that guided the selection and shaping of the materials that went into the play.

Although Shakespeare transcends Marlowe in that he eschews blatant use of Reformed doctrines in constructing his plots, it seems to me that similar assumptions about the mentality of his audience often underlie the characters and events by which he compels our sentiments. In *Hamlet*, for example, one again finds a man of surpassing excellence: scholar, swordsman, courtier, lover, philosopher, skilled judge of the arts, mirror of fashion, model of righteous behavior. He feels, he thinks, he delights in ways that transcend our own, and we respond with respect and love. Above all, he experiences the fears and diffidences that we do. As he is more perceptive and sensitive than we, we grant him the capacity to suffer more

---

[23] See the prefaces to *All for Love, Troilus and Cressida,* and *Sylvae,* and *A Parallel of Poetry and Painting,* in W. P. Ker, ed., *Essays of John Dryden* (Oxford, 1926), I, 191–192, 203, 260–261; II, 125–126.

keenly too, and his ability to master his feelings and to act despite them magnifies our esteem. Moreover, he has the imagination of genius. He knows and feels intensely what human life is and what its limitations are. And though he does not fear it, he knows death fully and what it entails, terrestrially and eternally, for himself and all he loves.

What, then, are our feelings to be when base, salacious evil has perpetrated a crime against Hamlet's blood and being, and when, though the criminals themselves would fain cease, a dark providence forces Hamlet to seek revenge and, in the process, knowingly to hurt those he loves? Even though one may question whether he is ready to act as is here suggested—I follow the later Hamlet and not the weaker figure of the First Quarto—the fact remains that when the play arrives at the last scene, Hamlet has, despite imminent peril, brought himself very close to accomplishing his ends. We rejoice when he escapes the King's toils; we hope that one word with Laertes will clear up the misunderstandings and rescue all. What suspense we suffer when Hamlet denies his forebodings and will duel, when he questions the length of the swords but is led not to examine them, when Gertrude whom he has won to his side takes a moment too long to die, when stupidity, ugliness, treachery, temper, and madness, all abetted by the inexplicable hostility of small events, bring to him his mortal scratch. How terrible to know that things could so easily have been otherwise and were not, that heaven could so use as marvelous an instrument as he and visit destruction upon him in the process with scarcely a hint of compensation. Once again, an admirable personality is caught in the predicament similar to that afflicting man as he appears in the Reformation views, and the audience is expected to see that, to understand Hamlet's own feelings, and to respond with sympathy and passion.

One could go on and on through many of the great tragedies in the era. There is *Romeo and Juliet*, for example, a juvenile romance in which love, incandescent with possibilities for happiness quite beyond the reach of most, is snuffed cruelly out by an alliance of good intentions, blunders, and eager love with cross and hostile stars. Or *Anthony and Cleopatra*, in which foolish but intense and sympathetic passion compounds with circumstance and selfish craft to bring low two brilliant and noble creatures. Or the malignant, cruel world of John Webster's *Duchess of Malfi*, where savage, inexplicable retribution falls horrendously out of proportion with the offenses that incur it. Perhaps the most heartrending appeal to the irrational mentality I have described is the death of Cordelia in *King Lear*. After the fierce old monarch has tried to provide for the future of his realm but ruined his plans with a foolish attempt to command love; after he has learned through fury, humiliation, anguish, suffering, and madness what it means to be dependent on those who pursue only self; after he is restored to his senses, rescued, and about to be returned to his throne—then, at the very moment when both spiritually and materially he is on the verge of enjoying a transcendent happiness in the love of Cordelia which he could never before have known, she is allowed to perish simply because of heedless delay occasioned by momentary distraction! In spite of the terrible price love has exacted, it is denied, and the old man dies, clutching the slain Cordelia in his arms, his cracked mind entertaining the vain illusion that she revives.

All this, is seems to me, is clearly designed to affect minds both sensitive to a notion of destiny operating on principles seemingly hostile to human standards of the right and just and predisposed to sorrow at spectacles of undeserved suffering at its hands. Perhaps the achievement of the new irrationality was to provide within a Christian context a place for the operation of Ate, or fate, and one rendered all the more awesome because it entails deliberate rather than frivolous or arbitrary exercise of divine power. One may feel, of course, that this was an idea the age could have found in Seneca or other classical authors. But Seneca and many other authors could easily have been "recovered" much earlier, had men wished. It seems just as likely that the new mentality found things in Seneca which preceding centuries had not judged so vital, and that one can readily hold that it was responsible for the Senecan vogue in Elizabethan England rather than the other way around.

The other kind of poetry to be affected by these considerations is what, for want of a better term, I shall call the "serious lyric." By serious lyric I mean a text that represents a single speaker engaged in a moment of reflection, action, or passion which threatens gravely to affect his happiness for good or ill. At least two species of this form are particularly relevant here, both of which flourished during the late sixteenth and the first half of the seventeenth century. The first is the elegiac, or funeral sort, which usually protrays a person caught in an instant of feeling occasioned by bereavement. One of the finest is Ben Johnson's "On My First Sonne":[24]

> Farewell, thou child of my right hand, and ioy;
> My sinne was too much hope of thee, lou'd boy,
> Seuen years tho'wert lent to me, and I thee pay,
> Exacted by thy fate, on the iust day.
> O, could I loose all father, now. For why
> Will man lament the state he should enuie?
> To haue so soone 'scap'd worlds and fleshes rage,
> And, if no other miserie, yet age?
> Rest in soft peace, and, ask'd, say here doth lye
> Ben. Ionson his best piece of *poetrie*.
> For whose sake, henceforth, all his vows be such,
> As what he loues may neuer like too much.

This is the speech of a good and gentle man reflecting the pain that the loss of a small son, in whom rest all hope and love, can bring. Throughout his plaint, the speaker assumes that the death was not happenstance—the son was but "lent," this must have been the "just" day. But the workings of fate, even in causing the pangs of feeling he suffers, elude his understanding. The piquancy of the portrait stems from this very puzzlement. He can readily see that in terms of this world death can be a blessing, but however strongly he feels obliged not to question the loss, not to mutter against Providence, such restraint is emo-

[24] Text from *Ben Jonson*, ed. C. H. Herford and P. Simpson, VIII (1947), 41.

tionally impossible for him. Bewildered, he can account for the death only in terms of the excess love and joy he had taken in the lad, and he comes to the paradoxical, though hardly comforting, resolve never again to take excess pleasure in things he loves. What affects us here is not the fact of bereavement itself, but the way it is seen: the pain, sorrow, and depth of feeling of a man who thinks that deprivation like his ought to be taken as a benevolent act, would fain see it as such, but who through the very limitations of humanity which he shares with us, can scarcely do so.

A similar kind of object appears in the elegiac section of Milton's *Lycidas*.[25] Although it is a much larger poem than Jonson's in that it represents a process in which a speaker passes from despair to happiness, the opening of the work is a masterful portrayal of an earnest, striving young shepherd-poet whose happiness is destroyed by what the death of his companion forebodes for his own endeavors. In Lycidas, the mourner has seen still another of his fellow poets, and his better at that, swept away by circumstances that he can view only as the operation of a totally perverse heaven, one that moves not only without regard to worth, hopes, or potential even for its own service, but seems to take away the best and leave the worst. For the mourner, who has scorned delights and lived laborious days for the sake of fame on the threshold of which he had believed that Lycidas and he had stood, the loss precipitates a moral crisis. What is the point of tending the "homely slighted Shepherds trade, / And strictly meditate the thankless Muse," when, just at the moment that "the fair guerdon . . . we hope to find,"

> Comes the blind *Fury* with th'abhorred shears,
> And slits the thin spun life. (*Lycidas*, 74–75)

All he has lived for seems therefore but vanity, and he bitterly calls in question divine providence. He will abandon the art from which he expected happiness to come, and, in seeking a

[25] Quotations from *The Works of John Milton*, ed. F. A. Patterson, I (New York, 1931), 79.

pittance of comfort, he is reduced to bedecking an imaginary bier in memory of his drowned friend.

Both Jonson and Milton present speakers experiencing the plight of man in Luther and Calvin's universe, where humanity, having no recourse for happiness but in the will of God, suffers intensely when the turn of events tempts even the strongest to call it into question. Like the tragedies, these poems depend for their effects on listeners with a lively capacity for perceiving the pathos of the situation and answering it with generous feelings.

The other species of this kind of poem is the devotional or "religious" lyric, which often portrays a person in a moment of intense feelings occasioned by anxieties past or present about the state of his soul and the availability of grace. Such a portrayal is characteristic of several metaphysical poets in England, none more than John Donne. So much emphasis has been laid on Donne's recusant background, his career as an Anglican clergyman, his affinity with the Anglo-Catholic tradition (which is responsible for the direction taken by much of the current study of Donne), and his supposed remoteness from Puritanism that one tends to forget that the Reformation even occurred, much less how fundamentally some of Donne's poetry falls within its traditions.

Yet look, for example, at the predicament of the speaker which Donne constructs in the first of the *Holy Sonnets* (1633):[26]

> As due by many titles I resigne
> My selfe to thee, O God, first I was made
> By thee, and for thee, and when I was decay'd
> Thy blood bought that, the which before was thine;
> I am thy sonne, made with thy selfe to shine,

[26] Texts from John Donne, *The Divine Poems*, ed. Helen Gardner (Oxford, 1964). As W. H. Halewood's *The Poetry of Grace: Reformation Themes and Structures in Seventeenth-Century English Verse* (New Haven, 1970) indicates, traditional opinions regarding Donne's theology are slowly changing.

Thy servant, whose paines thou hast still repaid,
Thy sheepe, thine Image, and till I betray'd
My selfe, a temple of thy Spirit divine;
   – Why doth the devill then usurpe in mee?
Why doth he steale, nay ravish that's thy right?
Except thou rise and for thine owne worke fight,
Oh I shall soone despaire, when I doe see
That thou lov'st mankind well, yet wilt'not chuse me,
And Satan hates mee, yet is loth to lose mee.

Now this is poetry that scholarship has linked with Jesuit meditative literature, particularly Saint Ignatius Loyola's and it may very well be that the logic of its organization and even some of its expressions follow the logic of the meditation. But the object that logic is used to portray is something else again. What Sonnet 1 presents is anything but a monument to the freedom of the will. It rings instead with the cry of a man who knows that the Lord works not only mercy but hands men over to Satan to work evil and seal their damnation. His predicament is not simply that he has resisted or slighted God, or wishes to repent, or insufficiently loves God or passionately desires salvation. No. Because he conceives of himself as one who by right ought to share in the glorious destiny to which all the acts and promises of God show mankind to be intended, and yet finds himself still in the power of Satan, he fears mightily what he suspects is reprobation, or may be. The creature who laments, "Oh, I shall soone despaire, when I doe see / That thou lov'st mankind well, yet will'not chuse me," is plainly one who, though he longs for nothing more, knows that he is not yet elect, knows that grace cannot be commanded or acquired, and that the strange ways of God carry the real possibility that from him individually grace may be deliberately withheld. The sonnet, in short, capures a man in an instant of passion felt by those who, until the moment of their summons, wander "scattered in the wilderness common to all."

Look as well at Sonnet 5:

If poysonous mineralls, and if that tree
Whose fruit threw death on else immortall us,
If lecherous goats, if serpents envious
Cannot be damn'd, alas, why should I bee?
Why should'intent or reason, borne in mee,
Make sinnes, else equall, in mee, more heinous?
And mercy being easie, and glorious
To God, in his sterne wrath, why threatens hee?
But who am I, that dare dispute with thee?
O God, Oh! of thine onely worthy blood,
And my teares, make a heavenly Lethean flood
And drowne in it my sinnes blacke memorie.
That thou remember them, some claime as debt,
I think it mercy, if thou wilt forget.

Suppose you wished to dramatize the question that Luther found unlawful to ask God: Why does "the Majesty" who lays "our destruction to the charge of human will" not remove "this fault of will in every man," or why does He lay "this fault to the charge of the will, when man cannot avoid it"? Can a better representation of a troubled soul in the act of raising this very question be imagined than that offered in the first eight lines? Luther's answer, of course, was that "though you should ask much, you never find out," and so it is in the poem too. What is really striking, though, is the thought that causes the impassioned murmurer to reverse his position and yield to the will and pleasure of God. The first line of the sestet puts on his tongue the text of Romans 9:20: "Who art thou that repliest against God?" And this question, we recall, is the very one that Luther (to say nothing of commonplaces in Calvinist creeds) used to stop the mouth of just such a railer.

If space permitted, similar points could be made about any number of Donne's other poems, such as Sonnet 10 ("Batter My Heart"), where the passion of the speaker stems from his realization of how completely dependent his regeneration is on the free grace and pleasure of God; Sonnet 4 ("At The Round Earths Imagin'd Corners"), which presents a sinner pleading for the grace to repent; or Sonnet 7 ("Spit in My

Face Yee Jewes"), with its expression of wonder at the "strange" love of God, who with seeming arbitrariness, as the allusion to Jacob's election over Esau makes clear, chooses odd and unfair ways to realize it. Even the speaker in "La Corona," who confidently proclaims the famous line "Salvation to all that will is nigh,"[27] is himself not nearly so certain of his power so to will and at the close prays God "with thine owne blood" to "quench thine owne just wrath" and to accept a garland of poetic tribute, not as something meritorious in itself, but only "if"—"if," that is—"thy holy Spirit, my Muse did raise." For the speaker is keenly aware that the Spirit may *not* have raised him, that the gift acquires merit only if it be the fruit of grace, and that he cannot even tell whether it is. His final utterance, "Deign at my hands this crown of prayer and praise," implies an ache that deftly touches the roots of human sympathy in us.

Nor are we confined just to Donne. Cast an eye on, say, Bishop King's "The Labyrinth" or Andrew Marvell's "The Coronet" or any number of pieces like "Midnight," "The Match," "Admission," or "Love-sick" from *Silex scintillans*, Henry Vaughan's monument to the operation of grace on the flinty heart,[28] and see what you find. Best of all, go (as Joseph Summers prompts us) to George Herbert's "The Altar," "Discipline," "Longing," or one of his loveliest, "Deniall," with its powerful *cri de coeur*, "O that thou shouldst give dust a tongue / To crie to thee, / And then not heare it crying!" Paradoxical as it may seem, even a work as patently "Puritan" as, say, Mil-

---

[27] Note, incidentally, that Donne says "nigh," not "assured" or "certain."

[28] Cf. esp. ll. 5–10 of Vaughan's "Authoris (de se) Emblema," in *The Works of Henry Vaughan*, ed. L. C. Martin, II (Oxford, 1914), 386:

> Surdas eram, mutusque *Silex*: Tu (quanta tuorum
>   Cura tibi est!) aliâ das removere viâ,
> Permutas Curam; Jamque irritatus *Amorem*
>   Posse negas, & uim, *Vi*, superare paras,
> Accedis propior [sic], molemque, & *Saxea* rumpis
>   Pectora, sitque *Caro*, quod fuit *Lapis*.

ton's sonnet on his blindness makes the 'hard" teachings of the Geneva Reformer gentler than most of these.

Whether Donne and Herbert, or Milton for that matter, agreed theologically with the doctrine of double predestination is not at issue here; it is easy to imagine Donne, for instance, tailoring personae to the prepossessions of his audience. But the hold of "Calvinist" doctrine over at least some of their art is at issue. What seems clear is that the effects after which such lyrics as we have treated strive, presume an audience sufficiently familiar with the doctrine to grasp the predicament in which the speaker suffers, highly sensitive to the emotional dislocation potentially inherent in such a plight, and readily capable not of rejecting the feelings rending the characters portrayed but of responding with sympathy to them. In a strange and powerful way, the dynamics underlying some of the finest metaphysical poetry written in Jacobean and Caroline England are "Puritan" in doctrine and force.

In works of this sort—that is, in the drama and in the lyric—then, one can trace some of the impact that Reformation preoccupation with the arcane "irrationality" of God exercised on the materials and imaginations of English poets and on the minds to which they attempted to appeal. Some may feel, of course, that the poets but played on proclivities innately present in all men at all times, and that a change of sensibilities had less to do with the emergence of such art than the genius of specific artists. This may indeed be so. But one should also point out that in the Western world, at least, such capacities as affect tragedy remained almost totally unexploited for the more than a thousand-year interval separating classical antiquity and the Renaissance. In *The Allegory of Love*, C. S. Lewis has remarked (pp. 3–4) that regardless of "how we mistake it for something natural and universal," the idealization of erotic love invented by eleventh-century troubadours effected a revolution that eight hunderd years later still touches us in matters ranging from our code of etiquette to our notions of romantic love. So too with the revolution reflected in the Augustinian Reformation set in motion 450 years ago by Luther's defiance at

Worms. We are so familiar with its legacy that we take it for granted as self-explanatory. But tragedy, to say nothing of the even more fragile lyric tradition, is not something "natural" or "universal" to all men; it has not always been so even to us. It has its origins, and, as it has been lost periodically in the West, we must not forget that it can also pass away, as it surely will when the mind of man changes sufficiently. To the "lunacy" of the northern Renaissance, then, one can pay this tribute: in the concept of the hidden God, the sense of awe at fate and destiny which antiquity once felt and used was brought back into the experience of Western man and placed at the service of poetry. "Mysteries," as Donne said,[29] "are like the sun, dazzling, yet plain to all eyes." From blinding revelation, the genesis of some of the noblest art ever formed.

[29] *Satire III*, vv. 87–88.

VII

THE IRRATIONAL AND LATE MEDIEVAL MUSIC

Gilbert Reaney

> The art of measured music is
> founded on perfection and
> therefore the art which uses more
> perfect values seems more per-
> fect. . . . The Ars Nova uses
> many and varied imperfections in
> notes, modes and measures. If it
> is more subtle than the old art,
> it does not follow that it is more
> perfect.
> —Jacobus of Liège

R *ATIO*, whether we call it reason, proportion, or merely discipline, had a special importance for the art of music in the Middle Ages. For one thing, proportion is the primary phy- sical basis of musical intervals, and from antiquity through the Middle Ages and Renaissance these proportional relationships were exemplified on the monochord.[1] Such proportions went back to a more general concept of number which coincided wonderfully with the numbers needed to produce the principal musical intervals. To quote Cassiodorus, one of the great medieval authorities, "The science of music is the discipline which considers numbers in relation to those things which are

[1] Cf. S. Wantzloeben, *Das Monochord als Instrument und als System* (Halle, 1911).

found in sounds, e.g., duple, triple, quadruple, and other proportions."[2] We, too, use the word "ratio" in the sense of proportion. Proportion to us implies balance, and perhaps that was why medieval composers set out their bass lines in equal segments, or at least in proportionally related segments. Proportion also implied measure in the Middle Ages: the measuring of intervals on the monochord, the measuring of note values in mensural music. A ratio is the relation of one number to another, and such relations rather than actual numbers were stressed in the Middle Ages. If we speak of 3/4 time, we are using a fraction derived from a proportional sign. In the Middle Ages 3/4 was a combination of triple time and duple prolation, the relation of semibreve to breve (3:1) and minim to semibreve (2:1).

Such opinions did not change radically from the sixth to the fourteenth century, though practical matters were given more space by theorists in the late Middle Ages. Marchetus of Padua, for example, defined music in the early fourteenth century as "that branch of knowledge which consists of numbers, proportions, quantities, measures, conjunctions and consonances."[3] The language is that of the early Middle Ages, but it can be applied to part music and monophony, to music in fixed rhythms as well as to plainsong. In the sixth century Boethius had said that the true musician was the one who understood the science of music by using his brain to think of the musical composition.[4] Boethius' authority was so long-lasting that even in the fourteenth and fifteenth centuries it was customary to devote the opening books of a musical treatise of any consequence to speculative theory, while practical music, plainsong, and polyphony came last. A good example is the clearly or-

[2] *Cassiodori Senatoris Institutiones*, ed. R. A. B. Mynors (Oxford, 1937), p. 144. Most of the English translations used in my article are taken from the pertinent sections in O. Strunk, *Source Readings in Music History* (New York, 1952).

[3] M. Gerbert, *Scriptores ecclesiastici de musica*, III (Sankt Blasien, 1784), 67 (hereafter cited as GS).

[4] *Boetii de institutione musica*, ed. G. Friedlein (Leipzig, 1867), p. 224.

ganized late fourteenth-century treatise, *Quatuor principalis musicae*,[5] where in chapter 1 we learn that the first principal section is devoted to music and its divisions (generalities about music), the second, invention and proportions (on the monochord), the third, to plainchant and its modes, and the fourth, to mensural music and descant.[6]

As an age of transition and new ideas, molded onto the old, it is hardly surprising that the fourteenth century provides many examples of the irrational in music, though on the surface everything is governed by the most rational thinking and techniques. For instance, from the early thirteenth century onward, we begin to find treatises wholly devoted to polyphonic music, though a genuflection toward the older theory may still be made by way of introduction. Jerome of Moravia included a number of these treatises in his own extensive work: the anonymous *Discantus positio vulgaris*,[7] *De musica positio*,[8] attributed to Johannes de Garlandia, Franco of Cologne's *Ars cantus mensurabilis*[9] and Petrus Picardus' *Ars motettorum compilata breviter*.[10] Still, the writers of such treatises seem to have realized that their procedure could be considered irrational. They did not want it thought that they had written only a conclusion but no beginning. They sometimes began, therefore, by referring to the topic that was supposed to come first according to the standard structure of treatises. A discussion of plainsong would normally precede one on measured music or polyphony. Thus, *De musica mensurabili positio* begins: "Having dealt with plainsong, which is called unmeasured

[5] C. E. H. de Coussemaker, *Scriptorum de musica medii aevi nova series*, IV (Paris, 1864), 200 ff. (hereafter cited as CS).

[6] CS, IV, 201.

[7] CS, I, 94 ff. New edition by S. Cserba, *Hieronymus de Moravia, Tractatus de musica* (Regensburg, 1935), pp. 189 ff. (hereafter cited as Cserba).

[8] CS, I, 97 ff.; Cserba, pp. 194 ff.

[9] CS, I, 117 ff.; Cserba, pp. 230 ff.

[10] CS, I, 136 ff.; Cserba, pp. 259 ff. New edition after all sources by F. A. Gallo in *Corpus Scriptorum de Musica*, 15 (Amsterdam, 1971), pp. 16 ff. (hereafter cited as CSM).

music, my present intention is to discuss measured music known generally as organum."[11] The idea is clearly to lead into the new material by means of a link to an existing series of lectures, or by using existing treatises, such as Guido of Arezzo's *Micrologus*.[12] An extreme example is Jacobus of Liège,[13] who began his *Speculum musicae*[14] as an attack on the moderns and then decided to add to his final book six others, the first five of which would be the necessary theoretical and speculative introduction. Indeed, even in book six, which is mainly devoted to plainsong, Jacobus continues his discussion of the monochord and its divisions according to the Greeks, Boethius, and Guido.[15] A realization of the full importance of this theoretical instrument from ancient times through the Middle Ages is essential to an understanding of the mathematical nature of the assessment of musical intervals and scales in those times.[16]

Order and discipline can, however, lead to rigidity, a constant danger in the Midle Ages. Music developed rapidly from the thirteenth to the fifteenth century, and irrational elements were bound to upset the symmetry built up by the theorists. The use of notation made it possible to indicate not only the melodic line, but also the rhythm of polyphonic music. Around

[11] CS, I, 175 (also p. 97); Cserba, p. 194.

[12] New edition by J. Smits van Waesberghe (Nijmegen, 1955), cited as CSM 4.

[13] Jacobus's real name has often been in doubt, though the acrostic drawn from the initial letter of each book of the treatise makes it certain that he was called Jacobus. His Liège origin was confirmed to me by Albert Seay in a personal discussion; apparently this qualification appears in an anonymous treatise in a fifteenth-century Italian manuscript.

[14] The last two books are published in CS, II, 193 ff.; the others are published in a 5-volume critical edition by R. Bragard (Florence, 1955–1968) (cited as CSM, 3).

[15] CS, II, 205 ff.

[16] For a thorough discussion, see C. D. Adkins, "The Theory and Practice of the Monochord" (Ph.D. dissertation, State University of Iowa, 1963).

the year 1200 the organa of Perotin employed a notation that made it possible to read individual musical phrases in a series of six so-called rhythmic modes.[17] The basic rhythm was triple, so that it seemed against *ratio* to have purely duple meter, in spite of the fact that the basic groups, equivalent to our quarter and eighth notes (or three eighth notes) tended to be grouped in pairs, as in a measure of 6/8 time. The note shapes were those of plainsong, and the rhythm was indicated by the number of notes in each plainsong unit, as well as by the number of such units in each phrase. Thus, a group of three notes followed by two-note units indicated trochaic rhythm (long-short-long, etc.) in 6/8, as in

The first revolution was that of Franco of Cologne,[18] who in the mid-thirteenth century subtly altered certain note forms so that note values could be read by the shape of the notes, as still happens today. This peaceful revolution, however, far from paving the way for a wider use of duple rhythm, confirmed the ascendancy of triple rhythm, and Franco's contemporary Lambertus could still say that a series of duple longs was impossible.[19] Even before Franco, however, musicians had realized that the single notes of plainsong, the virga ascending and the punctum descending, could represent the long and the breve of mensural music.[20] It was left for Franco to clarify the meaning of note groups.

It goes without saying that a doctrine so rigid as arbitrarily to exclude duple rhythms from independent existence could not go on forever. But the rigidity was partly a result of the

[17] Cf. W. Apel, *The Notation of Polyphonic Music, 900–1600*, 4th ed. (Cambridge, Mass., 1949), p. 220.

[18] Franco's *Ars cantus mensurabilis* is published in CS, I, 117 ff., and GS, III, 1 ff.

[19] CS, I, 271.

[20] Cf. Apel, *Notation*, pp. 282 ff.

notational system with which the doctrine was bound up. If an independent long note was made up of three short notes or breves, a long of two breves was incomplete, or imperfect. It was therefore as irrational to the thirteenth-century musician to think in duple longs as it is to us not to think in duple time. And yet duple rhythm must have existed before the thirteenth century. Unfortunately, since it was only in the thirteenh century that notation became sufficiently developed to express rhythm clearly, we can only make hypotheses about the use of duple rhythm before that time.

In the fourteenth century a new systematization of rhythmic theory was attempted by Philippe de Vitry in his treatise, *Ars nova* (c. 1320).[21] To judge from the extant manuscripts, Vitry introduced his new doctrine with a discussion of the *Ars vetus* of Franco Cologne.[22] It appears from the abbreviated and apparently earliest version of the complete treatise preserved in MS Paris (Bibl. Nat., lat. 7378A)[23] that Philippe de Vitry, like so many modern music historians, wished to preface his new art with a discussion of the current tradition: then he could go further. The need for a reexamination of rhythmic theory sprang from the gradual introduction of notes shorter than the long and the breve during the later thirteenth century. For Franco, the semibreve had the same relation to the breve as the breve had to the long, and thus three semibreves equaled a breve. But as composers introduced more and more semibreves to the breve, the longer values became slower, and finally more subtle and definite values had to be given to semibreves. Thus, while three semibreves were worth no more to Franco than a group of three triplet quavers in modern notation, they might be worth three dotted quarter notes in 9/8 to Vitry. Before the Ars Nova period, the semibreve was the only note form that

[21] *Philippi de Vitriaco Ars Nova*, ed. G. Reaney, A. Gilles, and J. Maillard (Nijmegen, 1964), pp. 13 ff. (CSM, 8). This work also appears in *Musica Disciplina*, X (1956), 13 ff.

[22] Cf. A. Gilles, "Un témoignage inédit de l'enseignement de Philippe de Vitry," in CSM, 8, pp. 52 ff. (also in *Musica Disciplina*, X, 35 ff.).

[23] Fols. 61v-62.

could represent values shorter than a breve, and obviously if there were three semibreves to a breve, they had to be longer than a group of nine semibreves to the same breve. In other words, the semibreve represented more than one value, and this situation was clarified by men like the anonymous writer called Theodoricus de Campo by Coussemaker. Living in the Ars Nova period, however, he was able to use Vitry's terminology and speak of minim value or imperfect semibreve value for the note that, as he says, the ancients simply represented as a semibreve. For him a note was a minim, not because of its shape, but because of its value. He simply says that the older musicians did not add a tail to the minim,[24] and it is a fact that older writers used the term *minima* of the semibreve without a tail, when it had the value equivalent to our eighth note.[25] When it was worth a quarter note, or a dotted quarter note, it was called an imperfect or perfect semibreve, according to Pseudo–Theodoricus de Campo,[26] and a *semibrevis minorata* or *minor* by Johannes de Garlandia the Younger, as quoted by Robert de Handlo.[27]

Vitry was sensible enough to realize that everything was made clear by the simple addition of an ascending tail to the minim. The semibreve was then worth either two or three minims acording to its position. In this Vitry followed the same principles as had related semibreves to breves and breves to longs. His *Ars nova*, however, went beyond the mere clarification of the shorter note values. He was mathematically minded enough to realize that, with groups of two or three notes, there are four possible combinations: 2×3, 3×2, 3×3 and 2×2. (In the notation of 1300 each one of these notes was represented by the semibreve, and all combined to fill the space of a single breve, occupying in modern terms one measure of either 6/8, 3/4, 9/8, or 2/4.) At a single stroke Vitry simplified this notion by adding an ascending tail to the second of each

---

[24] CS, III, 185. New edition by C. Sweeney in CSM 13 (Amsterdam, 1971) p. 42.
[25] CS, I, 389.
[26] CS, III, 186. Also CSM 13, p. 42 f.
[27] CS, I, 389.

group. Thus, the two semibreves of 6/8 were subdivided into two groups of three minims, the three semibreves of ¾ into three groups of two minims, and so on.

All this seems rational enough, yet with the emergence of a type of measure lacking all triple relationships, the much scorned duple rhythm had at last achieved acceptance. But nothing more. A survey of fourteenth-century compositions shows that duple rhythm was still the exception, except where it was combined with triple rhythm, as in 6/8 or 3/4. Only two of Guillaume de Machaut's twenty-three motets have 2/4 rhythm in the upper parts, though it occurs in a slightly higher proportion of his ballades, rondeaux, and virelais. Perhaps the incidence of 2/4 rhythm was low because polyphonic songs were the forward-looking compositions of the time. But also mensural notation had been based on a ternary unit since the time of Perotin. To eliminate ternary units altogether was a revolutionary idea which was not realized until the sixteenth century, and mensural notation continued to be based mainly on ternary longs, breves, and semibreves, except in the less popular 2/4 rhythm. Such a rhythm was still irrational for the fourteenth century, and when the basic mensuration had a binary origin, it was usually considered a trick whereby complex syncopations and other rhythmic subtleties could easily be notated, as in Philip of Caserta's *Par les bons Gedeons*.[28] No one seemed to realize how much simpler the whole procedure of notation was when binary units and an additive approach (the dot) to ternary values were used, as in our own present-day notation, than when ternary units implying subtraction for binary values were employed.

Vitry's rationalization was confirmed by Johannes de Muris in his *Notitia artis musicae* of 1321,[29] better known as *Ars no-*

---

[28] Transcription after MS Chantilly, Musée Condé, 564, fol. 45v, and MS Modena, Bibl. Estense, M.5.24, fol. 31, in U. Günther, *Zehn datierbare Kompositionen der Ars Nova* (Hamburg, 1959), no. 10.

[29] U. Michels, "Die Musiktraktate des Johannes de Muris" (Ph.D. dissertation, Freiburg-im-Breisgau, 1967), I, 3 ff. (now published in *Beihefte zum Archiv für Musikwissenschaft* [Wiesbaden, 1970]).

vae musicae.[30] To be sure, he stressed that "all perfection is implicit in the number three."[31] And he fell in with the accepted idea that duple rhythms were less perfect than triple, and therefore imperfect: "... the binary number, since it falls short of the ternary, also since it is thus of lower rank, is left imperfect."[32] But he speaks a good deal, too, of various new types of imperfection used by the moderns, such as the imperfection of the breve by the minim, and that of the altered breve by the semibreve.[33]

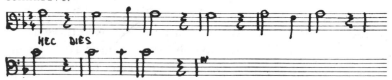

De Muris was not quite so specific about the combination of imperfect rhythms with other imperfect ones (semibreve plus minims, as in 2/4 or 4/4), but he did say that "music is sung with perfect notes in perfect time, or with imperfect ones in imperfect, whichever is fitting."[34] This comment may simply refer, however, to the use of the same note forms as binary values involved in maximodus (maxima and long) with those any event, just as Vitry had four prolations or types of measure, de Muris had four degrees of measure.[35] The two were not synonymous, nontheless. De Muris was simply relating the values involved in maximodus (maxima and long) with those employed in modus (long and breve), time (breve and semibreve, and prolation (semibreve and minim).[36] All these could be employed at one and the same time in the isorhythmic motet. Vitry, however, was primarily interested in semibreves and minims, which, as we have seen, were originally a form of semi-

[30] This title appears in MS Paris, Bibl. Nat., lat. 7378A, fol. 61*v*.

[31] GS, III, 292.

[32] *Ibid.*, p. 293.

[33] *Ibid.*, p. 296.

[34] *Ibid.*

[35] *Ibid*, pp. 293 ff. See also the table in Strunk, *Source Readings*, p. 177.

[36] GS, III, 293 ff.

breve. Thus, all of Vitry's so-called prolations would come under de Muris's degree four.

The new art of the early fourteenth century was rational to a high degree, for every unit was accounted for between 1, the smallest value or minim, and 81, the largest value or maxima. In perfect or triple measure, there were 3 minims to the semibreve, 3 semibreves to the breve (9 minims), 3 breves to the long (27 minims), and 3 longs to the maxima (81 minims). According to the combination of mode, time, and prolation, varied groupings of minims, semibreves, and breves were possible. Johannes de Muris's four degrees consisted of four groups of three in the proportion 3:2:1.[37] For example, his third degree (time) consisted of a perfect or triple breve, an imperfect or duple breve, and a semibreve, of which three equaled a breve. In the late fourteenth century Johannes Torkesey invented a triangular diagram[38] which made these relationships very clear. The left-hand side of the triangle showed all the duple note values; the right-hand side, all the triple ones. The apex was not the minim but the semiminim, a note known to Philippe de Vitry and possibly introduced by him.[39] The semiminim had become the basic unit by Torkesey's time, although theorists, when they would accept any note at all smaller than the minim, tended to be divided in their acceptance of a triple as well as a duple subdivision of the minim.[40] This ambiguity may account for the rather tentative use of the semiminim in practice in the fourteenth century; even in the early fifteenth century the semiminim did not exist independently but only as a subdivision of the minim into two or three smaller notes, or some similar idiomatic motif. At the other end of the scale of values was the maxima, and the base of Torkesey's triangle contained six

[37] *Ibid.*

[38] Cf. A. Gilles and G. Reaney, *Johannes Torkesey, Declaratio trianguli et scuti* (Nijmegen, 1966), p. 61 (CSM, 12).

[39] Cf. *Philippi de Vitriaco Ars Nova*, pp. 5, 23 (also in *Musica Disciplina*, X, 7, 23).

[40] The authors of the *Quatuor principalia*, for example, are opposed to the semiminim (cf. CS, IV, 257, 271).

maximas, which were joined by lines to the two sides of the triangle, so that all possible triple and duple values of all notes from the semiminim to the maxima were shown by numbers denoting the number of semiminims they comprised.

The new theory was combined with practice in the fourteenth-century motet, of which Vitry himself left a dozen or so.[41] His treatise *Ars nova* is in fact called *Ars quaevis mensurandi motetos* ("the art of measuring motets") in the abbreviated Paris version which may well be the oldest source of the work.[42] No other musical form of the period could express all the four degrees of mensural music at one and the same time, though to be sure maximodus was rarely employed. The natural development of the motet in the late thirteenth century had been in the direction of slower-moving bass lines and quicker upper parts, as more and more semibreves were pushed into the space of a breve.[43] After Vitry's rationalization, longs and breves were organized as never before in the lower parts, the tenors and contratenors, while a similar rigid plan soon became usual in the higher voices, the triplum and motetus. The difference was that the upper voices moved mainly in minims and semibreves.[44]

Motets had of course been organized formally and rhythmically in the thirteenth century. For example the motet *Quant voi revenir—Virgo virginum—Haec dies*[45] has a tenor arranged in three-bar groups in the first rhythmic mode (see music ex-

[41] See L. Schrade, ed., *The Polyphonic Music of the Fourteenth Century*, 1 (Monaco, 1956), 22, 48, 54, 60, 68, 72, 76, 82, 85, 88, 91, 87, 104, 106.

[42] *Philippi de Vitriaco Ars Nova*, p.69 (also in *Musica Disciplina*, X, 52).

[43] Up to nine semibreves to the breve. Cf. Petrus de Cruce, *Aucun ont trouvé—Lonc tans—Annuntiantes*, with up to seven semibreves in the triplum, in A. T. Davison and W. Apel, *Historical Anthology of Music*, I, 2d ed. (Cambridge, Mass., 1949), no. 34. The semibreves are transcribed as sixteenth notes in the modern transcription.

[44] Equivalent to our eighth and quarter notes.

[45] Easily available in Davison and Apel, *Historical Anthology of Music*, I, no. 32b.

ample, p. 201). This simple formula nevertheless is a variation on the basic first-mode formula, as in the following example:

In fourteenth-century terms, each of these three-bar groups is a *talea*, a stereotyped rhythmic pattern that appears several times in the course of the composition. The entire melody here contains four *taleae* plus an irregular cadential two-bar group: There are two statements of the melody, the *color* in fourteenth-century language, over which different music is sung by the triplum and motetus. In this instance there is less variety than later in the organization of the phrases, because the phrases end simultaneosly in all voices. After the first two three-bar groups, however, some subtlety is introduced by the two upper voices, which have two four-bar phrases. These are naturally equivalent to the two following three-bar groups of the *color* plus the two cadential bars.

This is a simple form of the development that took place in the fourteenth century. It ended in the complete rhythmical identity of each principal section of a motet, not only in the lower voices but in all voices. This was the so-called isorhythmic motet, and rhythmic complexity was cultivated. A new type of asymmetry often offset the prevailing symmetry, so that in the lower parts, for example, a twofold melodic statement might be superimposed on a threefold rhythmic statement. Moreover, the trend became more popular as the century progressed, moving from one type of measure to another in the upper as well as the lower parts. Thus, the triplum might begin in 6/8, continue in 3/4, and end in 2/4.[46]

---

[46] Cf. G. Reaney, *Early Fifteenth-Century Music*, I (Haarlem, 1955), 39 ff. (Johannes Carmen's four-part motet, *Venite, adoremus— Salve, sancta*, which probably dates from shortly after the beginning of the fifteenth century).

All this sounds quite rational, indeed, but of course development led to change, to anomalies, and to irrational proclivities. It was natural enough that isorhythm should be adopted by the lyric song forms, like the rondeau and occasionally the ballade. Machaut's first ballade,[47] a two-part work, is made up of two rhythmically identical sections, plus another three isorhythmic groups using a different pattern. And the isorhythmic rondeau, consisting of two rhythmically identical halves, occurs with noticeable frequency in the famous late fourteenth-century Chantilly MS, in which five of the seventeen rondeaux are isorhythmic.[48] But when we read in the actual poetic texts of composed ballades and rondeaux that the poets themselves, and often the composers as well, considered that all current rhythmic experimentation was wrong, unreason is obviously coming to the surface.

For example, there is the ballade *Or voit tout en aventure*[49] by Guido, from MS Chantilly. As one might expect, the music employs many new note forms and syncopations. Guido says, "Now look; I have used all the techniques at my disposal, since I must write in the new fashion, even though it displeases everyone. For it is really the opposite of good art, which is perfect. We work against nature when we undo what has been done well by Philippe de Vitry, who gave us a good example. And we leave what he has done for Marchettus the counterfeiter, whose art has no measure." Guido must have thought that Marchettus of Padua was responsible for all the new note forms and rhythmic complexities of his time, but Philip of Caserta is a much more likely candidate, for he discusses many of these things in his short but valuable *Tractatus de diversis figuris*.[50]

[47] F. Ludwig, *Guillaume de Machaut, Musikalische Werke*, I (Leipzig, 1926), Ballade 1; Schrade, *Polyphonic Music* (Monaco, 1956), III, Ballade 1.

[48] See my inventory of the codex in "The Manuscript Chantilly, Musée Condé 1047," *Musica Disciplina*, VIII (1954), 88 ff. (No. 60 is not isorhythmic. The present number of the manuscript is 564.)

[49] Facsimile and transcription in U. Günther, "Das Ende der ars nova," *Die Musikforschung*, XVI (1963), 117 ff.

[50] CS, III, 118 ff.

Marchettus stands at the beginning of the Ars Nova period in his treatise *Pomerium*,[51] while Philip of Caserta was writing well after the mid-fourteenth century. Certainly he discusses both the conflicting rhythm called *traynour* and the semibreve variants with both ascending and descending tails which are found in Guido's composition.[52] The extreme rhythmic variety possible with such techniques led to the idea that measure was in fact missing, an idea expressed in the texts of a number of compositions, for example, the anonymous *Je la remire sans mensure*[53] and Gilet Velut's *Jusqu'au jour d'uy*.[54] It is difficult to suppress the feeling that the most irrational feature of these compositions is the poetic text. Gilet Velut says he has spent his whole life up to now learning to speak (probably meaning learning to compose), but now it seems to be better to be silent, for one sees so many experiments made without weight, number, or measure.[55] Nevertheless, as in Guido's piece, the composer really lets himself go, employing lengthy syncopations and even passages in triple rhythm which conflict with the prevailing binary measure.

Strangely enough, Philippe de Vitry led the way to these eccentricities. Having added the minim tail to the semibreve, and apparently having invented the semiminim, he gave the impetus to the rapid multiplication of note forms which characterized the later fourteenth century. There were semibreves with tails above and below, others with hooked tails above and below, others with a hooked tail above and the normal one below, and so on.[56] Also, Vitry had employed red notes to

---

[51] The work has been variously dated before or after 1320, but most scholars have agreed within a year or two. The most recent suggestion of 1321–1326 is made by F. A. Gallo, *La teoria della notazione in Italia dalla fine del XIII all'inizio del XV secolo* (Bologna, 1966), p. 39, where a full bibliography may be found.

[52] CS, III, 121 ff.

[53] Preserved in two manuscripts: MS Modena, Bibl. Estense, α M.5.24, fol. 34; MS Paris, Bibl. Nat., fonds ital. 568, fols. 126v-127. A facsimile of the MS Modena is in Apel, *Notation*, p. 411.

[54] Reaney, *Early Fifteenth-Century Music*, II (Haarlem, 1959), 125.

[55] *Ibid.*, p. lxxi.

introduce duple rhythms where triple ones prevailed, and vice versa.[57] Colored notation was a great help in making possible the simultaneous performance of different types of measure in different voiceparts, for instance, four notes against six or nine—as it were, a kind of vertical four prolations matching Vitry's four used in the course of a single voice.[58] Such rhythmical conflicts, which could be made quite complicated by the use of syncopation and special note forms together with coloration, may well have been what was meant by the term *traynour* used in the *Tractatus de diversis figuris*.[59] Eventually there were white notes as well as black and red ones, not to mention hollow red notes, half-black and half-red notes, half-white and half-black notes, and so on. The intention was to clarify the meanings of note groups and single notes, just as Franco of Cologne had done, but by 1400 there were so many different note forms and such a lack of standardization in their meanings that composers almost unanimously abandoned all but the most usual notes. Transition composers like Cesaris seem to have begun with compositions in the older, more complex style, like his *Se par plour*,[60] and continued in the newer, simpler style which characterizes the early fifteenth century, as in *A l'aventure va Gauvain*.[61] Guillaume Dufay was the leading composer of the new generation.

Many of the theorists were not entirely pleased by the turn of events in the fourteenth century. They could see that the smallest note value in normal use was the minim, which was as it should be, for it was necessary to have a norm from which all other values were controlled, a least common denominator. Besides, as they saw it, you cannot have less than the least, and the

[56] See J. Wolf, *Geschichte der Mensural-Notation von 1250–1460*, I (Leipzig, 1904), 289 ff.

[57] *Philippi de Vitriaco Ars Nova*, p. 28 f. (also in *Musica Disciplina*, X, 28 f.).

[58] See CS, III, 121 ff.

[59] *Ibid.*, p. 123.

[60] Reaney, *Early Fifteenth-Century Music*, I, 22 ff.

[61] *Ibid.*, p. 21 f.

meaning of minim is "the least." To be sure, Philippe de Vitry had already invented the semiminim,[62] though he did not use it in his compositions. The anonymous authors of the *Quatuor principalia musicae*[63] flatly refused to believe that Vitry allowed the semiminim at all, but Jacobus of Liège knew Vitry's reference as early as the 1320s, shortly after the *Ars nova* was written.[64] Not that he approved of it. In fact, he has a whole chapter on the futility of adding tails to notes,[65] whether minims or semiminims. "If the ancients could distinguish one value from another without adding tails, why can't the moderns?"[66]

A later fourteenth-century English theorist, author of the *Breviarium regulare musicae*,[67] was unable to deny the existence of the semiminim, but, like Jacobus, he could see that it was wrong to call it less than the least; and so he cut the Gordian knot by calling the semiminim "minim."[68] Unfortunately, this designation is confusing to anyone who doesn't know the terminology, for the minim then acquires the name *minuta*, though the author of the *Breviarium* does allow the semiminim to be called *simpla* or *crocheta* as well as minim.

Pseud-Theodoricus de Campo devotes a whole chapter to the semiminim.[69] Essentially, he evades the problem of the ambiguity of the term "semiminim" by pointing out that, whether we call the smallest note value in use a semibreve, a minim, or a semiminim, it is still relative. And if the human voice could move quickly enough, the semiminim could be subdivided again. He was not to know that in the fifteenth century the fusa and semifusa would take the subdivision of small note val-

---

[62] See n. 39.

[63] CS, IV, 257, 271.

[64] CS, II, 419.

[65] Bk. VII, chap. 33, *Quod irrationabiliter moderni semibreves caudant* (CS, II, 416 ff.).

[66] *Ibid.*, p. 417.

[67] Possibly a certain Willelmus. See G. Reaney, *Breviarium regulare musicae* (Nijmegen, 1966), p. 6 (CSM, 12).

[68] *Ibid.*, pp. 24 ff.

[69] CS, III,190 ff. Also CSM, 13, 51 ff.

ues two steps further,[70] though it should be noted that the semi-breve with a semiminim tail above and below it already had the value of half a semiminim in the late fourteenth century.[71] Nevertheless, Pseudo-Theodoricus hit the nail on the head when he said that the question was a relative one, and Jacobus of Liège gave the musical example to show that the older values of long, breve, and semibreve could just as well be used as the newer ones—the semibreve, minim, and semiminim—apparently assuming that the long moves at the same pace as the new semibreve.[72] This would appear to be a remarkably early reference to the use of diminution in notation through-out a piece. It is clear that, as soon as long-breve notation began to appear old-fashioned and to be replaced by semibreve-minim notation, the field was open to use either notation as seemed most convenient to the composer. The lays of Guil-laume de Machaut are an obvious example of this predilec-tion.[73]

From a twentieth-century standpoint, the whole argument about whether a smaller value than the minim can be said to exist seems like a tempest in a teacup. But it was not unimpor-tant to decide which note value was the smallest one, what it should be called, and what was the justification for its defini-tion. Unfortunately, too much status was often accorded to a name. Since the minim was the smallest value, nothing smal-ler could exist; but in fact the semiminim already existed in theory. Jacobus of Liège may be adamant in saying that we should consider the thing rather than the name,[74] but he says it only to strengthen his own argument that the old notation was just as satisfactory as the new. The same is true of his discus-

---

[70] See Wolf, *Geschichte der Mensural-Notation*, I, 399; Adam of Fulda in GS, III, 360.

[71] See Anon. V in CS, III, 396 f.

[72] CS, II, 417 ff.

[73] See G. Reaney, "The *Lais* of Guillaume de Machaut and Their Background," *Proceedings of the Royal Musical Association*, LXXXII (1955), 25 f.

[74] CS, II, 419.

sion of imperfection. "The art of measured music is founded on perfection," he says, "and therefore the art which uses more perfect values seems more perfect. This is the art of Franco. The Ars Nova uses many and varied imperfections in notes, modes and measures. If it is more subtle than the old art, it does not follow that it is more perfect."[75] To be sure, the term "imperfection" implied a real lack of the value implied by perfection, though to us it is clear that in music imperfection referred to duple rhythms and perfection to triple ones. How can duple rhythm be inferior to triple? Here the word "imperfection" has led Jacobus to judge duple rhythm as inferior. He confuses perfect or triple rhythm with perfection as a value. "Reason follows the law of nature which God implanted in rational beings."[76] The hegemony of *ratio*, however, too often led to a dependence on accepted definitions.

Jacobus of course was a conservative, and in Book VII of his treatise he set out to defend the old art of Franco and Petrus de Cruce, not to mention their predecessors, against the moderns. His words, however, often ring true in the twentieth century, even as they reveal what he and his contemporaries saw as rational or the reverse. In chapter 44[77] he tells us how some of the moderns considered those who did not know the new art as ignorant and undiscerning. "They consider the old art as rude, and, as it were, irrational, the new as subtle and rational. It may be asked, what is the source of this subtlety in the moderns and this rudeness in the ancients? For if subtlety comes from a greater and more penetrating intellect, who are to be reputed the subtler: those who discovered the principles of this art and found out what things are contrary to them, but have scrupulously followed these principles, or those who protest their intention of following them but do not, and seem rather to combat them?"[78] Indeed, both theorists and composers have

[75] CS, II, 427.
[76] *Ibid.*
[77] *Ibid.*, p. 428 f.
[78] *Ibid.*, p. 428.

only built on the foundations of the old, and thus even Boethius should be given due credit. If the moderns find the old art irrational, Jacobus finds them just as irrational when they concentrate on the exclusive composition of motets and chansons, while the ancients delighted in measured organa, partly measured organa, organum duplum, conductus for two, three, or four voices, and hockets as well.[79]

The criticism may have been just, but it is only fair to say that in the early fourteenth century the motet, by a natural development, had taken the center of the musical stage. It was soon to be joined by mass settings in motet style, as well as those in descant, conductus, and simultaneous style.[80] Moreover, the chanson was to see a remarkable development in the hands of Guillaume de Machaut, with his polyphonic ballades, rondeaux, and virelais, not to mention the many monophonic lays and virelais in Ars Nova style. If Jacobus could speak of two-, three-, and four-part conductus, the fourteenth century could boast of its two, three-, and four-part ballades and rondeaux. Canonic songs are rare, but the three-part *chaces* of the Codex Ivrea and the Italian *cacce* represent another distinct pair of forms.

As further evidence of the conservative alarm over the decline of musical discrimination, one may cite the attack of Pope John XXII on the new school of composers in his bull *Docta Sanctorum* of 1324/25.[81] It is understandable that the Church would require modesty and decorum in its sacred music, and the Ars Nova with its tendency to quick and complex rhythms, hocketing, and even secular texts, did not please the Catholic hierarchy. John XXII was particularly offended by the way the plainsong, the foundation of church music, was used. Even today it seems unreasonable, even irrational or mindless, to take a Gregorian melody, compose new music over it so that the

---

[79] *Ibid.*, p. 428 f.

[80] See H. Stäblein-Harder, *Fourteenth-Century Mass Music in France*, Corpus Mensurabilis Musicae, 29 (Tübingen, 1962).

[81] J. A. Richter and A. Friedberg, *Corpus iuris canonici*, II (Leipzig, 1881), 1225 ff.

words are obscured, stretch out its notes to such a length that it is unrecognizable, and apply new and often unsuitable rhythms to it. But that is just what fourteenth-century motet composers did. How these motets were used in practice is a matter for speculation.[82] Some of them were no doubt used liturgically, but secular French motets, even though based on liturgical tenors, can hardly have been used in church. Even so, one of Pope John's complaints was that the Ars Nova composers did in fact make use of tripla and moteti in the vernacular (*triplis et motetis vulgaribus nonnumquam inculcant*).[83]

The logical way to complete the Mass or office would be with a polyphonic work based on a concluding chant. We may assume, for instance, that Guillaume de Machaut's exquisite motet *Felix virgo—Inviolata*,[84] based on a section of the *Salve, regina*, was intended for this purpose. Although it is isorhythmic, this four-part composition begins with a free introduction, an irrational element in the strict isorhythmic context. The lower parts, tenor and contratenor, are, however, the essential isorhythmic framework, and with complete logic Machaut states the tenor rhythm three times, each statement amounting to six measures in maximodus, Johannes de Muris's first degree. Within those six measures the mode is first imperfect for three measures, then perfect for three, while the contratenor employs the reverse procedure: the perfect, then imperfect, mode. The upper parts are in imperfect time and perfect prolation. Thus, all four of Johannes de Muris's degrees are applied here. Another rational procedure, diminution, appears in the contratenor and tenor of the second half of the piece. Hence all the notes and rhythms are the same as in the first half of the piece, but cut in half, as it were. This heightens the tension generally, and the upper parts, though they remain in 6/8, employ more hocketing, another procedure condemned by Pope John XXII.[85]

[82] G. Reaney, "The Isorhythmic Motet and Its Social Background," in *Kongress-Bericht Kassel 1962* (1963), pp. 25 ff.

[83] *Corpus iuris canonici*, II, 1256.

[84] Ludwig, *Guillaume de Machaut, Musikalische Werke*, III, (Leipzig, 1929); Schrade, *Polyphonic Music*, III, motet 23.

[85] See n. 83.

It has always been a source of wonderment to twentieth-century listeners that several different texts were sung simultaneously in fourteenth-century motets. A most irrational procedure, surely. Jacobus of Liège in fact mentions, in connection with the performance of some modern motets, that the text could not be heard (*littera perditur*).[86] One wonders, however, whether he was biased in favor of the older motets, which also made use of a number of different texts sung simultaneously. The newer ones presumably used quicker notes, hockets, and other rhythmic complications, so that hearing the text was more difficult than it had been in the thirteenth century. The nature of the procedure seems more disturbing when the triplum is sung in French and the motetus in Latin. A consideration of the medieval stage may help to clarify the conception, for often enough several scenes were depicted and even performed at one time in the Middle Ages. The usually wordier triplum commenting on the material of the motetus also brings to mind the medieval method of glossing a well-known text. An interesting example is the motet *Sub Arturo plebs—Fons citharizantium*,[87] with the tenor *In omnem terram exivit sonus eorum et in fines orbis* ("Their sound has gone out into every land and to the ends of the earth"). The motetus is a succinct history of music theory, begining with Jubal and Pythagoras, and ending with the composer of the motet, John Alan, while the triplum lists fourteen additional contemporary musicians, most of them in the service of the king of England, Edward III (1312–1377) or his son.[88]

What seems irrational and defective to the twentieth century may have been perfectly rational and complete in the fourteenth. Machaut's *Hoquetus David*[89] has not a word of text in

[86] CS, II, 432

[87] U. Günther, *The Motets of the Manuscripts Chantilly, Musée Condé, 564 (olim 1047) and Modena, Biblioteca Estense, M.5.24 (olim lat. 568)* (Tübingen, 1965), pp. l-li.

[88] *Ibid.*, pp. 49 ff.

[89] F. Ludwig and H. Besseler, *Guillaume de Machaut, Musikalische Werke*, IV (Wiesbaden, 1954), 21 ff.; Schrade, *Polyphonic Music*, III, 65 ff.; G. de Van, *Guillaume de Machaut, Double Hoquet* (Paris, 1938).

its upper two parts, and the tenor is based entirely on the melisma *David* from the *Alleluia Nativitas*. Textless singing was as common in the Middle Ages as it is uncommon today. When a plainsong sequence was sung, it was common to repeat each melodic phrase to the vowel *a*. In English motets it was the practice to exchange the upper parts, so that the first voice sang what the second had just sung, and vice versa. At such times one voice sang a text and the other often vocalized.[90]

The shortness of a medieval motet may seem strange to ears used to symphonies lasting up to an hour or more. Some manuscripts, however, may not yield up a complete piece. A motet may be only a part of a piece. Sometimes the plainsong extract used as a tenor may have been intended to be inserted in its context, the complete plainsong. This could be true of the Machaut motet *Felix virgo—Inviolata* mentioned above. It is almost certainly so with the presumably English motet *Balaam de quo vaticinans*,[91] dating from around 1300, which fits neatly per parts are missing, a Sarum Missal now in the Bibliothèque de l'Arsenal in Paris[93] gives a measured version of the plainsong for the two verses set elsewhere polyphonically.

It has become clear that *ratio* did not always imply reason in the Middle Ages. What is rational to one person is irrational to another. The man who reasons well is not always the most rational person. He is often arguing to prove a point, as was often true of the medieval theorists. Jacobus of Liège wanted to

[90] See the motet *Ave, miles celestis—Ave, rex patrone* in M. F. Bukofzer, *Studies in Medieval and Renaissance Music* (New York, 1950), pp. 30 ff. (also in D. Stevens, *The Treasury of English Church Music*, I [London, 1965], 55 ff.).

[91] Preserved in MS Montpellier, Faculté de Médecine H 196, fols. 392v-394v, and MS Oxford, New College 362, fol. 86 (motetus only). Transcription in Y. Rokseth, *Les Polyphonies du XIIIᵉ siècle*, III (Paris, 1936), nos. 340-341.

into the sequence *Epiphaniam domino*.[92] Even though the up-

[92] For a transcription including both sequence and motet, see Stevens, *Treasury*, I, 11 ff.

[93] MS 135 (see Stevens, *Treasury*, I, xviii).

defend the ancients against the moderns, but was mature enough not to oppose the good things the moderns had added to the old. Even so, he could not help condemning the moderns, but nevertheless his philosophy was sound. He realized that he could be wrong in what he had written, and we can see he made a mistake in condemning duple rhythms as imperfect, but as a man of his time he could not be expected to see how important duple rhythms would become. Six and a half centuries later, however, we may still perhaps agree with Jacobus's statement: "May what is rational, or more rational, and what accords most fully with this art of music be retained, and what is less reasonable be cast out. For both art and reason must have their place."[94]

[94] CS, II, 427.

VIII

MODES OF PERCEPTION OF REALITY IN THE RENAISSANCE

Marc Bensimon

O NE OF the axioms this study implies is that, consciously or unconsciously, man reacts in various ways to the primordial anxieties caused by the threat of death and the passing of time. Rather than actual perception, man's orientation toward spatial and temporal reality is the subject of investigation here. Perception of reality is generally considered to be the antithesis of imagination, yet imagination draws upon reality for its images, if only to deform or modify them. In this sense, then, it is similar to perception. Further, imagination structures these images according to strict exigencies of irrational dynamics.

Man's various ways of coping with his anxieties are not unrelated to his mind's final orientation, whether highly conscious or impulsive, toward outside reality; very often, imagination or action in *space* is but the translation of an emotion originating in a concern with time or ultimate fears. A simple, but nevertheless symbolically significant, example will illustrate the ramifications of this idea.

To calm growing impatience before the departure of a train, a person in a waiting room is driven by his restlessness to assume one or more of various attitudes. For instance, he may pace the floor and thus experience the vain and impractical satisfaction of wasting in action, in space, the time spent in waiting. Or,

221

motionless and lucid about his growing irritaion, he may on the contrary concentrate on it as if his suffering self were an object. An intimate dialogue involving an element of self-pitying dramatization could result. Exaggerating somewhat, his mind could entertain an inner drama of crucifixion, of passive suffering, humanity's lot, viewed against a large historical backdrop. Another way might be to watch the huge clock on the opposite wall. The mind's eye fuses, so to speak, with the running hand on the face of the dial; forgetting the passing of time, consciousness becomes space. The person may choose on the contrary to close his eyes; he will then hear more intensely the ticking of the clock and, becoming one with it, forget time to become time. Finally, he may decide to forget his irritation altogether and, listening to some tune, rhythmically mark time with his fingers. Such reactions, though normal and spontaneous, are nonetheless irrationally selected. Similarly, rational thought and the conscious choice of themes and myths, forms and colors, have fundamental irrational exigencies. This essay is an attempt to define some of these exigencies for a few figures of the Renaissance.[1]

I

In the middle of the fifteenth century, François Villon, a poor alienated soul, a thief condemned to the shameful death of the gallows, bitterly muses behind bars on the absurdity of the human condition that all men are condemned to die. The three

[1] Although in this paper I will treat some authors and subjects dealt with elsewhere in this book, I have deliberately set aside historic and social considerations. Also, precise geographical differences and the fact that certain phenomena or attitudes existed long before 1470 have been disregarded. Starting from that date (c. 1470), I am attempting to follow through in some hundred years of thought, literature, and art those threads that seemed fundamental and significant. Although my essay raises serious questions about former interpretations of highly "intellectual" themes or thought processes, I in no way claim to present a definitive, systematic, synthetic view of the Renaissance. With the exception of Cusanus, Ficino, Pomponnazi, and Machiavelli, philosophers whose fundamental importance to sixteenth-century French literature

themes so popular at that time—*vado mori, contemptus mundi,*[2] and *ubi sunt*—are soberly but brilliantly orchestrated by Villon. At the threshold of death, he finds with an ironic retrospective glance that his nostalgic consciousness can apprehend nothing sure. The past, a strange mixture of mythical and historical characters, has faded; worldly values are leveled by death: "The world is but deceit and illusion" (*abusion*). There is also nostalgia for knowledge, but the poet remains a mystery to himself. As for outside reality, grasped through an opaque screen of proverbs, ready-made truths, it yields only the hollow echo of logocentrism, just as does Villon's evocation of an absent paradise. With past and future blocked, so to speak, by hopeless walls which prevent the imagination from wandering, and with the anxiety caused by posthumous nothingness, physical decay can become reassuring in its tangibility. Minute details of physical turgidity, a motionless tableau of aged women, "poor silly crones/Dumped down on their haunches/All in a heap," before a fire become as hypnotic as the ever swinging bodies on the gallows in Villon's most famous ballad.

After a rhetorical appeal to the pity of those who will survive, Villon draws attention to the image of the swinging bodies whose flesh has already rotted away or been eaten. As for the bones, the poet's use of *we* to describe their turning into ashes and dust ("Et *nous,* les os, *devenons* cendre et pouldre") implies a magical unconscious gesture against the threat of nothingness.[3] Yet, beyond this, one would seek in vain a real gesture

---

is undeniable, the literary examples are drawn mostly from French authors. Bosch, Brueghel, Il Primatice, and Antoine Caron, well-known painters, supply examples most relevant for my essay. The translations into English are mine and so is the emphasis unless otherwise indicated.

[2] This theme is brilliantly analyzed by Donald Howard (see chap. 2, above).

[3] Cf. E. Morin, *L'Homme et la mort dans l'histoire* (Paris: Corrêa, 1951), p. 132: "Bones or bone powder remains in the last analysis the mystical product that, because of its indestructibility, is evidence of the soul; the bones or the effigies will be the supports of the cult given the dead. They will be the magical intermediate, the points of fixation, for the soul."

of revolt in Villon's ballad. Resignation, self-pity, and punishment are the lot of the thieves, the guilty ones, and indeed perhaps of all men. A tragic sense of inescapability prevails in this static but not motionless image of bodies swayed by the merciless whim of the wind. Sharp-beaked birds—magpies and ravens—have pocked the bodies, pecked out their eyes, and plucked their beards and eyebrows away. Whatever the ultimate significance of guilt may be, the concentration of symbols (gallows, birds, decaying flesh and bones, loss of eyes and hair) does express certain fears and conflicts at a primary instinctual level. It is beyond the scope of this presentation to study these symbols in depth, but Freud in his study of Leonardo, Neumann in his *Art and the Creative Unconscious*, and others[4] have alluded to the importance of threatening birds as symbols of a destructive Vulture-Mother. Their prevalence should simply be noted here.

Villon's inner drama is exteriorized in his *Débat du Cuer et du Corps*, where the poet's heart is broken at the sight of his body sulking in a corner like a whipped cur. The moral and physical prostration is blamed on Saturn, but the lucid author, even while questioning this fatalistic view, can find no motivation to surmount his sense of dejection.

Whether of Saturnine origin or not, the melancholia of Villon and his contemporaries, this *mal du Siècle*, is definitely connected with guilt and fears at the primary level. In *Saturn and Melancholy*, Klibansky, Panofsky, and Saxl reproduce a circular fifteenth-century miniature of the children of Saturn with, in the center of the wheel, a blindfolded man hanging from the gallows.[5] Charles d'Orléans's melancholic ballad, "In

[4] See, e.g., Jacques Schnier, "The Symbolic Bird in Medieval and Renaissance Art," *American Imago*, 14 (1957), 211–223.

[5] Raymond Klibansky, Erwin Panofsky, and Fritz Saxl, *Saturn and Melancholy* (London: Nelson, 1964), pl. 42: *The Children of Saturn;* single leaf from an astrological MS 1458, Anger-Museum, Erfurt. If an interesting parallel between the "hanged" and Saturn's children can thus be seen, another one, not less surprising, can be, and in fact has been, drawn between Saturn's children and Saint Anthony, the melancholic hermit. See E. Castelli's excellent essay on the many temptations

the Forest of Grievous Sadness," presents a lost, self-pitying wanderer groping about with his stick. It is a great pity, laments the poet, that it befalls him to be the man who knows not where he's going ("L'homme esgaré qui ne set où il va").

Hieronymus Bosch's *Wandering Fool* is marked by similar characteristics. The whole landscape is presented to the viewer as the symbolic winding road of life on which the alienated voyager—obviously a child of Saturn with his stick and his knapsack awkwardly but lucidly looks back. The same stage props appear again: the gallows stand ominously against the sky of the background; a dog in the foreground threatens the stranger; birds are perched on the strewn bones of a carcass. Bosch's characteristic fauna abounds, of course, in long-beaked creatures, demons who gulp down the damned; the numerous visions of Saint Anthony, be they by Bosch or others like Grünewald, express the same attitude before instinctual fears symbolized also by other threatening animals: cannibalistic werewolves, sharp-toothed ogres and witches.[6] The various scenes of life in Bosch's *Wandering Fool* are presented as little unrelated dramas.[7] Thus the meaning can come only from

---

of Saint Anthony: *Le Démoniaque dans l'Art* (Paris: Vrin, 1958), p. 4 n. 2. On the evolution of the concept of the Saturnian artist, see André Chastel, *Marsile Ficin et l'Art* (Geneva: Droz, 1954), III Saturne, pp. 163 ff. Ficino had already indicated means of escaping the pernicious influence of Saturn, and Leonardo rejected altogether the Saturnian curse.

[6] Castelli (*op. cit.*, pp. 42–43) notes that the saraband of the spiraling forms made by the dragonfly-serpents and other monsters lifting the monk in Lucas Cranach's *Temptations of Saint Anthony* (pl. 41) points to a circular conception of space. According to Castelli, this "theological motif" also appears in Martin Schöngauer's *Temptations*, where "the saints fly outside the magical circles that the demons draw when attempting to encircle them." For my study it is important to note only the presence of the circle associated with this theme, as with so many others (see n. 16, below).

[7] The use of drama is so intimately connected with a representation of reality in fifteenth-century art that Pierre Francastel, eminent sociologist and art historian, has written more than 200 pages on the significance of montage in the visual arts of Quattrocento (see Francastel,

the moral and symbolic explanation inferred by the painter or the viewer. The painting has no chronological narrative element. As in many other compositions of the master, the eye travels circularly; here it is from an allusion to death in the background to another one in the foreground. The traveler himself seems to be at the end of his journey: The same figure appears in the circular painting of the *Hawker* (*The Prodigal Son*).[8]

It has often been remarked that the *Testament* of François Villon, like much of fifteenth-century French literature, offers a fragmented vision of reality and breaks in chronology, since the diverse ballads written at different times are bound together only by eight-verse stanzas. Unity not only in the ballads but also in the stanzas is brought about by oft repeated rhythms, whose monotonous, incantatory quality seems to be a mode of bringing solace almost magically. In the ballads, the return at the end of each stanza of the last verse of the first stanza creates a special circular, rhythmical effect. Time in its strict chronological sense is denied (reality then is not so much experienced linearly as a succession of events); yet in another sense, time is spun aurally, as it were: the alternation of strong and weak beats has a rocking, lulling quality. Especially in Bosch's large compositions, it is likewise rhythm that gives unity to an otherwise chaotic reality. Despite the painter's lack of symmetry, despite the baffling variety of forms, rhythmic unity is achieved by the magic sense of color which, like fire, binds together heterogeneous elements.[9] Yearning for oneness, for total unity, is reached by subjacent harmony, orchestration, in a dramatic attempt to depict not only the human condition but also heaven and hell simultaneously.

Bosch's *Seven Deadly Sins*,[10] also a circular composition, represents the eye of God mirroring the seven mansions of sin,

---

La Figure et le Lieu [Paris: Gallimard, 1967]). It is my contention that in poetry as well, as we have just seen, a dramatic presentation of the self and of life is more prevalent than a chronological or lyrical one.

[8] Circular panel, Boymans–van Beuningen Museum, Rotterdam.

[9] See n. 24, below.

[10] *Tondo*, table top, c. 1475, Prado, Madrid.

thus summing up the human condition. The irony of the caption, "Beware of the eye of God," is further conveyed by the wheel-like design which leads the viewer's eye in an endless circle around the mansions. This composition, together with the rays, like so many spokes in the center, conveys the implacable futility sensed when destiny is experienced as a merry-go-round, or, to use a symbol then very frequent, as the wheel of Fortune.[11] While the plastic representation of the various scenes implies a visual apprehension of reality, the mind, when viewing it, must resort to mental motion as if that were the only way to transcend the dramatic spectacle of the human condition. Consciousness links together the heterogeneity of life's events through ceaseless circular movement. One is thereby constantly brought back to the point of origin. The mind adopts a transcendental and englobing perspective to find, perhaps, the center, the unity it yearns for.

Oneness, absolute, is also the goal of Bosch's contemporary, Nicholaus Cusanus, whose thought Ernst Cassirer in his brilliant *Individual and the Cosmos* had singled out as the focal point of Quattrocento philosophical efforts. Cusanus defines oneness as the ultimate, unattainable coincidence of opposites where the absolute minimum equates the absolute maximum, where the triangle becomes a circle, where the trinity becomes unity, and where movement and repose become synonymous. In this abstract, mathematical world, notions of time and space seem vain; they are not given direct consideration. From this point of view, one could say that the world of Cusanus, at least in his important work *De Docta Ignorantia*, is timeless and spaceless.

To be sure, there are geometric figures in Cusanus's work, and he does allude to the earth, sun, and stars. Yet their use, as will be seen, is subordinate to a very special attitude, the movement of thought itself: the dynamic mental process which by its own virtue expresses a fundamental relation to chronology.

[11] Note the central position of the wheels of Bosch's *Hay Wagon*; see also Cusanus: movement ("the connection between form and matter") compared to "an intermediate spirit" called "atropos, clotho, and lachesis."

Blissful unity is defined as a reunion of opposites, but this utopian fusion can be imagined only in an inaccessible future;
present reality is conflictual and antithetical.

So Cusanus, jumping on the merry-go-round, on the wheel,
flees from the static present reality and seeks to arrive at ultimate truth by means of relationships in motion. The key word
for Cusanus is not *watch*, *split*, or *oppose*, but *link*. The
student of Cusanus will have recognized the term *nexus*, so
obsessively used in his work. Between matter and form there
is a third term; between God potential and the Act, there is a
spirit conceived as a *relation*:

> If our holiest doctors have called unity, Father; equality, Son;
> and the connection, Holy Spirit, it is because they have pro-
> ceeded by making an analogy with perishable realities of this
> world, . . . for in the Son there is no more and no less human-
> ity than in the Father, and there exists between them a certain
> connection. Indeed, natural love *links* one to the other.[12]

The body of knowledge is also apprehended in its relationships. In addition, thought itself is conceived as a self-
measuring, self-reaching dynamic device: the mind becomes
aware of its own secretions, its own thinking processes in their
function of forming relationships:

> When I say "God is," this prayer moves forward by means of
> a certain movement. . . . First, I pronounce the letters, then
> the syllables, then the words, then, finally, the prayer. . . .
> Thus movement comes down imperceptibly from the univer-
> sal into the particular, . . . the same is true of all movement.[13]

Cusanus goes on to explain that what brings all things toward
unity in this relation of the particular to the universal is the
spirit, the movement of "amorous connexion," as he calls it,
in order that the "universe be one." This example reveals how
much the thinking process of Cusanus, drifting from the anal-

[12] *De la Docte Ignorance*, ed. L. Moulinier (Paris: Alcan, 1930), I, ix,
pp. 53–54.
[13] *Ibid.*, II, x, p. 148.

ysis of an utterance to an evocation of the whole cosmos, leans on the notion of *relation* and its synonym for him, *movement*.[14] Cusanus's world is one of perpetual quest, a constant dynamic becoming. Just as the image of the snake of time biting its own tail (a vicious circle) is drawn to evoke an eternal round,[15] the image of the definite circle or sphere, central to Cusanus's spiraling world, is used to describe the flow of time, which he conceives circularly. This mental process is similar to his game of squaring the circle (a favorite pastime of his)[16] or reconciling opposites:

> The circle is the perfect figure of unity and simplicity; . . . this unity is infinite, like the infinite circle. Therefore, as its power is, so to speak, perfectly one, it is also perfectly strong and infinite. And its duration is so perfectly one that the past is nothing else in it but the future; the future, but the present; yet they are duration perfectly one, or eternity without beginning or end; in effect, so large are the contents of the be-

[14] See n. 11, above.

[15] Tracing the evolution of representations of the *Ouroboros* from 1470 on would be most rewarding. Panofsky has, of course, contributed much to the study of Saturn's iconology. The snake itself undergoes some changes. Often represented in the traditional circular way in the fifteenth century, it straightens out and divides the picture into two symmetrical sections in Gafurius's harmonic cosmos in his *De Musica* (1496), which is discussed below. In the 1560s the snake's coils assume diverse positions, but the circular image of time disappears. For similar views cf. Eric Neumann, *The Origins and History of Consciousness* (Princeton: Princeton University Press, 1954).

[16] See Cusanus, *Compléments théologiques*, ed. M. Gandillac, (Paris: Aubier, 1921) pp. 451–452. See Bachelard's comments on the Jonas complex in *La Terre et les rêveries du repos* (Paris: Corti, 1948), pp. 148 ff.: "Whoever draws a circle is dreaming of a womb; whoever draws it in a square, giving is symbolic value, is building a shelter. See also, in C. G. Jung, *Psychologie und Alchemie* (Zurich: Rascher, 1944), p. 183, illus. no. 60: "The squaring of the circle, the reunion of the opposite sexes [die zwei Geschlecter zu einer Ganzheit zusammenfassend]," and Loeffler-Delachaux, *Le Cercle, un Symbole*, in Bachelard, *op. cit.*, p. 118. It seems more proper to note simply that the circle, along with the notion of cycle, evokes naturally a return to the point of origin.

ginning itself that the end is its beginning. Now all this is shown to us by the infinite circle without beginning or end, indivisibly eternal one and powerful to the maximum.[17]

One may note in passing that the very structure of this paragraph is circular. The famous analogy of the polygon within the circle must not be thought of as a static figure. For it to have meaning, one must imagine the *motion* caused by increasing the sides of the polygon. Even if infinitely multiplied, they will never coincide with the circle. What emerges from this image also is the unconscious desire to round off angles, to bind.

It is obvious that with so dynamic a concept Cusanus could not accept a static view of mystic fusion in the restful bosom of God.[18] His mysticism does not imply losing one's identity or seeing completely the light of God. The *via negativa* is not a straight path; when knowledge is rejected, when "the circle, the sphere, . . . are vomited," to use Nicholaus's own words, one can perceive this incomprehensible God, but only through a thick cloud, perhaps even by his very absence. God is like a timeless, eternal, thinking clock who in thought contains the succession of hours, but for whom six o'clock would not precede seven o'clock: they would be simultaneous. "The thought of the clock, which is eternity," says Cusanus, "seems as if it were folding all things in itself and projecting them outside of itself."[19] Perhaps the best and simplest illustration is his descrip-

---

[17] *De la Docte Ignorance*, ed. Moulinier, p. 83.

[18] See Georges Poulet's introduction to his excellent *Métamorphoses du cercle* (Paris: Plon, 1961), pp. xx-xxii, where he suggests that from Eckhart on, God, formerly static, becomes dynamic and overflows his own self; following Cusanus, Poulet remarks, most Renaissance thinkers allude to the image of the circle with its center but insist on the fact that the circumference is to be perceived as an expansion of the center. Robert L. Delavoy, *Bosch* (Lausanne: Skira, 1960), p. 24, notes the "image of the sphere recurs like an obsession in the work of this great visionary; and a cosmic referent will always be found to underlie the moral purport of each picture."

[19] Cusanus, *Traité de la vision de Dieu*, ed. M. Gandillac, (Paris: Aubier, 1921), p. 399.

tion of a pyramid whose base represents the darkness of man
and whose apex touches light and God, represented by the
base of another pyramid whose apex touches the base of the
first. This static figure would appear meaningless were not one
ready to imagine a motion from the base of one pyramid to the
base of the other, from man to God, God to man, *linking* them
together. This drawing was so fundamental for Cusanus that
he advised his disciples to apply the formula to "all objects of
research" as he puts it, so that this image may "lead them to all
secrets."[20] He warns, however, against identifying reality with
this type of imagery: "Supernatural light and supernatural
darkness are not to be seen with the naked eye." It has been
remarked that Cusanus evokes the symbol of the sun as a light,
but as on a photographic negative.[21] It is subdued like the light
in Bosch's *Way to Paradise*. This light is "excellent" since the
viewer can face it without being dazzled. In fact, solar imagery
seldom appears in Bosch and Cusanus. On the other hand, py-
romorphous symbols, imagery of burning fires, thermic sensations, are often present in both, as well as, incidentally,[22] in

[20] Cusanus, *Conjectures*, ed. M. Gandillac (Paris: Aubier, 1921),
pp. 159–160.

[21] M. Gandillac, "Le Rôle du soleil dans la pensée de Nicolas de
Cues," in *Le Soleil à la Renaissance* (Brussels: Presses Universitaires de
Bruxelles, 1965), pp. 348–349.

[22] See esp. *De la Docte Ignorance*, ed. Mouliner, III, ix, p. 204: "All
reasonable men are judged in Christ, just as are judged in fire the materials among which some are transformed in the image of fire: thus the
purest gold is burned to such a point that one no longer distinguishes
the gold from the fire. . . . When we see gold, silver, or copper being
melted in a very intense fire, we cannot tell the metals apart when they
have taken the form of fire. But, if this fire were in possession of understanding, it would know the degree of perfection of each of them and
the capacity to withstand an intense fire would appear different for
each, in conformity with the degree of perfection of each. There are
materials that, when submitted to the test of fire, remain indestructible,
are capable of light and heat, and can because of their purity be transformed into the image of fire." God is also compared to a glassblower
who shapes incandescent matter with his breath (*De la Docte Ignorance*, ed. M. Gandillac, [Paris: Aubier, 1921], p. 35, and Gandillac, *Le
Soleil à la Renaissance*, p. 348 nn. 2, 3).

Villon's poetry. In his *Bosch*, Delavoy observes: "Assuredly it is not due to chance that, from the *Hay Wagon* to the *Garden of Earthly Delights*, from the *Last Judgment* to the *Temptation of St. Anthony* the theme of fire so constantly recurs."[23] Quoting Bachelard's *Psychanalyse du feu*, Delavoy points out that fire here signifies need for change, evil. Bachelard himself insisted on the binding value of fire, on the syncretic attitude behind this symbol: "Thus sexualized fire is the *link between all symbols*. It *binds* matter and spirit, vice and virtue. It idealizes material knowledge; it materializes ideal knowledge."[24]

Not only does Cusanus linger on images of metal in fusion, but his amorous vision of God is described with similar imagery: "To see You is but to excite my sweet affection toward You, to enflame myself with love, to feed in the flames, and feeding, to give myself desires of fire and in these live coals to quench my thirst."[25] God of course is unknowable. He can have no name. *Theos*, we learn, is only the name of God as an object of quest by man: "*Theos* comes ... from *théoreô* or from *Théô*, that is, from the Greek verbs *contemplate* and *run*. He who seeks must indeed *run* by means of *sight* in order to be able to reach the Theos in the vision of all things."[26] In his *De Visione Dei*, Cusanus's quest for God, ending with this vision of fusion, begins with an amusing analogy which Cusanus found fascinating: he describes at length a painting by a contemporary, Roger de la Pasture, unfortunately preserved only as a copy on tapestry in the Berne museum. According to Cusanus, the All-Seeing One in this painting had the extraordinary ability of seeming to focus his gaze upon the onlooker regardless of the latter's position in the room. Should he move about, the gaze will follow him and "he will be astonished when he realizes that this motionless gaze was moving, and his imag-

[23] Delavoy, *Bosch*, pp. 77–78.

[24] Bachelard, *La Psychanalyse du feu* (Paris: Gallimard, 1938), p. 113.

[25] *Traité de la vision de Dieu*, ed. Gandillac (Paris: Aubier, 1921), p. 384.

[26] Cusanus, *Recherche de Dieu*, ed. Gandillac (Paris: Aubier, 1921), pp. 190 ff.

ination will not be able to comprehend how the gaze can *at the same time be in a different motion.*"

Cusanus goes on to describe the ultimate qualities of the vision of the Omnipresent. He states explicitly that to see this hidden God is to be seen by Him. The same mirroring relation found in Bosch's tondo, *The Seven Deadly Sins*, emerges: "By seeing me You enable me to see You, You who are a Hidden God . . . To see You is but to be seen by You . . . You tend to show Yourself to those who seek You, for Your eyes are open and never turn away from them. . . . Should I wander off, You allow me to have Your gaze upon me."

Further, Cusanus conceives of his life as a "voyage" with God as a "faithful companion." Again, sight and motion are intimately connected: "Wherever I turn my steps, I am always before You. Now, *to see* and *to move* are in You one and the same. You move with me, and You are in continual motion when I walk." It is clear that when *sight* is used by Cusanus and perhaps Bosch to support mental and spiritual speculation, it signifies *motion*. The other senses are also equated in God "so that all of theology *makes a type of circle.*"

Cusanus's dependence on all senses can best be illustrated by an amusing example: "One can imagine a perfect animal with senses and intelligence, a sort of cosmographer, who lives in a city with five gates [corresponding to the five senses]."[27] Messengers from all over the world bring him additional information; should you close one gate, some information would be lacking. "That is why our cosmographer does his best to keep all gates open in order to continue *hearing new relations* from the messengers, so that his description always *nears* the truth."[28] One may note in passing, in addition to the concern with cosmography, the persistence in this passage of the dynamic use of *relations*. Let us suppose, Cusanus continues, that, all information once gathered, the gates are closed; the cosmographer then thinks of God. God is apprehended "in the same *relation* to the whole world as that of himself to the map just drawn."

[27] Cusanus, *Compendium*, ed. Gandillac (Paris: Aubier, 1921) p. 540.
[28] *Ibid.*, p. 541.

The notion of relation, of proportion, is also important in Cusanus's conception of music. "Harmony infinite and absolutely precise," he says, "is a *proportion* in equality, but no living man can hear this harmony with his ear of flesh."[29] Moreover, one will recall the importance of *relation* in some musical pieces, as, for instance, in fifteenth-century chansons, a genre so popular then; in those called *fricassées* (or *quodlibet*), the composer would try to bring to a concordance in the same piece two voices, one singing in Italian and the other in French,[30] or to relate musically two texts with entirely different meanings. This phenomenon suggests that in poetry, painting, and music, as well as in intellectual endeavors, a similar desire to link fragments, to unite opposites, to bind, to round off, underlies these activities.

One of the masterpieces of Ockeghem, his *Deo Gratias*, composed of four rounds of nine voices, is impressive by the recurrence of at least two voices coming back for the conclusion with a paraphrase of the preceding piece, thus creating a solid circular structure. The same phenomenon occurs in poetry, where authors, seemingly oblivious of any poetic message, nevertheless convey a statement to their readers by means of homophony, alliteration, internal rhymes, and refrains, thus leaving their consciousness with a satisfying sense of circularity, of return to the beginning.

II

To what extent the mechanisms we are about to study stem from strong feelings of inferiority, from fears of being destroyed or gulped down by outer and inner monsters, from anxiety at the close of a turbulent century and the beginning of a new one, is hard to determine. There is a gradual pushing aside of the fabulous and monstrous fauna, which disappears

[29] *De la Docte Ignorance*, ed. Moulinier, p. 103.

[30] A desire to harmonize French and Italian appears in Jean Lemaire de Belges's *La Concorde des deux langages* with the terza rima, a "linking" rhyme, used as a sign of goodwill.

or is combatted rather than suffered. More and more exotic but recognizable animals, such as the rhinoceros and the giraffe, appear on the scene. Artists show a growing interest in them; kings and lords want to own them. The most impressive example, of course, is Dürer's celebrated rhinoceros (1515). Two years later the king of Portugal sent a live one for the pope's private menagerie; unfortunately, this exotic cargo sank off the coast of Genoa. Bosch included an elephant and a giraffe among the animals cohabiting peacefully with Adam and Eve in the Garden of Eden; at about the same time Lorenzo de' Medici kept a giraffe in his menagerie which a contemporary artist represented on a leash. Francis I welcomed animals as gifts, sent special missions to enlarge his collections, and kept in his presence, even when traveling, his lions, leopards, and other beasts.

Along with private menageries, aviaries also became fashionable, and natural historians such as Pierre Belon accorded birds special importance; he wrote seven books on the nature of birds.[31] His binary classification which intrigued late nineteenth-century scholarship and his strange illustration comparing the anatomies of bird and man both reflect a mental structure (to be analyzed below). Further, the growing passion for hunting is illustrated by the paintings and poems dealing with this sport; but, whether man dominated his wild beasts or was dominated by them, they must have played a very important symbolic role. One can muse over the sudden impulse that in 1583, a time plagued with bloodshed and guilt, drove the king of France, Henry III, to destroy his entire menagerie after a dream.

Heroic and triumphant though these mechanisms may seem—and in many ways they reflect a legitimate and healthy reaction—they are as disquieting as the fixity of an eye without eyelids, as unnerving as sharp-edged crystal objects that cast no shadow.

[31] See Pierre Belon, *Histoire de la Nature des Oyseaux* (Paris, 1555), and *Portraits d'oyseaux* (Paris, 1557). Belon excluded griffins and harpies "inasmuch as we do not admit their existence in nature."

In answer to Villon's statement of despair (*vado mori, contemptus mundi*, and *ubi sunt*), new themes, formulated in a heroic mode, are hurled at the world. Immortalizing fame, conquest, reordering of this world with its past extended and relived, and especially ubiquity are the new solutions. Ubiquity resolves, as we shall see in the following section, the problem of time by domination of space. One of the most striking examples is, of course, the vogue of astronomical clocks, showing time but also, and especially, the movements of the planets, the signs of the zodiac, the seasons, and so on.[32] One can venture that, whereas consciousness of time's passing was formerly experienced in terms of a circular rhythmic motion, it is now transformed into spatial perspective.

The same is true even of music, which undergoes a similar and significant change in conception. Progressively, duration or succession is replaced by simultaneity. Thirty years ago Lowinski's commentaries on the expansion of tonal space[33] described such a preoccupation with space. At the time when Magellan was circumnavigating the world, A. Willaert, notes Lowinski, explored the complete range of fifths for the first time in the history of music. The Neo-platonic academies revived Pythagorean philosophy and made fashionable the famous "musical theory" of the cosmos: above instrumental and inner, or *humana*, music reigned a third form, cosmic, or *mundana*, music.[34] According to this theory, the same intervals existed between the tones as between the planets, just as there was a constant relation between the beings in space and inner realities.[35] Analogies between perspective and the new polyphony, between architecture and music, were made. For

[32] See Politiano's description of the famous astronomical clock of Lorenzo della Volpaia, a marvel that everyone talked about (Chastel, Marsile *Ficin et l'Art*, pp. 96–97 and n. 16).

[33] Lowinski, "The Concept of Physical and Musical Space in the Renaissance," in *Papers of the American Musicological Society* (1941).

[34] André Chastel, *Art et humanisme à Florence au temps de Laurent le Magnifique* (Paris: P. U. F., 1961) p. 190.

[35] See Angelo Berardi, *Documenti Armonici*, who as late as 1687 compares the immobile earth with *cantus firmus* and the rotating plan-

Leonardo, music, *sventurata musica*, is unfortunate, condemned as it is to be subordinate to painting. The Renaissance appropriated and modified the Horatian concept of *ut pictura poesis*; Leonardo would have liked to say *ut pictura musica*. Harmony "moving in duration" is for him inferior to harmony "unraveling" in space. What seems fundamental to him in both arts is simultaneity of perception. What he appreciates in "proportion" and in "harmonic view of the whole" is that the whole can be seen "simultaneously, at one glance";[36] hence, there is immediate domination and possession of reality. This was, of course, a painter's idea of music; but, as we have seen above, the very concept of music is identified with space notions, so that, paradoxical as it may seem, one could almost say that early Renaissance music appeals mainly to the sense of *sight*. A critic, Febvre, has noted the importance of music and maintained that Renaissance men were governed much more by hearing than by sight because of the intensity of their emotional reactions.[37] A. Chastel has shown that this observation was erroneous and that it was based on the fact that sight is regarded as the "intellectual sense" and the others, especially hearing, as emotive. Renaissance man's emotions, though intense, were connected with sight. From a psychological viewpoint, voyeurism, sadism, and other intellectual distant pleasures seemingly devoid of feelings actually can be dictated by or can give rise to intense emotion. Indeed, some of the activities of the imagination described above, though intellectual, are motivated by deep irrational forces. It should be noted, however, that during the second half of the sixteenth century hearing and the other senses at least equaled or perhaps surpassed vision in importance; and melodic music progressively replaced the canons and polyphonic orchestration.

---

ets with the mobile parts: "una musica di Dio. è questa mole immense e visibile" (cf. D. P. Walker, *Musique et poésie au XVIe siècle* [Paris, 1954], pp. 16–28, and Chastel, *Art et humanisme*, pp. 209 ff.

[36] Lowinsky, *op. cit.*, p. 73.

[37] André Chastel, *The Crisis of the Renaissance (1520–1600)* (Geneva: Skira, 1968), p. 34.

Renaissance preoccupation with space, found even in the musical arts, the whole translation of time into locus, resembles the magic-like, though purely unconscious, gesture of some insane persons who systematically substitute conjunctions of space for conjunctions of time. Statements such as "I'll leave *when* the hour strikes" frequently become in their language "I'll leave *where* the hour strikes."

Noteworthy also among some schizoid attitudes are the obstinacy with which statements are elaborated in a rational and disarming logic and the persistence of the will to act even when the ultimate purpose for the action ceases to exist. Withdrawal then takes the specious appearance of rationality, voluntarism, and action.[38] Autistic, autonomous voluntarism finds its infinite expression in an ordering of reality down to its ultimate details to the extent that, intricately schematized, geometric designs, for instance, have long ceased to correspond to the object.[39] Art always presents a narrow and stylized view of reality; but in extreme cases, rather than a representation of fears or suffering, or an expression of vague yearning for fusion with the infinite, for instance, there can be complete destruction, by means of incisive lines, of the object and surrounding reality. One may recall with profit some of the series of drawings made by schizophrenic patients before and during a crisis. The drawings become more and more geometric, and background and object integrate so that the totality of reality becomes an abstract pattern. This tendency occurs in the murals of some Renaissance galleries where the ornamental design is so elaborate and complicated that the motif can hardly be discerned from the grotesques and other geometric lines. Duplicative symmetry—the space application of antithesis—and duality, together with the multiplication of analogies freely and at will, become the main modes of defining space. The symbol and the symbolized object become one. Quantification and limitless expansion are welcomed by consciousness. The main sense at

[38] I am leaning heavily on E. Minkowski's penetrating remarks in his *La Schizophrénie* (Paris: Desclée de Brower, 1953).
[39] *Ibid.*, p. 115.

work in the spatial world is, of course, the eye. This is all very evident in Marsilio Ficino's imagery and organization of reality, inner and outer, as we shall see imediately below. Also, sun worship, elevation, mountains, flying imagery, the cult of white,[40] gold, angels, and so on, often part of the magic rites of schizoids,[41] are found frequently in Ficino's works. This parallel drawn between what characterizes schizoid voluntarism, as just defined, and Ficino's imagery could be extended to a fundamental Renaissance attitude toward time and space.

Circularity and syncretism are also present in Marsilio Ficino's thought, which forces together both classical and Christian beliefs into a would-be coherent system. While there is no doubt as far as the history of ideas is concerned that the two philosophers are closely associated, it must be admitted, as Cassirer himself later recognized, that Cusanus's influence on the Florentine Academy was not so strong as had once been maintained. The *De Docta Ignorantia* and *Theologia Platonica* differ in spirit as well as in form and content.

Fundamentally, Cusanus spirals up freely from relationship to relationship toward the inaccessible. The physical universe and the world of geometry are used chiefly as a point of departure for his abstract, ever moving thought. Ficino's thought, on the other hand, presents a series of different facets,[42] of new analogies which, though clear and most symmetrical in themselves, complete or halt the progression of thought.[43] Essentials

[40] See n. 7, below.

[41] It goes without saying that *schizoid* here refers simply to a separationist or dualistic fundamental attitude toward reality, and nothing else.

[42] The presentation of reality by the juxtaposition of symmetrical opposites is the product of dialectical reasoning; but the dialectics is quite different, as Bachelard has pointed out, from dialectic imagination which seeks to apprehend all of reality and which finds more reality in the hidden than in the apparent. A third use of dialectics might well be the syncretic attitude of Cusanus in his desire to reunite the opposites.

[43] See Paul O. Kristeller, *Renaissance Thought* (New York: Harper & Row, 1961), p. 16.

can be distinguished only with difficulty from the multiplicity of minute details. Ficino's world is ordered symmetrically and hierarchically. To the twelve souls of the spheres (eight for the planets and four for the elements) corresponds a spatial hierarchy of beings: first comes matter, or the body, multiple and divisible; then the soul, mobile and indivisible; higher, the angels, immobile and divisible. Finally over the whole edifice rules God, immobile and indivisible. He corresponds to the single soul of the universe. Obviously, reality here is quantitative; space ordered anagogically and antithetically (e.g., division vs. oneness, motion vs. immobility) is indispensable to this system. One cannot sufficiently emphasize the importance of separation, of schism, for the imagination of the sixteenth-century man and his relation to the cosmos.

Quantitative space notions also dominate moral yearnings. Astrology plays a leading role, giving, so to speak, a "psychological face" to the planets and constellations and serving as a mirror of conscious and unconscious aspirations and conflicts. Correspondences of an extraordinary vitality become the pivot of man's relation to the cosmos and to time. Further, the cosmos is interiorized just as much as imagination "travels" in space. "Totum in nobis est coelum," Ficino claims. It is in infinite space, beyond ugliness and evil, that happiness can be had by man, this "restless wanderer":[44] "Seek yourself outside of the universe . . . to find yourself / . . . *fly yonder*, and what's more, *look yonder*. For when you're *yonder* you embrace all things with a glance."[45] His imagination goes even further; the following statement can hardly be called "intellectual": "Imagine that your mind grows to the point of occupying your whole body, . . . that the various limbs have disappeared, and that *your whole body is but an eye.* . . . It will receive a greater *abundance* of light; it will *embrace all things at one glance;*

[44] Man then is no longer conceived as a tired traveler at the end of his journey (Ficino, *Théologie platonicienne*, ed. R. Marcel [Paris, 1964], II, xiv, p. 270); he can ascend from ephemeral things to eternal ones (*ibid.*, I, xii, p. 202).

[45] *Ibid.*, I, vi, p. 227.

. . . it will *see them all together equally without moving*."[46] The cosmos comes under the power of this single eye which takes on a Cyclopean proportion. Man here is not under the eye of God; he is God, omnipresent. Simultaneity and quantitativeness, visibility, or immanence supplant then the realm of abstraction and transcendence. The invisible or infinite world, once yearned for, disappears under or is reduced to visible, symmetrical, or antithetical schemes of conquest and possession. This attitude is true in fact for Ficino and for many ideal models, theories, hypotheses in art, politics, science, and religion in the sixteenth century, especially for systems that "embrace the wind," to use Montaigne's outlook on his time.

The soul for Ficino has a rational and an irrational side. Whereas the rational soul is subdivided into upper and lower functions—and Ficino gives it two bodies, one astral and one material—the whole irrational soul is but a shadow. In this luminous universe, it has little place. No wonder then that the presentation of hell, so concrete in Bosch, is very limited and ambiguous; hell for Ficino is psychological. In solar mythologies, as we shall see, the realm of darkness remains sealed, at least in the early sixteenth century; later, night will be worshiped more and more. In the last analysis the *Theologia Platonica* leaves little to chance. Its extremely rigid order is maintained throughout by the principle of symmetry. Very fashionable in Neo-Pythagorean circles,[47] symmetry permitted the simultaneous evocation of two mutually exclusive and contradictory aspects of reality, with little regard for ordering reality in chronological sequence. Thus symmetry, and perhaps the whole idea of duality, lent itself to a space-conscious era. To be sure, dualism is inherent to all Platonic epistemology, where it is used as a separating device since it brings awareness of something beyond.[48] But, more than an intellectual concept, dualism, along with its spatial application, symmetry, became a

[46] *Ibid.*, I, xiii, p. 122.

[47] On this cult and its implication see Chastel, *Art et humanisme*, pp. 100 ff.

[48] Cf. Pétrement, *Le Dualisme chez Platon* (Paris: P.U.F., 1949).

deep-seated irrational mode of confronting reality. In fact, it has been sufficiently remarked that Neoplatonic systems insisted especially on the dialectic, the structure, the means, rather than the end. Similarly for Copernicus, later, the "main consideration" in determining the value of a cosmological system is whether it reflects the "exact symmetry" of the parts, that is, their harmony."[49] This geometric approach, of course, highlights the notion of system.

It has recently been pointed out[50] that if, at the turn of the century, Florentine Neoplatonism occupied the center of what is called the Renaissance myth, its idealism and speculative syncretism were inversely proportional to the uneasiness of the time. And, in a certain sense, this attitude is prevalent also in so-called realists such as Machiavelli or rationalists such as Pietro Pomponazzi. In fact, a quick glance at *The Prince* cannot but reveal that the composition as well as the presentation of argumentation reflects a systematically dualistic view. There, voluntarism and pragmatic reality, seemingly geared to each other, do not necessarily mesh. Every phenomenon, whether psychological, moral, or even metaphysical, is presented here with its opposite, its symmetrical counterpart. Thus, liberality and parsimony, cruelty and clemency, Fortuna and free will are juxtaposed and presented with terms like "the one *and* the other," "the one *or* the other," on every page. Bifurcation is a symbolic means of facing the flood of time or the onslaught of destiny.[51] Pomponazzi's *De Immortalitate Ani-*

[49] A. Birkenmajer, "Copernic comme philosophe," in *Le Soleil à la Renaissance*, p. 16. One may refer profitably to Walter J. Ong's excellent article, "Systems, Space and Intellect in Renaissance Symbolism," *Bibliothèque d'Humanisme et Renaissance*, XVIII (1956), pp. 222–239, particularly his remarks on the fact that "methods" of knowledge will eventually bring about "systems" of knowledge up to Galileo's *Dialogo*. It is my opinion, however, that at the turn of the century systems are becoming autonomous, egocentric, abstract modes of thinking which have, so to speak, abstracted space and time: in a sense, the Cartesian venture is just that.

[50] Chastel, *Art et humanisme*, p. 2.

[51] See in particular the famous example of the opposition of Fortuna and Free Will (*The Prince*, chap. xxv).

mae of the same year (1515) is a strange piece of logic. One would seek in vain chronological sequence of a synthesis. The only structure is a system of theses and antitheses, a system in which even-numbered chapters refute the odd-numbered ones. The autonomy of this activity reminds us of some of the intellectual games played by the humanists, for whom beauty or ornament perforce excluded functionality.[52] They could have included thought!

In my discussion of the snake of time, I mentioned Gafurius's famous table of correspondences with the Muses on one side and the planets on the other. What is particularly striking in this schematic representation of the "harmonic cosmos" is the division into two sections by a snake that resembles a staff or a sword more than a circular *Ouroboros* biting its own tail. As in the above-mentioned examples, symmetry eliminates or wards off time. The sun-god Apollo rules time in conformity with pre-Copernican traditions and, with his memory, intelligence, and foresight, presides over the tripartition of time symbolized by the three-headed snake.[53]

In a sense, symmetrical presentation reflects a heroic mode of coping with anxieties and time. When projected outward, inner ambivalence assumes naturally a double form. A symmetrical symbol that served to reify this abstract concept of one's relation to past and future time is Janus, a favorite of the Renaissance, often mentioned by Ficino. This solar god and god of war[54] gazes simultaneously at past and future. Thus the real concern—that of time—is suppressed, externalized as it is in space. In addition, the symmetry of his twin heads expresses the ambivalent, antithetical forms given the conflict.

Seen in this light, the remarks made by Carolus Bovillus, whom Cassirer calls one of the most "curious and characteristic

[52] Cf. Vinci's affirmation: "non può essere belleza e utilità."

[53] See n. 15, above. Cf. E. Panofsky's discussion of this symbol in *Meaning of the Visual Arts* (New York: Doubleday Anchor, 1955), pp. 146 ff.

[54] Cf. Poggio's frieze representing the priest of Janus opening the gate of his temple, as customary in wartime, to let out a formidable Mars (Chastel, *Art et humanisme*, pp. 219 ff.).

products of Renaissance philosophy," acquire new dimensions. This disciple of Lefèvre d'Etaples (indirectly influenced also by Cusanus and the Platonic academies) strives to show man as being not just a part of the universe, but a mirror, an eye. Yet he not only receives images but shapes them too. Further, Bovillus asserts that while reason is the power used by nature to return cyclically to itself, once the initial severance has occurred, real unity of self can be achieved only schizogenetically, that is, when the ego divides itself into two parts and reconstitutes itself through this division. *Splitting* is thus the way to subsequent unity. (*De Sapiente*, 1509).[55]

The picturesque figure of Silenus, master of Bacchus and ugly ornamental top of lovely perfume boxes, is also revived in the 1500s as a symbol of duality, of antithesis. Thus, Sebastian Franck can affirm that God decided to take the truth for himself and leave appearances to man; that is why, as he puts it, "All things have two faces ... and each thing is the opposite of what seems to be in the world: an upside-down Silenus."[56] For Erasmus, Silenus is much more. In the *Symposium*, Alcibiades had used the image to describe Socrates; Erasmus uses it to describe Socrates and also Christ. Elsewhere the images of appearance of truth dissolve under the ironic glance of Folly, lover of paradoxes and antitheses. Later, Rabelais likewise structures his work on ambiguity which is thematically announced in the first lines of his prologue by the same evocation.

The contemporary interest in the androgyne is also noteworthy because it signifies a visual and symmetrical response to the abstract concept of love. The yearning for the Beginning, the Golden Age of Creation, Oneness, or Love is expressed not by abstract and dynamic thought, not by a linear vision of prehistoric ages, but rather by the magical evocation of this symmetrical, bisexual figure. By its presence, it negates time and chronological thought. Antoine Héroët, a poet at the court of Francis I, who with his *Amye de Cour* had championed

[55] See Ernst Cassirer, *The Individual and the Cosmos* (Oxford: Blackwell, 1963), pp. 88 ff.
[56] In M. Foucault, *Histoire de la folie* (Paris: Plon, 1961), p. 37.

platonic love and courtly conduct modeled on Castiglione's *Cortegiano,* paraphrased in verse Ficino's translation of Plato's *Symposium*;[57] the "monster," as he says, owed its perfection to its duality in oneness. Bisexual, it reveled in guiltless narcissistic bliss and in the assurance of its strength. But, contemptuous not only of men but also of Jupiter, it was split in two and condemned to seek forever its better half.[85] In a rare representation,[59] the androgyne is a symbol of alchemy. The androgyne possesses a sword; the standing figure dominates a dragon, also double. A crown, like a saint's halo, like the solar rays, visibly symbolizes purity and glory, but also power.

As Panofsky has keenly remarked,[60] Apollo surpasses Jupiter in popularity, and the sun-god becomes identified not only with a fused notion of justice (*Sol Justitiae*) and invincibility (*Sol Invictus*), but also with Christ. The Christ figure in turn can be found riding the lion ,the sun's zodiacal mansion, and thus acquires such warlike symbols as the sword.[61] Astrologers within the fold of the Church interpreted the conjunction of Jupiter and the sun to prophesy in this age of popular nervousness, disquietude, and hope the advent of a new religion or the Golden Age,[62] unless the latter was still in existence as the earthly paradise, as some continued to believe, as Columbus

[57] *L'Androgyne,* ed. F. Gohin (Paris, 1909), p. 85, vv. 149 ff.
[58] *Ibid.,* v. 173.
[59] *The Crowned Hermaphrodite,* in C. G. Jung, *Symbols of Transformation: An Analysis of the Prelude to a Case of Schizophrenia* (New York: Harper Torch Books, 1955), pl. XVIII.
[60] *Meaning of the Visual Arts,* pp. 258–259.
[61] " 'Christ as Sun-God and Supreme Judge' would seem to be the title which does justice to the iconographical attributes as well as to the mood of Dürer's engraving" (*ibid.,* p. 263). An interesting example of cosmic imagery with an evocation of the sword may be found in Michelangelo's vision of a three-trailed comet, a silver sword turned toward the Orient, a sword the color of blood toward Rome, and a sword of fire toward Florence (E. Steimann, *Michel-Angelo im Spiegel seiner Zeit* [Leipzig, 1932], in Chastel, *Marsile Ficin et l'art,* p. 171 *n.* 19).
[62] Chastel, *Art et humanisme,* pp. 341–351.

thought, somewhere in India, at the highest point of the cosmos, at that very place where at the time of the creation the sun had first shone.[63]

If the sun with its 128 rays is the symbol of God's all-seeing eye in Bosch's *Seven Deadly Sins* with its inscription, "Cave, cave, Deus videt," the eye of God looking at man is really a mirror in which man sees himself. If the spectator in Cusanus's example is under the ubiquitous eye of God no matter where he stands,[64] in Ficino the inverse attitude appears: man does not mirror God; he is God. The whole cosmos comes under the power of his one embracing eye, as we have seen.[65] It may appear paradoxical to speak in the same breath of Ficino and Calvin (or Luther); yet recent scholarship destroys the older notion of a glorious pagan Renaissance of which austere theologies would be but the counterpart.[66] Disquietude[67] and quest for new modes of life are the common denominator of those two attitudes which in effect have many more similar underlying points than is usually recognized. Without alluding to the intellectual or spiritual contents of Calvinistic or Lutheran doctrine, one may easily conclude from their rigorous code of ethics that self-humiliation does not exclude Promethean aspirations. Driven by the notion that failure signifies not being among the elect, the moral self is mobilized to conform to an austere pattern. Stiffness of will parallels other

[63] See M. Mollat, "Soleil et navigation au temps des découvertes," in *Le Soleil à la Renaissance*, pp. 92–93.

[64] *Traité de la vision de Dieu*, ed. Gandillac, pp. 376–377.

[65] *Théologie platonicienne*, ed. Marcel, I, vi, p. 69.

[66] See J. Boisset, *Erasme et Luther, libre ou serf-arbitre* (Paris: P.U.F., 1962), pp. 13 ff. Boisset shows that nothing is more erroneous than the traditional picture that opposes a frivolous and pagan Renaissance to an austere religious reform. See also *Courants religieux et humanisme à la fin du XVe et au début du XVIe siècle* (Colloque de Strasbourg, 1957); and F. Simone's article in *Pensée humaniste et tradition chrétienne au XVe et au XVIe siècles* (Centre National de la Recherche Scientifique, 1950).

[67] See Boisset's description (*op. cit.*, p. 14) of the differences and similarities between Erasmus's and Luther's anguish.

heroic attitudes of the age.[68] An enraged Luther issues a call
to arms: "The hour of the sword has come." An intransigent
Calvin also takes up his pen to fight the real foe: the spiritual
libertine, not, as one might think, the Catholic.

Calvin's *Institutes of the Christian Religion* is filled with eye
imagery and with allusions to the sun. Further, for him, infinity
and simultaneity blend. He expresses amazement that the "infinite multiplicity of stars" could have been created "in one
moment." Elsewhere, giving a view of the greatness of God, he
ventures into a long description of the relativity of whiteness:

> Just as the eye, which sees only black things, decides that what
> is actually of a dark whitish color or else half gray is the whit-
> est thing in the world. . . . If we look on the ground or if we
> contemplate the things around us, we are convinced that our
> sight is firm and clear; but, should we raise our eyes straight
> toward the sun, the power exercised by our sight on this earth
> is confounded and dazzled by so brilliant a light . . . that we
> must admit our good sight is too weak and feeble to look at
> the sun. Thus it is with our intellectual faculties. . . . What
> pleased us before under the color of justice will seem to be
> soiled with great iniquity; . . . what deceived us miraculously
> in wisdom's shadow will show itself to be extreme madness.[69]

This passage summarizes many of the aspects of the theme we
have been describing: the eye, space, whiteness,[70] the sun, dualistic or antithetical modes. The latter process is also somewhat

---

[68] Perhaps oddly or paradoxically enough, much more than the
Erasmian attitude or that of Montaigne, where the quest for true
knowledge ends with humility.

[69] *Institution chrétienne*, ed. J. Pannier (Paris, 1936), I, 41 ff.

[70] Ficino shuns darkness: "Sight is naturally made for and likes
clarity, light. . . . It longs to draw enjoyment from light but in moving
through the friendly element without being lost in it. All colors that
contain more darkness, that is, more black than light, do not allow it to
expand, and the visual ray does not find pleasure at will, but when there
is a more dazzling color than black, it expands too broadly and is dis-
persed by an invisible voluptuousness" *De Vita*, III, 21, in Chastel, *Marsile Ficin et l'art*, p. 104).

disquieting; there may be mention of this "beautiful master-piece of the universe" which can be contemplated at one glance in its length and width, but aside from this one infallible "mirror," God is invisible.

Closer to Calvin both chronologically and intellectually than is usually realized is Saint Ignatius of Loyola, founder of the Jesuit order. With his *Spiritual Exercises* (1540), codified devotion reaches its peak. His voluntarism is also expressed, not by a sword but by the principle of obedience "like a stick in the hand of an old man," or by the motto "contemplation in action," which signifies a fusion of *sight* and *action*. To be sure, Loyola continues a mystic tradition familiar to him. The Flemish Mombaer had already utilized visual disciplinary devotions to encourage prayer, as seen in the use of a *chiropsalterium*, or psalmodic hand, of a *cantichordium* where each musical note corresponds to a vowel.[71]

In the Renaissance, thought itself and memory also become dependent on spatial points of reference (*loci* and *imagines*). Cusanus uses the portrait of the All-Seeing for didactic spiritual purposes, yet with Loyola these exercises acquire special importance; for him, abstract concepts are to be visualized. Actual places *must be seen* with the eye of the imagination: "Viendo el lugar," as he puts it. The *composición de lugar*, or composition of place, allows one to summon to the imagination, by means of each of the five senses, hell, paradise, or eternity. Consciousness then finds in the visualization of eternity a means of satisfying temporal preoccupations. Later Saint Theresa of Avila insists upon the importance of visualizing every word of a prayer, complaining that all too often a recitation degenerates into a mechanical ritual: "If you recite 'Our Father, which art in Heaven,' visualize the Father, the Heavens."

Without going into an abstract and complicated question of theology, it may be suggested that, when symbolism becomes obsolete, man turns toward nature for a new interpretation and for psychological support. In other words, man makes use of the visible world and gives it a revitalized symbolic value. Thus,

---

[71] For Rabelais's spatialization of sound and language, see p. 256.

it might be much more accurate to say that in sixteenth century man relates not to the principle of immanence, but that he seeks transcendence in the visible. This might help to explain the insistence on the concreteness of the value of water in baptism or on the actual presence of Christ in the bread and wine of the Holy Sacrament.

The refusal to deal with the invisible suggests a negation of darkness, of sleep. The symbol of wakefulness is, of course, the watchful Argus who with his hundred eyes, is frequently evoked by poets and painters. He is sometimes also called *bifrons* and is represented with two heads. He can see behind his back. Daylight and action typify his domain (like Hercules, he is an invincible giant); but this all-seeing divinity (Panoptes) depends for his strength on remaining awake, since he must be charmed to sleep to be slain. Sleep and darkness are here synonymous with death, a common enough Virgilian term but one that Renaissance poets will not forget. In a mural painting by Pintoricchio,[72] Hermes is lulling Argus, the keeper of the nymph Io metamorphosed into a cow, to sleep. The scene recalls in its peacefulness a pastoral from Sannazaro's *Arcadia*. The symmetry of the composition is emphasized by a forked tree. Placed in the middle of the painting, the tree expresses plastically the conflict between the forces of nature (Hera) and of Zeus, the supreme power. But victory, it must be noted, can come about only through deceit. The sword in the corner of the painting suggests deceptive calm. The episode portrays a moment lasting in time, "the lulling of Argus," and the consequential death of Argus is only intimated. Thus again chronology is subordinated to space and to the plastic representation. It suffices to contrast Rubens's versions of the same theme[73] to grasp the different relation to chronology and reality. Rubens represents Hermes with his sword drawn and his body and arm ready to plunge the weapon into Argus's slumbering form

[72] *Argus Lulled by Hermes*, Borgia Aparments, Vatican, Rome, in *Il Pintorrichio*, ed. Enzo Carli (Milan; Electa Editrice, 1960), pl. 77.

[73] *Argus Slain by Hermes*, Royal Museum of Art, Antwerp, Roger, in A. D'Hulst, *Olieverfschetsen van Rubens* (Antwerp, 1968), pl. 44.

sprawled against a tree. The assymetrical baroque composition enhances the dynamism of the action and its imminent violence, thus rendering pictorially the narrative element. Moreover, the symbolism of Argus's loss of power, or the triumph of dream life (or blindness ánd death), is further emphasized by the fact that Argus has lost his monstrous attributes: he has but two eyes.

Pintorricchio's Argus, on the other hand, has a body completely covered with eyes. No less than Ficino's evocation of the limbless creature metamorphosed into a gigantic eye, the sight of an anthropomorphic Argus with a hundred eyes antagonizes the mind, which rebels when confronted with a human figure covered with apertures suggesting the lips of as many wounds. Does the artificiality of the treatment, its lack of integration, not suggest the fictitious nature of the mythical experience? Does its nature not indicate that the symbol has become an object of fascination in itself?

This hypothesis explains perhaps the vogue of poetic games and contests. In some of them, indeed, as in the *Blasons du corps feminin*, a part of the body of a lady is isolated. Poets thus laud the atttributes of an eye, an eyebrow, a mouth, or a breast by repeated analogies. Obviously, the eye, symbolizing love, is the gate to the soul and a choice object of worship. These aesthetic constructions express distance and alienation rather than intimate possession. In one of them, for example, the eye of the lady is synonymous with the sun, and the poet's soul becomes nature; his poem describes the power of this solar goddess to regulate in the poet's soul the various seasons with their prevailing meteorological conditions! The multiplicity of visual images in this poem obviously destroys somewhat narcissistically the object it wants to capture, regardless of the incantations.[74] What poets capture is surface, not depth, just

> Eye, not an eye, but a golden sun.
> Eye, like God, by my eyes honored.

[74] For example, Antoine Héroët's "Blason de l'oeil," in Albert- Marie Schmidt, *Poètes du XVIᵉ siècle* (Paris: Pléiade, 1953), pp. 311–312.

Eye that could with its position and shape
For ten years more cause a battle to last.
Eye depriving me of the glance owed me,
Seeing me better than were it looking at me.
Eye without which my body is useless.
Eye through which my soul is distilled.
....
Eye beautiful and clear like the azure sky.

like the painters or even, for that matter, the alchemists, whose complicated and secret formulas mask an essential alienation from inner reality.[75] Their anxious scrutiny wanders from surface to surface apprehending reality from without, from the "tip of the eyes," so to speak. It never focuses on an organic center or establishes intimacy with it.

One is reminded of the intricate and bizarre cubistic figures of Dürer. In his *Geometria*, Lorenz Stöer gives reality so geometric and abstract a quality that it no longer *represents* any object at all; rather, it *becomes* an object. The surfaces of walls and ceilings are invaded by grotesques and ornamentation that, though clearly defined, symmetrical, and geometric, have no focal point. The eye cannot rest or make distinctions between object and background. This "mad vitality," as Chastel puts it, reflects depth from which it is alienated. Alienation from depth or from certain feelings is in effect synonymous with the desire to possess not only space with the eye but also, by implication, nature and time. Travel leads to a form of exile; in the Renaissance, exile, whether voluntary or not, was fashionable. Geographical alienation is rendered by Rabelais when he isolates various ways of life on so many islands. Social and even psychological alienation is frequent among poets and artists of the Renaissance, although the tendency is to normalize folly by generalizing and internalizing more and more; exorcism wanes as madness is no longer conceived in terms of outside demons who enter the soul to possess it. Witch burning and torture do not cease, however, and obsession with death, which

[75] As Jung and Bachelard would put it; see Bachelard, *La Terre et les rêveries*, pp. 49–51.

accompanies alienation, takes on the special form of having to see beneath the flesh, to see through it. If the fascination with anatomical dissection which in fact developed during this period must be called accidental, it can at least be said that illustrations[76] that map the human body take on as fantastic an appearance as the contemporary navigators' surface representations of the earth. Even the hereafter is visualized in what is considered one of the masterpieces of French Renaissance sculpture: Ligier Richier's standing figure which is but a view of bone through flesh. It shows, as late as 1544 (almost 100 years after Villon), René de Châlons's desire to be portrayed, not peaceful, as he appeared on his deathbed, but as he would look three years later with the bones protruding through his decaying flesh.

It could be objected, with truth, that anatomical dissections also served life. Yet it is no coincidence that the scalpel is the instrument of miracles performed on human life by Ambroise Paré, one of history's most famous surgeons. That he devised new medical instruments and methods to remove cataracts so as to restore sight, comes as no surprise. In addition to his accomplishments as a pioneer oculist, Paré is known also for practicing plastic surgery; for the facial symmetry of those who have lost an eye he suggests "another eye artificially made of gold or silver."

Thus the eye is everywhere present in the enterprises of Renaissance man. It would indeed be an endless task to analyze, for example, all the montages of contemporary love imagery and psychological discourse where the eye plays a dominant role, both in veneration of the lady from afar and in the lover's submission to her lethal gaze, so prevalent in Platonic and Petrarchan verse. This activity is usually rather narcissistic, for the poet does not really see the lady whose charms he supposedly wishes to praise. One of the first poems of his *Délie* (1544) sums up Maurice Scève's situation: The poet's eye has no specific direction (*girouettoit*, "was

---

[76] See, for example, the anatomical engravings from Charles Estienne's *De dissectione partium corporis* (1545).

My eye, too ardent in errors of youth,
Moved freely about, hardly prudent, unaware.
Behold—O delightful fear of fears!—
My love's gripping sight, like a basilisk
Piercing body, heart, and reason destitute,
Penetrated into my very soul.
    Hard was the blow that, though no sharp-edged blade,
Makes, the body still alive, the spirit lifeless,
Pitiable offering before the sight of thee, O my Lady,
Now become the idol of my life.[77]

pivoting like a weathervane"). The glance of the beloved, like
that of the sight of the Medusa, transforms the lover into a
petrified worshiper of his lady. The latter, despite the poet's
allusions to the moon, is a solar divinity. Here she is identified
also with a mythical snake whose sight is lethal. As if these
symbols did not suffice, her glance is also compared to a penetrating sword.[78]

As suggested earlier, there is indeed a relation between possession with the eye, distance, and sadistic activities, especially
when the sword is involved. The cruel imagery of Scève's poem, by no means exceptional, arises in the context of an idealized love. The same cruelty occurs in its natural counterparts,
—sadism, voyeurism, necrophilia, and so on—which flourished
in misogynic works of the period. These two extremes are
frequently juxtaposed in Marguerite of Navarre's ambivalent
Heptaméron. Witness, as a product of idle travelers' imagination, the story of a valet who fancied he could obtain favors
of the lady of the house and who stabbed her some twenty times
in the kidneys before raping her. The whole episode was, of
course, viewed by a child hidden under a bed.[79]

[77] *Délie*, I, in *Poètes du XVIᵉ siècle*, p. 75.
[78] Even in Rabelais the sword is an important element, although one
basic ingredient is lacking in the main character, Panurge: courage.
Brother John and the giants themselves, though mock heroes in many
ways, lead many a battle with swords, sticks, etc., against fantastic enemies, giants, and mock monsters (*andouilles*).
[79] *Oeuvres complètes*, ed. P. Jourda (Paris: Garnier, 1962), I, 6.

In its realistic dimension, Marguerite's work mirrors the two attitudes toward women prevalent among her contemporaries: idealization and debasement. Ample evidence of growing fears of succumbing to the domination of the opposite sex can also be found in literature and art. Women are portrayed sword in hand, whether they are Amazonians, well-armed virgins, priestesses, or witches; whether the woman portrayed is Judith, Salomé, or Delilah. Alexander's mistress humiliates Aristotle in sixteenth-century representations of the old fabliau: Brueghel's Mad Meg moves about, sword in hand, towering completely out of proportion to the other figures, the incarnation of elemental malevolence.

A revisitation of Rabelais's work might not give the modern reader only the satisfaction of finding the celebrated enthusiasm for life which usually accompanies a definition of Rabelais's humanism of this "generation of laughter," as it is often called. Laughter covers up tears and consuming grief, and a profusion of forms and details is juxtaposed less as the expression of pedantic knowledge than as a verbal outpouring as gratuitous as the quest of his antiheroes or, for that matter, as all the activities of mankind. His work reflects life like a grotesque mirror, with, as he says, "an incredible disregard for all that which men commonly do, such as *watch, run, sail, fight, travel, toil,* and *turmoil* themselves." Hence, for Rabelais, human life is also essentially sight and action. He himself views it from afar. His corrosive ironic distance which reduces everything to the same denominator stems from a psychological attitude that would have to be described, medically speaking, as perversion and revolt. Rabelais, though molding himself against the very structures we have just defined, is the *enfant terrible* of the sixteenth century. To be sure, his giants as well as the world in which they evolved were realistic: no incident in Rabelais's grotesque work could intimate belief in a supernatural or fantastic reality. When the cosmos becomes incomprehensible, explanations—no matter how fanciful—come immediately to the rescue. In a sense, we are kept in familiar territory, in broad daylight; hell, when it is evoked in one instance, a mock resuscitation scene, is amusingly reassuring and implies no descent into some possibly frightening inner abysses. Religion, alchemy, astrology, devils, magic, and hermetic practices are as frequent in Rabelais's work as they must have been in his time, but they are viewed from the outside and ridiculed.

Yet his satire is only a point of departure for his invention, and it should be stressed that Rabelais is as much a creative genius as his contemporaries, no matter how negative, uncommitted, and subversive his irony may show him. His mockery, which spares no one, not even the reader, and his evocation of giants, as huge and benevolent as the cosmos (which, once frightening, becomes reassuringly small and familiar because of the very size of the giants), are indeed means of warding off inferiority and fear. These anthropomorphic giants pursue one central activity:—intake of food, drink, windmills, sometimes excrement, pilgrims, and even the author himself. The themes of gigantism, swallowing, and being swallowed are really one and the same. (The whale episode, evocative of Jonas, may suggest other digestive ventures.) The whole humanistic program, in fact, where the disciple is to become a "bottomless pit of knowledge," and indeed the ultimate answer at the end of the quest, "Trink," may have a similar significance. As for Rablais's outpour of scatology, Gallic flavor or national tradition hardly suffices to explain it. There is, of course, a relationship among sadism, manducation, coprophiliac pleasure, and anguish before time. Kronos has teeth, and his fears are not unlike those that give birth to the creation of friendly giants.[80] Voluntarily or not, then, Rabelais seems to relish his perversion, unable or unwilling to seek transcendence, elevation, or hier-

---

[80] For an interpretation of the ogre rendered harmless and benevolent, see G. Ròheim, *The Gates of the Dream* (New York, 1952), pp. 366 ff. See E. Panofsky, *Studies in Iconology: Humanistic Themes in the Art of the Renaissance*, repr. (New York: Harper, 1962), pp. 82 ff.

archy, as the free associations in this chirping of the drinkers show:

> I never drink without thirst, either present or future. To prevent it, as you know, I drink for the thirst to come. I drink eternally. This is to me an eternity of drinking, drinking of eternity. . . . I drink, for fear of dying. Drink always and you shall never die. If I drink not, . . . I am stark dead without drink, and my soul *ready to fly* into some marsh amongst frogs: the soul never dwells in a dry place. If I could get up as well as I can swallow down, I had been long ere now very high in the air. . . . The great God made the planets, and we make the platters neat.[81]

The pun concluding the passage, "Dieu a fait les planètes et nous faisons les plats nets," might well summarize Rabelais's attitude. We find here parallel construction, reflecting a macro-microcosmic relation, but ironized. The accent is placed on Renaissance concern with (1) the cosmos and (2) the return to the very beginning—of life or of the world—and Rabelais's concern with licking his plate clean, thus equating by a vertical relation the demiurge and man (God-we), the cosmos and intake (*planètes—plats nets*), as a main activity of godlike giants, resulting in a disrespectful attitude toward the Creator, the creation, and man himself in an ironic pulverization of language by means of the pun.

Another instance of language made visible, reminiscent of mnemonics, occurs when the querying travelers, wandering from isle to isle, from one alienating truth to another, are frightened by mysterious explosions which turn out to be frozen sounds and words thawing in the Arctic spring. The enigmatic prayer to the oracle of the Divine Bottle is also transcribed on Rabelais's own manuscript in the shape of a container.[82] In nei-

[81] *Gargantua*, ed. Louis Moland, 2 vols. (Paris: Garnier, 1950), I, 23–27.

[82] It does seem significant that in this prayer, the bottle—the end of all quest—is the container described as full of mysteries. Significant also is the fact that the mystery-containing bottle, end of all quest, is a parody of all containers, just as *Trink* signifies *intake* (but in an ironic

ther instance, however, does language lead to lyrical soaring.[83]
There can be no elevation in the world of Rabelais, and no
descent, either: his is an art of surfaces. In one instance,
however, evoking the famous plant, pantagruelion (be it hemp,
asbestos, or some moral or psychological quality of man),
Rabelais prophesies the conquest of space by future generations. In the words of the Olympian gods, frightened by man's
boldness,

> They may contrive a way ... to pierce into the high aerial
> clouds, get up into the springhead of the hail, make an inspec-
> tion of the snowy sources, and shut and open as they please
> the sluices from whence proceed the floodgates of rain; then,
> prosecuting their ethereal voyage, they may step into the
> lightning workhouse and shop; ... then ... they will ... in-
> vade the territories of the moon, passing through both Merc-
> ury and Venus. ... Some will take up a lodging at the Ram,
> ... some at the Lion Inn, ... others at the Scorpion. ...
> [They] will set themselves down at table with us, drink of
> our nectar and ambrosia, and take to their own beds at night
> for wives and concubines, our fairest goddesses, the only
> means whereby they can be deified.[84]

To be sure, Rabelais is only half serious about the "space program." As we have seen, descent into hell as well as ascension
into space is quite foreign to his imagination. Yet, in the above
passage as elsewhere, he is poking fun at a real activity that
might have been the main attraction of a space-conscious
sixteenth century, one that we may wish to consider a Renaissance legacy to our own age: flying.

---

way), that is, a return to the breast, the womb. Hence the *unnatural*
birth of the giants, the breaking of the chains and the cradle by the
Hercules-like giant in infancy, the manducation, the misogynic attitude, and hence also at a higher level the alienation from nature and the
attraction it exercises on the author, which explains in part his ambivalent or ambiguous attitude toward the quest.

[83] *Ed. cit.*, II, 206–207.
[84] *Ibid.*, I, 614.

Examples of this natural or unnatural activity, as one may wish to call it, abound. The history of aviation counts many examples of early imaginary flight; for example, there is frequent mention of magic boots or "swift-foot apparatus" for rapid locomotion in the air in Tibetan records of Buddhist saints.[85] Despite Leonardo's lack of success in creating a flying machine, the Renaissance could be called a space age also because of the importance it attributed to space and flying.

When concrete projects fall short of realization, imagination and dreams come to the rescue. It is beyond the scope of this essay to discuss the various theories about the deeper motivations that give birth to the desire to kick the earth with one's heels and soar above it to view it in "monarchical contemplation."[86] It may mean escape from concrete reality or sublimation, reaction to uterine regression, expression of superiority, or simply man's way of relating to what is *above* him. In any event, separation, positively or negatively polarized, from terra firma or from nature, or freedom from gravity, is axiomatic to the desire to fly.[87] Elevation, in motion or position (a privileged viewpoint from which the omniscient can contemplate the cosmos), may satisfy this desire.[88]

To return to our contemporary parallel, schizoid attitudes often include sun worship, obliteration of time, and imagery of

[85] B. Laufer, *Prehistory of Aviation*, Field Museum of Natural History Anthropological Series, XVIII, no. 1 (Chicago, 1928), p. 54.

[86] Bachelard's expression in *L'Air et les songes* (Paris: Corti, 1950), p. 282. Flight in Bosch's paintings is different. Castelli had already noted (*op. cit.*, pp. 43–44) that for Bosch "it is . . . a false elevation, a takeoff toward darkness."

[87] It is evident that all that is said here may equally well be applied to a certain cult of the mountain which includes, among other things, the sense of power, of challenge, and of purification (see Bachelard, *L'Air et les songes*, p. 282). It is then especially significant to mention here the *temple d'honneur et de vertu* situated on an inaccessible hill with an arduous path leading to it so plastically described by one of the forerunners of the Pléiade, J. Lemaire de Belges. One has to wait for Montaigne to find the negation of height.

[88] See n. 109, below.

space and flying, as a schizophrenic patient believed: "I stand for the solar principle.... White is the spiritual principle;... the sun according to the current conceptions is like a ball of fire. ... My brain alone can capture the pure waves from the sun."[89] Another recounted that "a priest took me up into the air. I just flew through and ... up in the sky I found an angel, a woman called Angel Love. She had yellow hair and a body of gold and wings made of feathers."[90] The same patient explained on another occasion that he was so happy he flew into space like the sun.[91]

Alluding to Icarus, one of the most frequently evoked mythological characters in the sixteenth century, Ficino lauds man, the "lord of all things, who tramples the earth, furrows the sea, rises up in the air on huge towers, not to mention Daedalus's and Icarus's feathers. He knows how to make fire ... [but] man needs celestial power to rise up to heaven and measure it. With his supracelestial mind, he goes beyond the skies."[92]

The whole Promethean program of the Renaissance cannot be discussed here, but is should be noted that the anagogical process of the age, the aspiration to reach higher levels, whether physical, moral, or metaphysical, is fundamental to the whole Renaissance structure we have just defined, and that the notion of physical space inherent in it becomes increasingly important. For example, the voluntaristic desire to surpass oneself in wisdom, virtue, and knowledge is expressed by a most popular myth, that of the Temple of Honor and Virtue, plastically described by poets and situated atop a mountain of extremely difficult access. The imagery of Neoplatonic love (ladders, wings, etc.) expresses a similar physical desire to soar in space; fame and glory are represented with wings, and poets often fancy themselves as swans—a guarantee of immortality. Ronsard, for instance, says: "Just like Horace,

---

[89] Minkowski, *op. cit.*, p. 230.

[90] Ròheim, *op. cit.*, p. 86.

[91] *Ibid.*

[92] In Chastel, *Marsile Ficin et l'art*, p. 60; see also *Théologie platonicienne*, ed. Marcel, II, iii, pp. 24–25.

transformed into a swan, / I make flight that frees me of death."[93]

Plato in his *Republic* had a special punishment for astronomers who lingered on the study of the visible skies: they should be changed into birds because they liked the sky so much.[94] Many Renaissance men indeed deserved this fate. With its concern for origins and birth, astrology was extremely important in the sixteenth century, as we have already seen. As pointed out in John Burke's essay (above), the Hermetic view, though it fought the idea of a predetermined life, was still a prisoner of the struggle. Astrology was important also because it offered the reassurance of identifying with a circular destiny, solidary of a solid and visible cosmos whose eternal movements were known. According to Calvin, the vogue for astrology was so prevalent that the intelligentsia were "practically bewitched" by it. He was sufficiently alarmed to write the *Treatise against Astrology* (1549), in which he condemned those dissatisfied with the "useful human sciences" recently "resurrected" by God. His belief was that if one applies himself to "good and useful things, one will have no leisure time to transport oneself into the air, to flit among the clouds without touching heaven or earth." Yet he does not completely abandon the visible sky; he respects what he calls "natural astrology" and concedes that "when God wants to extend his hand in order to make some judgment worthy of memory, he warns us sometimes by means of comets."[95] "To flit among the clouds" was really not hollow rhetoric: it expressed a real belief among the learned as well as among common folk. For instance, it seems that flying to the sabbat became standard practice for witches during the Renaissance. Some of the persecutors accused the witches of using such evil means of locomotion, and in some courts it was debated whether flying to the sabbat was to be considered a

[93] "A son Retour de Gascongne," in *Oeuvres complètes*, ed. G. Cohen (Paris: Gallimard, 1966), II, 746.

[94] See Pétrement, *op. cit.*, p. 142.

[95] Calvin, *Traité ou Avertissement contre l'astrologie*, ed. A. Angliviel (Paris: Cluny, 1962), pp. 27, 34.

more heinous offense than walking to it. "It was reported that witches attending the larger assemblies sometimes darkened the sky as they passed overhead."[96] The witches themselves believed, in good faith, that they flew. Group hysteria can explain their conviction, but it has also been proven that, in the sixteenth century, witches knew of aconite, capable of producing cardiac retardation, and other herbs that provided alkaloids for the fabrication of love potions, flying ointments, and other hallucinatory drugs. Modern experiments with some of these drugs have established their efficacy.

Participation of the learned in such practices is difficult to assess. But, whether on wings affixed with wax or on a forked stick or broom, whether with drugs or in religious visions where one experienced levitation and speedy flights through the heavenly spheres, imaginations were actively engaged in space activities.

Ficino's theories on divine rapture and contemplation of the spheres and heavenly regions (with or without soul-elevating love) were often used not only by his disciples, such as Nesi with his *poema-visione*, but also in French sonnets that exploited the theme of ascension through love. Toward the 1550s, interest shifted to cosmic literature: hymns and poems that exposed scientific knowledge, especially meteorology, one of the pastimes of the sixteenth century. For example in his *Amour des Amours* (1555), Jacques Peletier du Mans, a leading poet, philosopher, scientist, and mathematician, published ninety-six love sonnets in the Petrarchan tradition, followed by an unusual second part where, upheld by the force of his love as by a strong pair of wings, the poet departs on a cosmic exploration, flies over the Mediterranean and Mount Olympus, and then enters the sublunar and planetary regions. The poet's main interest seems to be the scientific one of giving an explanation of the causes of lightning, hail, rain, frost, and other meteorologic phenomena, using the most traditional sources (Seneca, Pliny, and Lucretius).

[96] See R. E. L. Masters, *Eros and Evil: The Sexual Psychopathology of Witchcraft* (New York: Matrix House, 1966), pp. 150–155.

As early as 1551 Ronsard himself gave Queen Marguerite of Navarre's body the same honor Ovid had given Caesar: she is transformed into a star and thus allowed to continue contemplating France. Her soul, however, returns to take its place near God. Unlike us, "poor and weak" without knowledge of our birthplace, she can see the earth below and know the causes of cosmic phenomena. This is her ultimate felicity, her final and eternal reward. Happiness here seems to be equated with rational knowledge and understanding of the cosmos. We can thus understand the popularity enjoyed by Macrobius's commentary on the *Dream of Scipio* in the sixteenth century. Ronsard indeed drew on Macrobian tradition for his lines on the cosmic voyage undertaken by the soul when it leaves the body (during sleep) to "learn all the secrets of the heavens including how lightning is made, as well as the clouds, hail, frost, and so on."[97] It is not specified whether these aerial dreams were physically induced or were poetic fictions. In any event, little room is left for fusion with a god of love. Rather, this intellectual program implies distance, possession with the eye. Personifying Philosophy in a hymn of praise, Ronsard describes her as one who "spies on the nature of the great God," who can with one "single clever glance" grasp the whole endless expanse of sky. Just as a witch pulls down the moon with her charms, he says, Philosophy brings the sky to earth and places it in our hands like a toy. Here also Ronsard lingers on the merits of a philosophy that was able to discover nature's secrets, particularly those of the weather. Another hymn praises philosophers who can chase flatterers from the king's table. To illustrate, Ronsard evokes with beautiful imagery the combat, by sword, of the winged, golden-haired twin sons of Boreus against the flying Harpies trying to starve poor Phineus, hungry and blind.[98]

Like Botticelli, like Brueghel and many of his contemporaries, Ronsard evokes the seasons, glorifies summer and the sun with its golden chariot, and personifies the hours as maidens,

[97] "L'Excellence de l'esprit de l'homme," *Le second Livre des Poèmes, in Oeuvres complètes*, ed. Cohen, II, 466 ff.

[98] "Hynne de Calays et de Zethés," in *ibid.*, II, 125 ff.

just as Il Primatice had done when painting for the Ulysses Gallery at Fontainebleau the dance of the hours in a harmonious circle suggesting the movement of the spheres.[99] The whole cosmos is set in motion by Ronsard and *takes flight*:

> O round and vaulted heavens, lofty dwelling of God,
> Rolling your huge sphere so swiftly
> On its two jutting axes, that the wingèd speed
> Of eagles and of winds could not rival yours.[100]

Many invisible winged creatures fill the air during the Renaissance. As late as 1555 Ronsard devotes a long hymn to demons, describing their nature, habits, and so on, and even relating a personal night encounter with these frightful spirits against whom only the sword prevails. The cult of the sun and daylight, the Herculean dimension acquired by visual possession of the cosmos, and magnificent flights on the wings of imagination are Ronsard's expression of an aggressive and heroic attitude before time. An eminent critic recently showed the therapeutic role of the sun for this Saturnian poet, concerned with warding off nefarious astral influences.[101] It should be pointed out that an increasingly ominous future added to Ronsard's own growing anxieties.

III

In the early 1550s Du Bellay had proclaimed a new poetry and had called language written in a "higher and better style" the "wings" of heavenly immortality. Then, only three years after

---

[99] Louis Dimier, *Le Primatice* (Paris: A. Michel, 1928), pl. XVI.

[100] "Hynne du Ciel," in *Œuvres complètes*, ed. Cohen, II 190.

[101] G. Gadoffre, "Ronsard et le thème solaire," in *Le Soleil à la Renaissance*, p. 568: "So that his invocation to air, light, cosmos, love, music, and the hot summer are not the literary expression of a certain form of 'dolce vita,' but an effort to ward off by means of sun and light the threats of the forces of darkness." See also G. Gadoffre, *Ronsard, par lui-même* (Paris: Seuil, 1960), pp. 78–80.

the publication of Ronsard's quasi-epic hymns, Du Bellay presented in *Regrets* (1558) a collection of mournful sonnets expressing plaintively a new form of melancholia and dissatisfaction.[102] Heroic defiances of Fortune, immortal glory, cosmic exploration are now no longer valid for the poet. His frequent poetic use of the terms like *now, no longer* indicates real changes.[103] Du Bellay conceived of present reality as a series of unpleasant, incoherent, insignificant events. They are experienced passively or suffered. Past activities have been rejected. The future is far away, both in time and in space. As for antiquity and its heroic mythology, with figures like Perseus who dared to kill the Medusa, Hercules, the twins, and others "formerly" so heroic in love and war, its evocation serves only to magnify his own shortcomings, to "make the problems more real" in 'love's games." Elsewhere, comparing himself to Ulysses and other heroes, Du Bellay deplores his own vulnerability. He chooses to identify not with the twin heroes but rather with blind Phineus and deplores having no one to chase the Harpies.

> Who will chase from me these greedy Harpies?
> Who will soar for me once more toward heaven
> To bring back my senses and return my eyes to me?
> And who will enable me to eat my food in peace?[104]

The tone differs radically from Ronsard's triumphant hymn of "Calays et Zethès." In a corrupt and decadent Italy which bears little resemblance to the ideals forged by enthusiastic French humanists and whose ruins are no longer viewed with the interest of an archaelogist but as a sign of decay, Du Bellay, voluntarily exiled, yearns with nostalgia for his parental home. The suffering and frustrated traveler is like the mariner who "as his only treasure brings back herrings instead of gold in-

---

[102] A literary pose, to be sure, but a new fashion.

[103] "Now Fortune rules over me, / And my heart which once knew no master / Is now slave, plagued by a thousand evils and regrets" (*Les Regrets*, in *Poètes du XVI⁰ siècle, ed. cit.*, pp. 448–449)

[104] *Les Regrets*, in *ibid.*, p. 480.

gots." He lives his alienation in two modes: temporal and spatial. Happiness and sadness are curiously interwoven with present and future times in pessimistic lines where the poet's wishes are justified and at the same time proven vain by the sight of ruins to be ("triumphant arches at whose soaring points the very heavens marvel" which slowly turn to ash). Therefore, he concludes, his "sad desires" should "live happy because if time ends such hard things it will also bring to an end the torments he is now enduring.[105]

Around 1558, in *The Fall of Icarus*, Brueghel expressed in a coherent and harmonious seminatural landscape a mosaic of elements belonging to different times and places: a sixteenth-century plowman, a rocky Mediterranean coast, imaginary mountains, a caravelle, Icarus, and so on. A sense of organic unity between man and nature is conveyed to the estranged viewer through the plastic quality of the painting itself, its rhythm, and especially the subject in the foreground: a man of the earth. Antithetical to this is the presentation of a Lilliputian Icarus whose ambitious flight is no longer placed high on the scale of values and whose fall indeed goes unnoticed, as Auden said so beautifully in his "Musée des Beaux-Arts." Another curious element is the lighting: the foreground is sunlit while the sun is already setting on the horizon. Sunless days, dark days, twilight, characterize this particular moment. Daylight is less valued as heroic attitudes are replaced by the nostalgic presentation of former heroes—Icarus, Phaeton, Ixion, Prometheus—with emphasis placed on their passivity, their humiliation, or their defeat. Desportes also uses the theme of Icarus but emphasizes the desirability of the fate of the hero fallen into the sea. In contrast with earlier treatments, the theme is presented as a narrative along chronological lines.

New meaning is given the hackneyed theme of the blinding glance of the lady. Unlike the eagle, the poet closes his eyes and solicits the dark cover of sleep, night, or death. The complicity of night allows for passivity and ambiguity. Visibility and action, as we have seen, had been ultimate values; negation of

[105] *Antiquitez de Rome*, in *ibid.*, p. 421.

sight shows the deflation of heroic attitudes, self-emasculation. In a comtemporary play, Robert Garnier's *Les Juifves*, the king of the Jews is at the mercy of Nebuchadnezzar, the cruel Babylonian king who identifies himself with the sun and God: "No matter how great the Lord is, I shall be no less; he commands over lightning, thunder, winds, hail, frosts, and moving stars."[106] The inflexible Nebuchadnezzar selects a refined torture for his victim: privation of sight. Even Ronsard, inevitably caught up in the fury of religious hatred, calls upon God's wrath to strike the guilty with blindness:

> Grant that the serpents of the hideous Furies
> Stir in their minds panic terrors,
> Grant that in full daylight their vision be troubled,
> Grant that each blow as two blows be felt,
> Grant that dust becloud their eyes.[107]

The Protestant d'Aubigné depicts the children of Mother France as tearing out one another's eyes.[108]
Earlier, language had been descriptive of the cosmos. It had served to name visible objects; words themselves had become visible objects. Rhythm had provided an imitative support for plasticity: Ronsard's sentences exploded with thunder or waved sinuously like golden curls around the head of his Venus or his Cassandra. The poets, inspired by the gods, even the Hermetists, had had faith in the creative, magic power of language, a humanistic instrument of knowledge, of re-creation of the world. The Tower of Grammar, the lofty Temple of Virtue, are now replaced by the symbol of confusion of language, the Tower of Babel.[109] The persistent evocation of the destruction

[106] Ed. L. Pinvert (Paris: Garnier, 1922), vv. 189 ff.

[107] "Discours des misères de ce temps," in *OEuvres complètes*, ed. Cohen, II, 549.

[108] *Les Tragiques*, ed. H. Weber (Paris: Gallimard, 1969), p. 24, vv. 114 ff.

[109] Cf., for example, the *Hill of Knowledge* (Florentine School, fifteenth century), Jean Lemaire de Belges's *Temple de Vertu* (see H. Franchet's chapter in his *Le Poète et son oeuvre d'après Ronsard* (Paris:

of soaring symbols in Du Bellay's dream evoking the fall of Rome, in his *Antiquitez de Rome* (1555), had intimated this shift.[110]

Critics have not failed to note that the lack of vigor and incisiveness in Desportes's love sonnets reduces all imagery to mere rhetorical verbosity. They have pointed out, however, how the musicality of his verse saved him from oblivion. Indeed, language achieves an autonomous melodic rhythm independent of meaning. It becomes a charm; it lulls the ear. The aural takes precedence over the visual. When vision remains the privileged sense, it is made to serve the cause of outrageous sadism, violence, or exhibitionism, as in those savage poems of Agrippa d'Aubigné where, for instance, he rips open his stomach. Often, fear and guilt dull the eye, or else introspective interests find vision less useful than darkness, tactile sensations, or silence as a means of finding oft unnamed intimacy.

Saint John of the Cross, in his ambiguous *Noche Oscura*, evokes the secrecy of night which prevents seeing and being seen. For him, night leads more surely than daylight to the sensuous pleasures of the blind caress of the wind, to the rustling scent of the cedars. These feelings culminate in the suspension of all senses, in total abandon and oblivion. The mysterious and mystic world of Saint John is permeated with an obscurity that "gives more reality to what is hidden." Antonymy or even ineffability replaces enumeration, so frequent earlier: "I penetrated there, I knew not where, and I remained, unknowing, surpassing all knowledge." Saint John's strange *Mountain of Perfection* is a paradoxical admonition:

Champion, 1922). Brueghel's tower (of several painted at this time) is of 1563. M. Scève, in his *Microcosme* (1561), describes at length man's industry in constructing the tower, but the passage ends on the thundering noise of the sudden destruction of Babel struck by an irate God's lightning bolt. Jean de Sponde (see below) also evokes those "who undertake to conquer the heavens which they cannot fight," but he refers to those "alabaster faces with ebony souls," thus alluding indirectly to the destruction of the cursed biblical cities.

[110] See n. 105, above.

To arrive at tasting everything, desire to taste nothing.
To arrive at knowing everything, desire to know nothing of
  anything.
To arrive at being everything, desire to be nothing of
  anything.

No less paradoxical is his graphic version of Mount Carmel. Its resemblance to a mountain is dubious; it suggests depth rather than height. Language and visuality are defeated or bypassed in this kingdom of darkness; blindness becomes a value.

In his religious *Stances of Death*, Jean de Sponde orders his eyes sealed to worldly life:

My eyes, cast your dazzled gaze no more
Upon the shining rays of the flaming life,
Be sealed, be covered with darkness, O my eyes;
It is not to suppress your habitual strength
For I shall make you see lights much brighter,
But, emerging from darkness, your sight will be far keener.[111]

D'Aubigné's long poem, *Les Tragiques*, narrating the martyrdom of the Protestants, culminates in a Last Judgment where the Catholics in hell are deprived of their five senses. The elect, with bodies fully resurrected, shall regain their five senses, now purified.

Thus in this second life, immortal,
We shall have the same senses we had,
But, being of pure act, they will be made of action
And shall not bear infirm passions:
They shall be pure and belong to pure subjects, to God
  they shall go to take
Light, smell, taste, touch, and hearing.

In his last paragraph, in the best mystic tradition of late sixteenth-century and early sevententh-century Baroque literature, the poet suddenly enters into a state of total ecstasy, of

[111] *Stances de la morte*, in Schmidt, *ed. cit.*, p. 890.

fusion with God; he is completely blinded, deprived of all his senses, in a swoon:

> Wretched that I am, no longer can I to my eye
> Bring down the eye of heaven; I cannot bear the sun.
>
> . . . .
>
> My senses have no senses, my spirit from me flees away
> My ravished heart falls silent, my mouth is speechless:
> All dies, the soul flies away, and taking anew its place
> In ecstasy it swoons in the bosom of its God.[112]

Much earlier, in 1568, Brueghel's painting illustrating the biblical parable that "the blind led by the blind are doomed to fall" presented blindness more negatively and pessimistically. The blind are shown falling into a ditch or a river where they will presumably drown. This work has been compared to a futuristic painting or even to a slow-motion film sequence. Both in the *Noche Oscura* poem and in Brueghel's painting, supposedly the first in the sixteenth century to express "acceleration of motion," the chronological dimension has become important. (The use of clocks, increasingly common, also reflects growing concern with duration, the existential "passing," the flow.) The disproportionate length of the painting, the strong oblique descending lines, the colors, and the rhythms also lead the imagination to deny individual differences, to assume that the same person is captured at different moments in time and in different places in space. The blind are cut off from the sky. The vacuity of their eyes expresses tragic hopelessness. Their walking sticks lead them only toward inevitable doom and mark the futility of man's endeavor.

Furthermore, the painting is truly futuristic because of its prophetic nature. In it, consciousness becomes identified not only with motion in time but also with time to be. The blind symbolically calls upon his other senses in vain: his fall is bound to occur. Future time is thus telescoped, made imminent. D'Aubigné achieved the same curious effect by his sudden shift from prophetic narration to the present tense in the final lines of *Les*

---

[112] *Les Tragiques*, ed. Weber, p. 243, vv. 1200–1218.

Tragiques where ecstasy and spiritual truth abruptly replace sensory knowledge. It is as if the apocalypse and the beatific vision predicted for a not too distant future (1660!) were suddenly upon him.

History replaced the panoramic screen of mythology on which nations had viewed their antiquity. As we have seen, the androgyne that fascinated early sixteenth-century poets, along with many other symbols, had become more important than what it symbolized. Similarly, antiquity itself took possession of the minds of Renaissance poets and painters more as decor or as a setting than as history. In fact, it masks an absence of concern for linear historical order, past and future, as witnessed by the curious settings of Antoine Caron's paintings and Ronsard's "Ode à Michel de l'Hôpital," one of the most celebrated odes where he lingers on a tableau of the Olympian gods. As for his *Franciade*, it is a known fact that he soon lost enthusiasm for it and for the legend of Trojan ancestry.

Speculation on the philosophy of history and teleology are replacing poetic reveries about the Golden Age and the Creation. When man cannot face the force of time, he can at least flee with it or run ahead. Perchance this new linear awareness of time gives importance to melodic music. Simultaneous perspective, ubiquity, is condemned by Montaigne: "The soul that has no established viewpoint gets lost; for, as they say, he who is everywhere is nowhere."

Visual perception is less important than tactile and digestive imagery in another passage of the *Essays* where Montaigne condemns curiosity: "I fear our eyes are bigger than our stomachs, and our curiosity greater than our ability. We embrace all, but grasp nothing but the wind." This ability is tested by the author of the *Essays* and expressed in terms of movement, the movement of a groping blind man: "My conception and judgment walk only gropingly, staggeringly, . . . limpingly, and when I have advanced as far as possible, yet, unsatisfied, I see more country, with clouded and troubled eyes, and I can't make out anything."[113] Movement is often oriented downward.

[113] *Essais*, ed. M. Rat (Paris: Garnier, 1962), I, xxvi, pp. 155 f.

Slow motion with increasing momentum, anticipating Galileo's formula of constant acceleration, like that of Brueghel's painting, appears frequently in Montaigne's *Essays*: "Since you are in the ditch, it matters little who set you in motion; you always go to the very bottom: the fall stirs itself, rushes itself, and precipitates itself, all by itself."[114] Even self-knowledge is described as an inner movement toward oneself: "The others always look outward; I turn my sight inward; I plant it, I entertain it there; others look in front, I look into myself. I study myself unceasingly, I keep watch on myself, I savor myself. The others are headed elsewhere, . . . they always go forward; . . . as for myself, I roll myself into myself."[115]

Not only does Montaigne emphasize descent into oneself, but he also vehemently opposes all attempts at ascension, condemning them as presumptuous and bestial "Fanatic madness," he calls the urge to substitute complicated machinery, colored wheels, and ropes for an adequate scientific explanation of the cosmos. Striving to be angelic results in beastlike behavior. As for cosmonauts, he remarks: "The most fragile and yet proud creature is man: he feels and sees himself lodged here in the mud and excrement of the world, tied and nailed to the worst, the deadest, and most rotten part of the universe, at the lowest level . . . of the celestial vault, . . . and yet he goes and in imagination plants himself above the circles of the moon and brings the cosmos under his feet. It is by the vanity of this same imagination that he equates himself with God."[116]

Little hope is left to man. He cannot rise toward God. God is invisible. When Montaigne does speak of divine grace, he always refers to it as descending upon man without the latter's participation. Bosch's or Cusanus's "vision of God" is no more. The instrument of God's grace is his hand usually piercing through a cloud from above, as shown in so many emblems, engravings, and paintings. But this hand, God extends only "extraordinarily."[117] Alone, man cuts a pitiful figure. Lost in

[114] *Ibid.*, II, xxxi, pp. 125 f.
[115] *Ibid.*, II, xvii, p. 61.
[116] *Ibid.*, II, xii, p. 496.
[117] *Ibid.*, II, xii, p. 680.

a stormy sea with a broken helm, as Brueghel paints him, as Du Bellay, Desportes, Sponde, Montaigne, and even Ronsard in his later years lament, he is exposed to the winds of passion and strife. Thus humiliated, he can wait in darkness for the spiritual sun to rise. Meanwhile, for chronological reasons, he is denied his very reality, since the "judging and the judged" are in "continual change and motion." "Nothing really is," says Montaigne translating Plutarch, except God, and this, in a sense, also because of time:

> But then what really is? That which is eternal, . . . what never had birth, nor will ever have an end; to which time never brings any change. . . . For time is indeed a mobile thing which appears as the shadow of ever fluid and ever flowing matter, without ever remaining stable or permanent. . . . It would be a sin to say of God, who is the only one thing that is, that he was or will be. For those terms represent declinings, transitions, . . . wherefore we must conclude that God alone is.[118]

[118] *Ibid.*

IX

FOLLY, MELANCHOLY, AND MADNESS: A STUDY IN SHIFTING STYLES OF MEDICAL ANALYSIS AND TREATMENT, 1450–1675

Robert S. Kinsman

For indeed who is not a fool, melancholy, mad?
Qui nil molitur inepte, who is not brain-sick?
Folly, melancholy, madness, are but one disease,
delirium is a common name to all.
—Burton, *"Democritus to the Reader,"*
The Anatomy of Melancholy

IN THE first essay in this volume devoted to the darker visions of the Renaissance, Lynn White posits a double thesis, both parts of which provide points of reference for my own views on the changing names for, and the shifting outlook on, those deep and basic manifestations of mental or psychic deficiencies and disturbances: folly, melancholy, and madness, to use the then prevailing terms. Professor White regards the period from 1300 to 1650, conventionally labeled the "Age of the Renaissance," as the most psychically disturbed era in European history, its symptoms revealing terrible anxieties, some of which sprang from the mounting acceleration of cultural change. He further argues that the worst of the deep spiritual and psychic cleavages of the time were healed at the end of the period by "the emergence, in the minds of the ordinary people, of an absolutely novel . . . attitude toward change."

While hesitating to examine too closely the accuracy of the

phrase "absolutely novel," one can easily advance examples of changing attitudes in the outlook of medical science at the end of the Renaissance, the third and fourth quarters of the seventeenth century, the period of time I have loosely indicated by rounding off the date at 1675. Some of these attitudes are quite literally based on carefully accumulated fresh observations; some of them, as in the changing view of madness, are based on new "images" in which the dynamics of "animal spirits," for example, are expressed in terms of heating and circulation rather than in terms of dryness or hardness.

In 1651, to cite one instance of discovery from observation, Nathaniel Highmore, a physician of Sherborne in Dorset, had printed *The History of Generation*, "the first published observations based upon microscopic examination of the chick blastoderm."[1] In the same year, approximately two months before Highmore's history appeared, William Harvey finished an inquiry quite different from the one he had conducted in *De motu cordis* (1628) by publishing *De Generatione Animalium*. In it Harvey furnished a thorough and accurate description of the chick embryo, demonstrating in particular that the cicatricula or blastoderm was the embryo's point of origin. How much Harvey is still under the sway of the past, however, is shown in his description of the ovum as the "primordium vegetable or vegetative incipience, understanding by this a certain corporeal something having life *in potentia*; or a certain something existing *per se*, which is capable of changing into a vegetative form under the agency of an internal principle."[2]

Within the next quarter of a century one notes the rise of an imperfect yet increasingly sophisticated medical empiricism. It more and more profited, as Charles Bodmer remarks, from the century's "declining, richly vitalistic Aristotelian rationalism" and its rising "mechanistic rationalism with its roots in ancient

---

[1] Charles W. Bodmer, "Embryological Thought in Seventeenth Century England," in *Medical Investigation in Seventeenth Century England* (Los Angeles: William Andrews Clark Memorial Library, 1968), p. 11.

[2] Cited in *ibid.*, pp. 15–16.

Greek atomistic theories of matter."[3] Shifting rationales and sharpened incentives for recording personal observation resulted in Thomas Willis's new mode of viewing the problem of mental deficiency—fools and folly, *stupiditas* and *stultitia*— in *De anima brutorum* (1672) and in Thomas Sydenham's "curious observations" (1682) derived from the "testimony of [his] senses"[4] concerning the special hysteric aspects of the older melancholy, observations suggesting that melancholy and mania almost merged. By the first quarter of the eighteenth century, a slow displacement of terms and attitudes had occurred, differentiating melancholy into "hypochondria" and "spleen" (for men only, so to speak), "hysteria" and "vapors" (for women only), all four actually forms of one and the same disease. Thus, forty years after Sydenham's treatise, Richard Blackmore could publish a *Treatise of the Spleen and Vapours or Hypochondriacal and Hysterical Affectations* (1725), whereas Robert Burton, approximately forty years before Sydenham's observations, had included hypochondriacal or "windy" melancholy as one of the three "particular" species of melancholy and had established a special subsection for "Maids', Nuns', and Widows' Melancholy."[5]

For the final example to justify the notion that 1650 to 1675 marked the end of an era—the resort to a new outlook, the dependence upon a new central image—let us include the founding in Paris of the Hôpital Général (1656). Its establishment was noticed in England in the shift of Bethlehem Hospital (Bedlam) to new quarters on a large piece of land near London Hall on the south side of the lower quarter of Moorfields, in July 1676. The design of the building was

[3] *Ibid.*, p. 5.

[4] These phrases are Dr. William Cole's taken from his epistle to Sydenham written at Worcester on November 17, 1681, and cited in *The Entire Works of Dr. Thomas Sydenham, Newly Made English from the Originals ... by John Swan*, M.D. (London, 1742), pp. 331–332.

[5] *The Anatomy of Melancholy*, ed. Holbrook Jackson (Everyman ed., 1964), I, 414 419 (Pt. I, sec. 3, mem. ii, subsec. 4). The fifth edition of this monumental and idiosyncratic work, the last within Burton's lifetime (d. 1640), was printed in 1638.

allegedly taken from the Chateau de Tuilleries, an act of large-scale imitation which, we are told, so infuriated Louis XIV that, in revenge, he ordered a plan of Saint James's Palace "to be taken for offices of a very inferior nature."[6]

As Michel Foucault very aptly comments, the decree that established the Hôpital Général is a genuine landmark. Formal, large-scale confinement replaces small-scale hospitalization; the enforced wandering of the mad is replaced by their enforced immobility:

> The great threat that dawned on the horizon of the fifteenth century subsides, the disturbing powers that inhabit Bosch's painting have lost their violence. . . . Madness has ceased to be —at the limits of the world, of man and death—an eschatological figure. . . . Oblivion falls upon the world navigated by the free slaves of the Ship of Fools. Madness will no longer proceed from a point within the world to a point beyond, on its strange voyage. . . . Behold it moored now, made fast among things and men. Retained and maintained. No longer a ship but a hospital.[7]

The Fool and Folly, 1450–1650

If ever an image or a non-religious icon dominated an age, the widespread image of the fool surely prevailed in the late Middle Ages from Brant's *Narrenschiff* and its horde of descendants, among which one finds *Cock Lorellas Bote* and *The Mad Men of Gotam*, to Erasmus's sophisticated and equally popular mock encomium, *Laus Stultitiae*.[8] In late Middle English, *Fool* and *folly* have a wide spread of connotations, ranging from

[6] Thomas Bowen, *An Historical Account of the Origin, Progress and Present State of Bethlehem Hospital* (London, 1783), p. 5 n.

[7] Michael Foucault, *Madness and Civilization: A History of Insanity in the Age of Reason* (1961), trans. from the French by Richard Howard (New York: Mentor Books, 1967), p. 39.

[8] See Walter Kaiser, *Praisers of Folly (Erasmus, Rabelais, Shakespeare)* (Cambridge, Mass., 1963), pp. 3–5, for his application to the fool of the Tainean "personnage régnant," and pp. 9–10 n. 8 for a brief but useful bibliography of Nicholas of Cusa.

fool as designating a person deprived or bereft of reason, "stupid," "ignorant," or "natural" (i.e., congenitally defective), to *fool* as one temporarily bereft of reason from beer or buffets, or *fool* as one who through an impious carelessness or physical indifference is imprudent in his religious or sexual practices. A fourth and special, and better-known, denotation for *fool* is that of court jester professionally counterfeiting the ways and reactions of the other "fools" in order to entertain, a deliberate buffoon kept by a king or a nobleman for his amusement: "a fole sage / þat hadde his witt forlorn." Between the two extremes of the village idiot and the court jester lie many fine and perhaps confused gradations. Nonetheless, I dismiss the metaphorically foolish, the lightly foolish, the proud, the vainglorious, the ridiculous, to confine myself to two types of fools: the philosophical or Christian fool and the *stultus*, or the socially subnormal person, defective of judgment, with whom I shall deliberately confound the *stupidus*, or dull-born.

The concept of the "Christian fool" and "Christian folly," it goes without saying, has a philosophic and religious basis. As if deliberately done for our convenience, Nicholas of Cusa set down his ideas on these subjects in 1450 in his book *Idiota de sapientia*. Reflecting his far greater work, the *De Docta ignorantia* of 1440,[9] the *Idiota* takes for its thesis that God is best known to us through the simplest objects of sense experience. Their message is more accessible to the simple than to the learned.[10] In a dialogue form, the book uses several speakers in its philosophical fiction. They are brought together by their interest in the summer influx of pilgrims into Rome during the jubilee year of 1450. In Book III, in particular, we find subtly present Nicholas's doctrine of learned ignorance (or, as he would have it, the *coincidentia scientiae et ignorantiae, seu doctae ignorantiae*). As its first chapter heading indicates, we shall

[9] For a modern translation of this work, see Germain Heron, trans., *Of Learned Ignorance by Nicolaus Cusanus*, with introduction by D. T. B. Hawkins (London: Routledge & Kegan Paul, 1954).

[10] See Eugene F. Rice, Jr., "Nicholas of Cusa's Idea of Wisdom," *Traditio*, XIII (1957), 345–368.

discover why a philosopher must come to the *Idiota* to learn something of the nature of the mind.

The Philosopher, watching the pilgrims stream over a bridge, wonders that he can find so much uniformity of faith in so wide a diversity of bodies. To his queries, an Orator (representing the humanistic activity) responds, "Certainly, it must needs be the gift of God that Idiots do more clearly see and reach by Faith, than Philosophers by Reason."[11] The Orator then leads the Philosopher to the Idiot, "an admirable man" dwelling at the Temple of Eternity (originally dedicated by Titus Attilius Crassus to the mind). There they find him making wooden spoons; from their discourse with him they paradoxically learn how "Divine simplicity complicates all things." Nicholas of Cusa would have us understand that, as Proverbs 1:20 tells us, Wisdom dwells in the highest because it is equated with the Second Person; yet it cries aloud in the streets because the creation is eloquent testimony of the First Person. The Creator spells out the book of Nature which is more readily legible to the layman than to the learned man whose mind is clogged with obfuscate knowledge.

Though we wrench it out of its proper chronological order, let us turn to Erasmus's *Praise of Folly* (*Moriae Encomium* or *Stultitiae Laus*), published in 1511, before discussing Sebastian Brant's *Narrenschiff*, printed in 1494 and first translated into English (from Latin and French intermediaries) in 1509, just two years before the appearance of Erasmus's mocking oration. For our purposes, Erasmus's work is more immediately related to the epistemological tradition of Cusanus than is Brant's, although it develops "Christian folly" very skillfully from the idea that the fool, the *stultus*, is specially favored in God's creation, even if closer to the animals than the angels, because he preserves innocence from a conscious knowledge of sin. Speaking of "that class of men whom we generally call morons, fools,

[11] *The Idiot. Translated (1650) from Nicholas of Cusa, Idiota* (1450), with introduction by W. R. Dennes, in California State Library Occasional Papers (Sutro Branch), Reprint Series #19 (San Francisco, 1940), p. 25.

half-wits, and zanies," Folly remarks: "They do not feel shame or fear, they are not ambitious, they do not envy, they do not love. And finally, if they should approach even more closely to the irrationality of dumb animals they would not sin, according to the writers of theology."[12]

We must remember that Folly is presenting a consciously softened yet distorted version of things in her ironic self-laudation, and we must try to sense the deeper problems of those "innocents" who must be sought out, given food, kept warm, embraced, and given physical aid. It is in a splendidly gratuitous comparison with the plight of those unfortunates—still innocent—that Christian folly (the madness of a god in man's image and the unreason of the sacrifice) takes on heightened meaning:

> What do all these things cry out to us if not this, that mortal men, even the pious are fools? And that Christ in order to relieve the folly of mankind, though Himself the wisdom of the Father, was willing in some manner to be made a fool when He took upon Himself the nature of a man and was found in fashion as a man?[13]

How carefully Dame Folly points out that Christ himself has enjoined folly and dissuaded from learned wisdom by using as examples children, lilies, mustard seed, and sparrows!

Turning back now to Sebastian Brant's *Narrenschiff* (1494), we find ourselves moving somewhat closer to a realistic examination of the *stulti* and the *stupidi*, although religious and philosophic overtones are by no means lacking in the satire. For example, in the 107th poem of his collection, "Of Reward for Wisdom" (*Von Lon der Weisheit*), through allusions to Luke 18:16–17 ("Suffer little children to come unto me," etc.) and Matthew 11:25 ("I thank thee, O Father, . . . because thou hast hid these things from the wise and prudent, and hast re-

[12] *The Praise of Folly by Desiderius Erasmus*, trans. Hoyt H. Hudson, 4th ptg. (Princeton, 1947), p. 48.
[13] *Ibid.*, p. 116.

vealed them unto babes"), Brant makes it quite clear that worldly, secular wisdom, uninformed by grace or conscience, is seriously defective:

> And Socrates, who through their creed [Pythagoras's and
>   Plato's]
> Won lasting fame and honor's meed
> Yet could not picture bright and clear
> The real wisdom dwelling here,
> Wherefore of them the Lord did say:
> "Their knowledge, skill, I'll toss away
> And wisdom, too, who here are wise,
> Let children have it— this their prize."[14]

Similarly the fools of the Schluraffen Ship (#108) are aimlessly voyaging, "For none of us sees wisdom's light." The narrator urges men of sense to avoid the endless journey of these "lazy apes" and "haste to wisdom's shore":

> Who's wise will get to shore with ease,
> We've fools enough apart from these.
> The best is he who'll always know
> What he should do and what forego
> Whom no one needs to drill and teach,
> Since wisdom he himself does preach.[15]

Brant's poem, although quite obviously deficient in structure when compared with Erasmus's beautifully wrought satiric oration, has a rugged power of its own, derived in part from its vernacular propinquity to the *narr, tore, affe, esel,* and *gouch* of late fifteenth-century Germany (read "western Europe"), and in part from its literary and visual device of manning a ship. However imperfectly realized, the construct concentrates a

[14] *The Ship of Fools by Sebastian Brant,* trans. into rhyming couplets with Introduction and commentary by Edwin A. Zeydel. (New York: Columbia University Press, 1944; Dover Editions, 1962), p. 348. See also #8, "The Teaching of Wisdom," a paraphrase of Proverbs 8.
[15] *Ibid.,* p. 354.

variety of experience. Thus we find rich men with bells on their foolish ears, unable to hear the tattered beggars chattering from the cold; a shipload in itself of crafty or slipshod artisans (carpenters, masons, tailors, printers); a boatful of "coarse fools; knights and clerks who sin with sword and pen, and cooks and waiters who transgress with pan and pot." As Brant himself confessed in a poem written for the public appearance of Erasmus's work in 1511, he was "satisfied to have carried in his ship *vulgares stultos*, common fools who speak dialect and belong to the lower classes of society."[16]

We must not ignore the significance of the 114 woodcuts that accompany the poem, for they bring us closer to the medieval outlook on besotted fools. Interestingly enough, as we shall see in a moment, the recto page preceding the prologue shows on its upper half a cart of fools under the title "das Narren schyff" and on its lower half, under the title "Ad Narra goinam," a distant boatload of fools and a nearer grouping to whom some of the "dizzards" (as Burton would call them) of the main vessel are calling *har noch* ("come along") while others are singing *Gaudeamus omnes*. Midships of the main vessel sits a "Doctor Griff" with a long lance in hand. This Doctor Grabit, as we might modernize it, is a Satanic caricature of Brant's, who with the fools in his "clutches" must yet remind his passengers and clients of their essential folly (cf. the woodcut to #76 in which he is shown pinching the ear of "Ritter Peter"). Beneath this woodcut we read the impetuous legend "Zu schyff, zu schyff bruder. Ess gat / ess gat." On the verso we see the Ship of Fools from a different angle, with the pennant of Doctor Griff this time at the masthead, and *Gaudeamus* still rising in the air.

---

[16] Ulrich Gaier, "Sebastian Brant's *Narrenschiff and the Humanists*," *PMLA*, LXXXIII (1968), 268. See Thomas G. Benedek, "The Image of Medicine in 1500: Theological Reactions to the *Ship of Fools*," *Bull. Hist. Med.*, XXXVIII (1964), 329–342, for sermons based on certain sections of Brant's work, one in particular by John Geiler (1445–1510), based on #38 with its discussion of the body-soul and reason-religion dichotomies.

Beneath the woodcut, which is labeled "Gen[s] Narragonien [sem]," we find sardonically edited Latin verses from Psalm 106 AV, (Ps. 107):22, 26–27: "They that go down to the sea in ships, that do business in great waters. . . . They mount up to the heaven, they go down to the depths: their soul is melted because of trouble. They reel to and fro, and stagger like a drunken man, and are at their wit's end." What is purposely left out is verse 28: "Then they cry unto the Lord in their trouble, and he bringeth them out of their distresses," so that, as Burton remarks, "You may give that censure of them in general which Sir Thomas More once did of Germanus Brixius' poems in particular: *Vehunter / In rate stultitiae, sylvam habitant furiae*" ("They sail in the bark of folly, they inhabit the grove of madness" [H. Jackson, Everyman ed., I, 112]).

The conceit of a fool's ship as such, although not always used to verbal advantage in Brant's poem, even if visually prominent in its illustrations, was an innovation. It apparently reflects, directly or ultimately, the practice in western Europe of sending the insane and lunatic on pilgrimages by boat to the shrine of Saint Dymphna in Gheel, near Antwerp. According to Christian legend, Dymphna was the daughter of a seventh-century pagan king of Ireland.[17] Secretly baptized by Saint Géréborne, to whom her mother entrusted her when dying, she fled with the saint into Flanders to avoid the incestuous desires of her father. He, excited by lust and pricked on by two demons, traced her down to her place of refuge in Gheel and beheaded her and the saint. Since her father had been possessed by devils, she became the patroness of the possessed, and, later, the epileptic when, in the thirteenth century, her body was allegedly discovered in Gheel and a number of epileptics and lunatics were thereupon restored to health. One might note, by the way, that the town was famous in the early nineteenth century for its superior mental institutions, a reputation that has continued to the present day. Dymphna's legend was celebrated in a series of eight panels executed by Goswyn van

[17] See Louis Réau, *Iconographie de l'Art Chrétien* (Paris, 1958), III, i, 407–408.

der Weyden in Antwerp in 1505 and in a retable of sculptured wood depicting nineteen scenes from her legend done locally by Jan van Wavre in 1515. She is represented with a sword in her right hand and with a chained demon at her feet.[18]

Dymphna's legend may well have been confused with that of Saint Ursula, the beautiful British maiden demanded in marriage by a pagan king but granted a three years' respite. During that time she collected a host of 11,000 virgins whom she trained in Amazon-like exercises before sailing up the Rhine to Cologne and thence to Basel. There they moored their ships and set out on foot to Rome to do homage to their bridegroom, Christ. On the homeward trip from Basel, however, they were all put to the sword by the Huns at Cologne. A sermon of the 1470s, entitled *Disz ist ein hubsche predig gethon uff S. Ursula tag, sagt von dem geistlichen narrenschiff . . .* , describes twenty-one fools and introduces, as a twenty-second character, Christ, who, crossing the seas dryshod, exhorts the fools to leave their vessel and board the ship that follows him, Saint Ursula's Ship of Penitence.

The point behind this disquisition is surely that the ship is a symbol of forced expulsion, of ritual exile, or of truly desperate wandering. Fools and lunatics often wandered the countryside like wild animals, seeking shelter in stables or sties. As Foucault points out, the custom of expelling the mad was frequent in medieval Germany: ". . . in Nuremburg, in the first half of the fifteenth century, the presence of 63 madmen had been registerd; 31 were driven away; in the fifty years that followed, there are records of 21 more obligatory departures; and these are only the madmen arrested by the municipal authorities."[19] The insane who were native to other communities were often expelled and sent back to the place whence they had originally come, often after they had been incarcerated and whipped before their expulsion. From 1400 to 1450, half of the sixty-two insane listed in Nuremburg were transported; from 1450 to 1500, twenty-one out of thirty-three were dispatched else-

[18] *Ibid.*
[19] *Madness and Civilization*, p. 19.

where.[20] At times the mad were handed over to river boatmen to be rid of them. In Frankfurt, in 1399, a naked madman was turned over to sailors for deportation; in the early years of the fifteenth century a criminal madman was similarly driven out of Mainz. Foucault records that a stubbornly foolish blacksmith of Frankfurt was twice deported and twice returned before being shipped to Bad Kreuznach for good.[21]

In a different sense, the mad were treated to a sort of ritual exile. Although ecclesiastical law did not deny them the use of sacraments, access to the church proper was forbidden them. Again in Nuremberg, this time in 1421, even though the Church could take no action against a priest who went mad, a mad priest was expelled by the city, "as if the impurity [were] multiplied by the sacred nature of his person, and the city put on its budget the money given him as a viaticum."[22]

One must not imagine, however, that the only way the late Middle Ages handled their fools and madmen was through physical expulsion. Just as the terms "folly," "melancholy," and "madness" overlap almost to the point of synonymy, so the harmlessly mentally defective and the dangerously ill were sometimes confined and huddled together. Burton tells us in *Anatomy of Melancholy*, in a subsection headed "Dotage, Madness, Frenzy, Hydrophobia, Lycanthropia, Chorus Sancti Viti, Ecstasis" (Pt. I, sec. 1, mem. i, subsec. 4) that "Dotage, fatuity, or folly" is a common name, "as some will have it," for such afflictions as phrenitis (which differs from madness and melancholy in its inflammatory quality) or lycanthropy, (wolf madness). He points out that "Madness, frenzy and melancholy" are "confounded" by Celsus and other writers and himself defines madness as a "vehement dotage, or raving without fever," far more violent in its "horrible looks," actions, and gestures than melancholy. It should not surprise us then that there were also places of detention for dolts and madmen in European cities.

---

[20] Cited by George Rosen, *Madness in Society: Chapters in the Historical Sociology of Mental Illness* (Harper Torchbooks, 1969), p. 140.

[21] *Madness and Civilization*, p. 19.

[22] *Ibid.*, p. 20.

For example, one can find in the testament of a certain Gerd Sunderberg of Lübeck (1479) that funds were set aside for the institutionalized care of "den armen dullen Luden." Or one learns that in 1523, almost a quarter of a century before Henry VIII was to grant Bethlehem Hospital to the mayor, commonalty, and citizens of London for the relief of the sick, lame, and impotent poor, one Stephen Gennings, "merchant taylor" of London, set aside £40 in his will to help purchase the patronage of the decaying hospital. These benefactors, in a way, may have unwittingly reversed the basic "metaphor" of exile implicit in the Ship of Fools and, by aiding established hospitals to specialize in the lunatic, may have unconsciously devised a sort of countervoyage in which madmen were shipped into confinement, as at Gheel, "in the holy locus of a miracle"[23] or within the sanctuary of a religious house. By 1650 the basic "image" is thus shifted from ship to shore, from boat to hospital, from exile outward to inward confinement.

As an example of the metaphorical shift, one has merely to mention that *Cock Lorelles Bote* of 1506 or 1508 still utilizes the ship image and lists fools of all types although of the lower classes. Their imaginary voyage extends from London's underworld throughout all England. With Robert Copland's *Hye Way to the Spytell House* (1535–1536), however, in the lapse of a quarter century the metaphor has shifted from ship to hospital. In this poem, at least, the order of philosophic Christian humanist fools has been displaced by a realistically portrayed procession of paupers and beggars, crooked, lame, and blind, pock-eaten "flesh and rind," breechless and barefooted, stinking with dirt and ragged in tattered clothing, saying "Good master, for your mother's blessing, Give us a halfpenny towards our lodging."[24] The hospital is probably Saint Bartholomew's, for reference is made that this sanctuary provides chambers for those sorely afflicted with shrewd wives, "Or else they should be lodged in Bedlam."

[23] *Ibid.*

[24] See the edition of the poem by A. V. Judges, ed., *The Elizabethan Underworld* (London, 1930), pp. 1–25.

As part of the growing sixteenth-century ingathering of the poor fools, we shall have to note that not until 1575 (18 Eliz. cap. 3) was legislation passed to establish houses of correction, the result of the growing desire to reclaim the virtuous poor through "training" over and beyond the offer of shelter. This is the result of the strongly prevailing notion that those served by the commonwealth should pay for themselves. The notion of the outward journey, the expulsion, persisted throughout the sixteenth and into the seventeenth century, nonetheless, in the "passing on" of the burdensome poor. As A. V. Judges summarizes this related phenomenon: "Most authorities are agreed that the English law of settlement did not attain its full vigour and flavour until the passage of 'An Act for the better relief of the poor of this Kingdom' in 1662 [please note the date] and some are of the opinion that that year saw its birth."[25] Any person who seemed likely to be a burden, or was in fact receiving what we should today call relief, was summarily removed from a parish in which he had not yet spent forty days to the last place in which he (and his family) had sojourned for that minimum length of time.

In 1600, to leap half a century beyond the *Hye Way*, appeared the English translation of Gazoni's *L'Ospedale de passi incurabili* (Ferrara, 1586) under the title, please note, of *The Hospital of Incurable Fooles*. Although its title indicates clearly the shifting currents of attitude toward the disposal of the mad, the book nonetheless displays an inner continuity with the humanist concept of folly. Indeed, the preliminaries to the translation represent Dame Folly, matron of the hospital, making a curtsy to Madame Fortune. The translator, Edward Blount, preserved the literary strain of encomiums to folly by dedicating his version to his most "Neere and Capriccious Neighbor," John Hodgson, better known as "John of Paul's Churchyard," a noted eccentric of the time.[26]

Although we here encounter reminders of the older fifteenth-

25 *Ibid.*, p. xxxii.
26 See William E. Miller, "*The Hospital of Incurable Fooles*," *SB*, XVI (1963), 204–207.

century Order of Fools, the list of inmates is far from conventional. We find "Alaine Fooles and naturals," to be sure, along with shallow pates and "ninnie hammers"; we find the stupid and "half dead" side by side with the "notted, grosse and loblolly-lams." The "lunaticall and Fooles by season" of the seventeenth "discourse" are near neighbors to the furious, brutish, or "bedlam sort" of the twenty-fourth discourse, devoted to fools "outrageous and fell."

Among the frenzied fools of the first discourse we have a reminder, quite accidental perhaps, of the watery exile of reason. One Talpine of Bergamo is a "delirant foole" who suffers, so the diagnosis goes, from a certain inflammation of the organic parts of the brain "which induceth a kind of dotage and grieuvous percussion of the minde" [please note the metaphor]. In an appeal to the signory of Venice the Bergamese had leaped into a well to show that he would at least preserve this part of his inheritance. In jest, he was offered lordship over the sea. In his next appearance before the signory, he reminded them that there was a deep discrepancy between being an admiral who had saltwater for his ships to sail on while he, without favorable court action in the lawsuit, could not even have "the fresh water of a well."[27]

Having indicated, nonetheless, that the walls of the "Hospital" had begun to displace the sides of the "Ship" as the convenient and, indeed, appropriate divider of the foolish and the mad from the sane and purposeful, perhaps it is time to turn to a real hospital of the times—to London's "Bedlam"—for an examination of a less literary mode of ingathering the medieval mad.

Bedlam, the "Great Confinement," and
Willis, "On Stupidity or Foolishness," 1400–1675

The Hospital of Saint Mary of Bethlehem, or simply Bethlem Hospital (Bedlam), was not a particularly active institution in

[27] I have taken the anecdote from the microfilmed version of *The Hospital of Incurable Fooles*, STC 11634, sig. C2.

the fifteenth and sixteenth centuries. Records of a visitation by the king's clerks in 1403 show that it had become an asylum principally for the insane, although not exclusively so, for in March of that year there were three sick persons lying in, along with six madmen. These inmates contributed to their own support or were partly supported by relatives, the amount of the contribution varying. The highest rate mentioned was 12d. a week paid by a merchant of Exeter, who had been a patient there for six weeks.[28]

The management of the hospital appeared to be in the hands of the porter, one Peter Taverner, a sorry hospitaler indeed. He had rendered no account of his stewardship for years; instead of distributing alms he had used the money to buy fuel and had made the poor pay for their fagots, while he turned over the best of the contributions in kind to his wife. He had disposed of the hospital beds and other goods, perhaps to offset debts that stemmed from his passion for dice and draughts, although he must have floated himself in nearly constant solvency by selling ale at his house within the close.

In 1454, at approximately the beginning of the period covered by this essay, Bethlehem Hospital was let to farm. By 1529 its headship had become a sinecure, if the appointment of George Boleyn, a layman, to the post is any indication. In 1547 it was transferred to the city; in 1557 it was placed under the care of Bridewell Hospital. In 1598, to judge from the inspection report of its board of governors, there were twenty inmates: fourteen private, six charity. The insane were kept belowstairs, "loathesomely and filthily."[29] Abovestairs were eight rooms for the servants and (please note) the poor.

In 1632 commissioners appointed to investigate the management of the hospital found it as badly run as it had been in 1403. The twenty-seven "distracted persons" (there had been thirty

[28] I have based my account of Bethlehem on the *Victoria History of London*, ed. William Page (1909), I, 496. See also W. S. C. Copeman, "The Royal Hospitals before 1700," in *The Evolution of Hospitals in Britain*, ed. F. N. L. Poynter (London, 1964), pp. 27–42.

[29] The report is cited by Robert R. Reed, Jr., *Bedlam on the Jacobean Stage* (Cambridge, Mass. 1952), p. 16.

the year before) were each technically allowed 2s. a week, but since the master, none other than a Dr. Crooke, spent most of the allowance on himself, and his steward appropriated the gifts in kind (unless bought back from him at an extortionate rate), the inmates were nearly starved.[30] Needless to say, there is very little indication that measures had been taken to try to effect "cures." The inmates seemed, to repeat my metaphor, inward exiles, objects indeed, so that Lord Percy with the Lady Penelope and her two sisters on February 6, 1609/10, might record that he and his little party had seen the lions in the Tower, "the show of Bethlehem, the place where the prince was created, and the fireworks at the Artillery Gardens."[31]

In 1644, closer to our terminal date of 1675, there was some notion of enlarging the hospital, but the Civil War rendered the project impossible, especially since sick and wounded were quartered there. Then, as I have earlier mentioned and shall again repeat, by 1675 the "Great Confinement" had so totally set in, the old metaphor of expulsion had been so completely internalized, that the increased number of applicants (shall we call them such?) made larger quarters necessary. So a new hospital was built, on a new site in Moorfields. In 1632 the number of inmates was twenty-seven, not a noticeably larger number that the twenty of 1598. In 1667 it was fifty-nine. Surely, one may argue, as I am about to, that changes in "medical" attitude and analysis seem likely to have accounted in part for the doubling of the number of patients entered annually into Bedlam. More systematic confinement may also have indicated that a custodial arrangement was beginning to prevail, behind which lay increasing confidence that it was within human powers systematically to effect cures. No longer must fools or madmen be shipped out, either for riddance or for recourse to the shrine of Saint Dymphna, let us say, for miraculous cure.

Although we lack abundant, firsthand, medical evidence of the specific treatment of the foolish and the lunatic in such a hospital as Bedlam, we may turn to some of the encyclopedias

[30] *Victoria History of London*, I, 497.
[31] Cited by Reed, *op. cit.*, p. 22.

of the time to trace general notions of the causes and treatment of madness.[32] Andrew Boorde, in his *Compendyous Regimente or Dyetary of Health* (first ed., 1542),[33] lumps several "causes" together when he "advertises" (warns) that

> euery man the which is mad or lunatycke [subject to the un-predictable, extrahuman influence of the moon and all that the "moon" rules remote from the center of God's Provi-dence], or frentyckc [from inflamed brain matter] or demon-yacke [from demonic possession] to be kept in sauegarde in some close howse or chamber where there is lytel lyght. And that he have a keper the which the mad man do feare.[34]

Boorde also warns against such persons being permitted to have shears, knives, or edged tools lest they take their own lives and specifically admonishes against their being permitted to have painted clothes or walls, or pictures of man or woman, fowl or beast, "for suche thynges maketh them ful of fantasies." Such a fear depends on a definition of madness similar to that given by the medieval encyclopedist Bartholomew de Glan-ville who, in his *De proprietatibus rerum*, following Plato per-haps, considers madness an infection of the foremost cell of the head with privation of imagination. Melancholy, on the other hand, he defines as an infection of the middle cell of the brain with a resultant privation of reason. This latter distinction he further complicates by noting that melancholy, ordinarily a quiet affliction, masters the soul out of dread and sorrow.

The types of madness were treated on a symptomatic basis of contraries controlling contraries. The frenzied, because of their infected imagination (and here the *imago* is the image-

---

[32] I have tried to avoid standard histories such as Gregory Zilboorg's *History of Medical Psychology* (New York, 1941), since they tend to highlight the exceptional achievements of such undoubted giants as Paracelsus (1493–1541), usually in terms of their anticipation of mod-ern psychological "truth." I am, rather, tracing shifts in accepted atti-tudes and am trying to rely on evidence contemporary to the times.

[33] I have used the edition of 1562, STC 3381.

[34] *Ibid.*, sig. H4v.

recording part of the brain), manifested in their casting about of eyes, their wagging of the head, their stretching and casting out of hands, their "grinding and gnashing togethers of the teeth," must be starved down by a drastically reduced diet (they were fed crumbs of bread many times wet in water) and kept from pictures, as one early sixteenth-century version of Bartholomew reads, "lest [they] be tarred with woodnesse [madness]."

In contrast with this chilly stilling of the frenzied, one can find a gladsome contrast in the treatment accorded those who, we would say, were mad with "depression." They were to be "refreshed & comforted, & withdrawen from cause & matter of dread and busie thoughts." They were to be "gladded with instruments of musick & some deale be occupied." But, at the last, if the purgatives and electuaries also prescribed did not suffice, they were to be "holpe with craft of Surgery," presumably not as in Bosch's painting *The Cure of Folly* (in the Prado, c. 1490?). In that satirical painting, which attacks the folly of "worldly" healing under the lettered banner "Meester snyt die keye ras" (The master [surgeon] cut out the stones), Bosch depicts a bit of cranial surgery. A fat burgher offers his forehead to the lancet of a charlatan wearing a funnel for a hat. The surgeon is extracting a swamp tulip (cant for money); beneath the satiric scene we read "Myne name is Lubber das" (i.e., "gelded badger").[35]

As I have mentioned earlier, the late medieval treatment of the mentally defective and the mentally diseased seems relatively undifferentiated and further blunted by the similar reception given lazars and unemployables. When, in 1540, London's originally monastic hospitals of Saint Thomas and Saint Bartholomew's were surrendered to the Crown, such numbers of the sick poor were turned out that the streets were crowded with "lazars and lame." Observing this social calamity, Sir

---

[35] The etching by Pieter Brueghel the Elder, entitled *The Witch of Malligem*, similarly satirizes the removing of stones from the head as a cure for insanity. See C. C. Fry, "Sixteenth Century Cures for Lunacy," *Amer. J. Psychiatry*, CIII (1946–47), 351–352.

Thomas Gresham, the lord mayor, petitioned Henry VIII that
the city should have governance of these two hospitals and three
others, including Bethlehem, to staff them and support them "so
that all impotent persons not able to labour shall be relieved, but
also that all sturdie beggars not willing to labour shall be pun-
ished."[36] Almost sixty years later the statute of 1597 (39 Eliz.
cap. 4) was to add little new concerning vagabonds and rogues.
Offenders were to be stripped naked from the waist up and "bee
openly whipped untill his or her body be bloody," then be sent
forth "the next straight way to the parish where [they were]
borne."[37]

With the passage of the Poor Law Act of 1601, however,
lunatics, as persons unable to work, were eligible for poor relief
and could apply to justices of the peace for allowances. In 1607,
by act of Parliament, dangerous lunatics could be admitted to
the houses of correction already established.[38] By 1650, this
early seventeenth-century social legislation had shaped a notion
of community care and thus a change of attitude toward the
"distraught," although not entirely offsetting the urban trend
to confinement. Thus, in 1641, the vestrymen of a parish were
ordered by a justice of the peace to care for a man whose wife
had appealed to the justice for assistance. Her husband had fallen "by God's Judgement and Visitation into a lunatic frensie
and distraction of his witts . . . hee lyinge bound in Cheanes
and ffeathers [fetters?], every of the neighbor fearfull to come
neare unto him in his fitts . . . both night and day in most
fearfull terrible shriekes and shoutinge."[39] In 1651 another justice of the peace ordered churchwardens and overseers to care
and provide for a man who had fallen into a "Lunacy and

[36] Cited by Copeman, "Royal Hospitals before 1700," p. 31.

[37] Cited by Thomas R. Forbes, *Chronicle from Aldgate: Life and
Death in Shakespeare's London* (New Haven and London, 1971), p.
181.

[38] For this fact and for the material in this paragraph and the next, I
am indebted to A. Fessler, "The Management of Lunacy in Seventeenth
Century England: An Investigation of Quarter-Sessions Records,"
Proc. Roy. Soc. Med., XLIX (1956), 901–907.

[39] Cited in *ibid.*, p. 903.

Violent distraction" and to ease him of his chains. And in 1669 an enlightened justice added to a court order which admitted a madwoman to a house of correction that she be kept there "without whippinge."[40]

At the same time older religious attitudes toward the mad were being advantageously incorporated into the spirit of the law, for such legal commentators as Dalton (1635) and Coke (1648) agreed that lunatics could not be held responsible either in criminal or civil cases, for they were "innocents" who lacked knowledge of good or evil. Hence lunacy was a state of involuntary ignorance in contrast, say, with drunkenness, which induced a voluntary ignorance or besottedness.

It is tempting, without surrendering totally to the fatal temptation of prolonged digression, to reflect on certain analogues between the treatment of the lezers or leprous and the mentally deficient or diseased. It is not entirely accidental that when in 1632 Vincent de Paul reorganized Saint-Lazare, the most important of the former leper houses of Paris, he arranged to change its functions to receive "persons detained by order of His Majesty."[41]

Like the wandering or exiled fools or madmen, lepers had roamed at large, at least in mid-fourteenth-century England. In 1346 Edward III issued an edict expelling all the lepers residing in London for fear that they were seeking deliberately to contaminate one another so that "to their own wretched solace, they may have the more fellows in suffering."[42] "Leprous" was almost as broad of application as "foolish," often meaning little more than "miserable" or "afflicted." In Isaiah 53:4, where the later King James Version speaks of the man of sorrows as "stricken," Saint Jerome in the Vulgate translated the Hebrew *naga* as *leprosus.* John Wyclif at the end of the fourteenth century applied the English word "leprous" to the same passage. Since this passage was thought to foreshadow the Christ, in their

[40] Cited in *ibid.*, p. 904.

[41] See Foucault, *Madness and Civilization*, p. 45.

[42] Cited by William MacArthur, "Medieval 'Leprosy' in the British Isles," *Leprosy Review*, XXIV (1953), 16.

zealous belief that their Lord had walked the earth as a beggar and leprous outcast, noble ladies in a religious fervor are recorded at times as washing the feet or embracing the bodies of lepers. Or as Burton remarks of his own need to anatomize melancholy and thus help others from a fellow feeling, like "that virtuous lady did of old, 'being a leper herself, bestow all her portion to build a hospital for lepers,' " he would bestow his all —time and knowledge—for the common good of all.[43]

Although leprosy was pandemic in Europe from 1000 to 1400, and although approximately 2,000 lazar houses were built in France and 326 in Great Britain (285 of them in England),[44] there is evidence that late in the period, at least, lazar houses, like other small, religiously endowed hospitals, were by no means exclusively reserved for lepers. Much like the Bedlam of the first half of the fifteenth century, Sherburn, founded for sixty-five lepers, provided shelter in 1434 for thirteen poor men and *no* lepers. Accommodations were then specifically set aside for a minimum of two lepers, but were not used because "ther cowlde not so many laiseris be found in that part of England."[45]

While a variety of factors, social and economic, may have contributed to the decline of leprosy, it is quite possible that a long acquaintance with "leprosy" resulted in stricter diagnosis. The result was that "many sufferers from other diseases were excluded, who under the usual loose system of assessment would have been accepted as lepers."[46] In the time of Edward IV, for example, one Johanna Nyghtyngale of Brentwood was accused of "leprosy" and served with the writ *De leproso amovendo* (directed against a lazar or leper "dwelling in any Town, and he will come into the Church, or amongst his Neighbors where they are assembled, to talk with them to their Annoyance and Disturbance"). She appealed to the king.

[43] See "Democritus to the Reader" *The Anatomy of Melancholy*, (Everyman ed.), I, 22.

[44] Figures from R. G. Cochran and T. Frank Davey, eds., *Leprosy in Theory and Practice* (Baltimore, 1964), p. 5.

[45] Cited in *ibid.*, p. 6.

[46] MacArthur, "Medieval 'Leprosy,' " p. 7.

Under his warrant she was examined by a commission including certain physicians of skill and was pronounced free of any blemish of leprosy.[47] It is possible that the extensive ulcerations of advanced scurvy, for further example, may have been misdiagnosed; as Sir William MacArthur points out, intractable skin diseases, cutaneous ulcerations, and deformities could then have been diagnosed as leprosy. In fact he cites a medical treatise by John de Mirfeld of Saint Bartholomew's in which the only symptom of leprosy described was an offensive sweating from the armpits (see footnote 42).

My brief digression is intended to have a point. Granted that a pandemic disease can disappear over time, we can guess from our own experience with loosely used terms such as "the flu" and "a virus" that new terminologies and new "trends" had developed. Along with larger attitudes toward the diseased—exile, then confinement—new skills in and new styles of diagnosis had emerged. In fact, the seventeenth century, to make my digression completely exemplary, was genuinely perplexed by the disappearance of old diseases and the emergence of new ones. Leprosy had dwindled; the *sudor anglicus* (sweating sickness) was thought to be only 200 years old. Scurvy and rickets were new; syphilis was only about a century new. Yet such a skin disease as ringworm or tetter, despite its resemblance to the "French crown" or *corona Veneris* of the new syphilis, reminded the early seventeenth century of the old dread disease—leprosy. As the Ghost tells Hamlet, when the poison coursed through his veins, "a most instant tetter [bark'd] about, / Most lazar-like, with vile and loathsome crust, / All my smooth body."[48] The big problem was to determine whether these new diseases were genuinely novel or had merely gone long unobserved, whether they were the workings of nature or of man's imagination.

One can find several instances of new disease specifically

---

[47] Cited in *ibid.*, p. 17.

[48] I was reminded of this interpretation by F. N. L. Poynter's article, "Medicine and Public Health," in *Shakespeare in His Own Age*, Shakespeare Survey 17 (Cambridge, 1964), p. 164.

labeled as such in the first three quarters of the seventeenth century. The fevers of 1661, as described by Thomas Willis (about whom more in a moment), were called "New." Similarly the ague epidemic in 1679 was known as the "New Disease," the "New Ague," the "New Fever," the "New Ague Fever," and in one county, Derbyshire, as the "New Delight."[49] It is as if, as we shall later see in the shift from the single diagnosis of melancholy to more multiple diagnostic indications for specifically differentiated diseases, that sometime in the sixteenth or early seventeenth century pathology began to lose a traditional vagueness. Particular entities began to be given form and "diseases" replaced "Disease."

During the epidemic of 1661, to illustrate my point, the English physician Thomas Willis (1621–1675) sought to set down the symptoms of the "New Disease" that had so suddenly and so silently seized the city of London. Among his problems must have been that of determining a mosaic pattern from the "facts" reported by the mortality bills and the elements of disease which he had himself witnessed in manifold permutations and combinations. The results of his observations were not published until 1667, under the Latin title *Pathologiae cerebri, et nervosi generis specimen. In quo agitur de morbis convulsivis et de scorbuto.* Whether it was an epidemic of meningitis or influenza with encephalitic complications or typhoid is still debated.[50] Willis, nonetheless, instills fresh insight into old terms as he describes the epidemic. Its onslaught was marked by "a heavy vertigo, a tingling of the ears, and often of a great tumult and perturbation of the brain." When fever was kindled, the next stage of the disease he compares with "a frank Phrensie, or deep Stupidity, or Insensibility." In the seventh or eighth day of the siege, he describes the swimmings of the head, the leapings up of the tendons, and the convulsive motions of the limbs.

[49] Lloyd G. Stevenson, " 'New Diseases' in the Seventeenth Century," *Bull. His. Med.*, (1965), 8, citing Charles Creighton, *A History of Epidemics in Britain* (Cambridge, 1891), II, 332.

[50] See Donald G. Bates, "Thomas Willis and the Epidemic Fever of 1661: A Commentary," *Bull. Hist. Med.*, XXXIX (1965), 393–414.

I mention Willis's observations to prepare for a return to my original point of departure: new attitudes toward "new" diseases or "old" in the mid-seventeenth century are based on new needs for differentiation and on new observations. Thus it is fitting that Thomas Willis, one of the pioneers in neuroanatomy, neurophysiology, and neuropathology and discoverer of the eleventh cranial nerve, should present a new view on mental deficiency (an understanding of what characterizes one type of "folly," that of the *stolidi* or *stupidi*) and on a form of "madness," schizophrenia (rendered by Willis as *stultitia*, significantly enough).

In 1672, three years before his death in 1675 (the year in which Bethlehem Hospital was moved into larger quarters), Willis had R. Davis of Oxford publish his *De anima brutorum* ("Two Discourses on the Souls of Brutes"). His chapter, "Stupidity or Foolishness," was to prove influential. In 1698, for example, it was reprinted in toto by J. J. Manget in his *Bibliotheca medico-practica* (Geneva: Chouet). Of modern interest should be the fact that in its Latin original the Greek word *psychologia* appears frequently, stiffly translated by Samuel Pordage in 1683 as "doctrine of the soul."[51] Of even more interest for this essay is that Willis ingeniously modified Gassendi's argument on animal souls in order to avoid conflict with ecclesiastical authorities and religious dogma—a shift in outlook, as it will turn out. Whereas Gassendi had claimed that animals must have souls because, like humans, they showed evidence of reason, memory, and other mental traits, Willis attributed these characteristics to a corporeal soul, or soul of brutes, under the

---

[51] Although I have consulted Pordage's translation of the *Two Discourses* in *Dr. Willis's Practice of Physick, being the Whole Works . . .* (London, 1684), I have relied heavily on Paul F. Cranefield, "A Seventeenth Century View of Mental Deficiency and Schizophrenia: Thomas Willis on 'Stupidity or Foolishness,'" *Bull. Hist. Med.*, XXXV (1961), 291–361. Willis may be among the first Englishmen to use the term, but *psychologia*, as Zilboorg points out, had been used as early as 1590 by Rudolph Goeckel as part of a title: *Psychologia: Hoc est de Hominis Perfectionem*. In 1594 Goeckel's pupil Otto Casmann published *Psychologia Anthropologica*.

control of a rational soul, placing God, as Dewhurst remarks, "completely beyond the realm of anatomical speculation."[52] By postulating twin souls, moreover, Willis was able to speculate on certain much bruited aspects of neurology and what we might term psychiatry, aspects previously believed to be properly within the sphere of theology.

As summarized by Paul F. Cranefield, Willis's doctrine of mental deficiency may be analyzed as follows. Stupidity (or *morosis*) proceeds from a damaged imagination and memory, further impaired in these centers of the brain by faults of the animal spirits and mechanical defects of the brain itself. In the brain center that Willis labels "Imagination" is seated the rational soul. From the imagination and the memory are supplied the notions or occasions of all things that the mind beholds or contemplates. When their corporal functions are mechanically defective, to use Willis's metaphor, the eye of the intellect is veiled or dulled or wholly darkened. Thus the reason for foolishness or stupidity may be found in the mechanically defective relationships between those "forekindred" centers—imagination and memory.

Following Willis as interpreted by Cranefield, let us look at some of the ways in which these functions or their relationships may be impaired. Let us examine in particular the animal spirits that are the immediate organs of both the "callous bodies," or the middle of the brain (imagination) and the cortical marrow of the brain (memory).

A defect in animal spirits, be it of excess or of deficiency, is bound to upset imagination and memory. If the animal spirits are of a "preternatural" (abnormal) disposition, they will ultimately cause the individual to be marked by "Phrensie," melancholy, or madness. If they are exhausted (lacking in "volatile salts"), these essential spirits will be almost drowned and overwhelmed by the "watery" and "terrestrial" and thus produce dull or "phlegmatic" reactions, to use the terminology of humoral psychology.

[52] Kenneth Dewhurst, *Thomas Willis as a Physician* (Los Angeles: William Andrews Clark Memorial Library, 1964), p. 14.

Willis also ponders mechanical or physical defects of the brain. A nicely shaped head will allow the animal spirits to be poured with an equal efflux to either side. A flattened head, or a sharply pointed head, will result in a fault of animal function, "for these kinds of Brains, like distorted Looking-Glasses, do not rightly collect the Images of things, nor truly object them to the Rational Soul."[53] If the texture of the brain is too thick or "Earthy," it is likely that its clumsy fabric will help form "Plowmen" and "Rusticks." Or if the pores and passages of the brain are too loose or too strait, they may on the one hand produce the aimless person of excessive heterogeneity of interests or, on the other hand, shape a mind with "too little store of matter for a good plenty of Spirits." In certain instances one can detect the combination of dull and torpid animal spirits with an "evilly conformed" brain. Behind such mechanical or physical defects may be detected poor or impaired heredity, injury or serious disease, dietary excess (if I may so describe "frequent drunkenness"), violent and sudden passions, or (and I should be enrolled as witness to this), the ripeness and declination of age, disposing some to foolishness.

As Cranefield, following F. H. Garrison,[54] points out, Willis's capacity for "close, careful, clinical observation" may be seen in his distinction between *stultitia* and *stupiditas*, both socially subnormal types of mental deficiency. The foolish are socially subnormal although they apprehend simple things well, dextrously, and swiftly; they have good memories but defective judgment; because of defective judgment, they reason badly and make poor inferences; they show their folly in awkward gestures and gesticulations. The stupid, on the contrary, are defective in apprehension and memory and therefore are defective in judgment; they are thus bound to dullness in behavior and simplicity in countenance and bearing.

In the opinion of at least one historian of medicine, Willis, through his powers of observation and recording, has presented

[53] Cited in Cranefield, "A Seventeenth Century View," p. 295.

[54] *An Introduction to the History of Medicine*, 4th ed. (Philadelphia, 1929).

"a fairly good and very early description of simple schizophrenia."[55] Cranefield compares Willis's description of the powers and defects of the "fool" with Bleuler's list of the characteristics of the schizophrenic. In the clumsy abstraction of modern psychological jargon, Willis has discovered the following: "The foolish have contact with their environment (they apprehend); they remember; but they have a loosening of associations; finally, they show bizarre motor behavior."[56] Willis's comments on the ability of the foolish to apprehend things "well enough, dextrously and swiftly" may be compared with Bleuler's statement that "Lucid schizophrenic conditions show no disorder of consciousness, if the latter is conceived as implying a loss of sensory contact with the environment." Similarly, Willis's observation that the foolish "compose or divide their notions evilly, and very badly infer one thing from another," has been paralleled with Bleuler's note that, with schizophrenics, "associations lose their connections." This last observation, Cranefield remarks, is "most striking," for even today a psychiatrist cannot differentiate between mental deficiency and schizophrenia until "the presence or absence of the schizophrenic thought disorder can be established."[57]

Willis classifies stupidity by its various degrees of severity and works out a corresponding scale of social possibilities. In descending order he proceeds from the high-grade defective, who cannot handle "letters" (i.e., cannot read or write easily) and thus is unfit for "liberal Sciences" although able enough for the "Mechanical Arts," to those who are unable to cope with liberal sciences or mechanical arts but can "comprehend" agriculture. Beneath these are those barely able to eat or to earn a living in the ordinary sense of the phrase. And then come "merely *Dolts* or drivelling Fools" who "scarce understand anything at all, or do anything knowingly."

Significantly anticipating the change in sociological outlook

[55] Cranefield, "A Seventeenth Century View," p. 313.
[56] *Ibid.*
[57] *Ibid.*, p. 314.

effected by Pinel and other eighteenth-century reformers, Willis suggests that ameliorative treatment is possible but should be reserved for those in the first two categories. For them a "master" (teacher) and a physician working together can devise a treatment, after a trial period. The master, through frequent care, can speed and sharpen the slow and torpid spirits of the high-grade fool by perpetual exercise. The physician can administer medical remedies — a course in chemotherapy? — which may purify and volatize the blood and the animal spirits. Thus he may prescribe coffee, spirits (alcoholic!), or elixirs. Other means of applying "drugs" are suggested, the most notable being the use of a quilted cap in which are stored and sewn petals of the lily of the valley and rosemary, along with nutmeg, cloves, and cinnamon.

In suggesting that a rank, a grade, or an order of fools need not climb the cordage of a ship sailing off into exile or be given temporary harborage in hospitals originally founded for the physically ill, but can hope for improvement through a special education which is to be the joint responsibility of a teacher and a doctor, Willis is opening up new horizons.

There are other contributions, both physiological and psychological, to be found in Willis's *Two Discourses on the Souls of Brutes*. Physiologically Willis begins a new epoch in the study of the localization of function by placing perception in the corpora striata, imagination in the corpus callosum, instincts in the midbrain, vital centers in the cerebellum, and memory in the cerebral cortex, that "shelly part of the Brain [which] is the seat of Memory and the porch of Sleep." Psychologically, he suggests in his clear but nonetheless metaphorical prose that psychological impulses are dependent upon nerve impulses produced in anatomically ascertainable paths.

Every moment of equilibrium is tentative and tenuous, the uneasy balance of opposing forces. In certain ways Willis's views on individual prescriptions for fools ran counter to the larger pressures to gather them in and confine them. When Bethlehem Hospital was transferred and the "New House" erected, it was hoped that the facilities would be adequate to

provide for the incurable and dangerous, since in the limited
quarters of the old hospital "it [had been] impracticable to re-
serve room for those forlorn beings, of whose return to the
comforts of a sound mind there were no hopes."[58] Such comprehensive facilities for all the seriously afflicted were apparently not to be realized in England. There the western European
movement of the "Great Confinement" was not so specialized
or so intensive as in France, where, following the success of
the founding of the Hôpital Général (1656), a royal edict
prescribed on June 16, 1676, the establishment of an *hôpital
général* in each city of the realm. Nor was Bedlam ever to shut
up within its walls 6,000 persons (or 1 percent of the population) as the Hôpital Général did in Paris, shortly after its foundation.

To be sure, at the opening of the seventeenth century, houses
of correction were established in Great Britain, in which trades
and crafts were to be taught. By mid-century they had been
largely displaced by workhouses. An act of 1670 defined the
status of workhouses, authorized officers of justice to collect
taxes and administer funds to keep them operating, and entrusted their control to justices of the peace. By the end of the
century there were a number of them functioning in England;
by the end of the eighteenth there were 126. It would take
John Howard's enormous energy, before the nineteenth century turned, to investigate hospitals and prisons to find out that
behind common walls were sequestered spendthrifts, debtors,
unemployables, and the insane. As Foucault very penetratingly
remarks:

> The act which, by tracing the locus of confinement, con-
> ferred upon it its power of segregation and provided a new
> homeland for madness, though it may be coherent and con-
> certed, is not simple. It organizes into a complex unity a new
> sensibility to poverty and to the duties of assistance, new
> forms of reaction to the economic problems of unemploy-
> ment and idleness, a new ethic of work, and also the dream of

[58] Bowen, *Historical Account*, p. 7.

a city where moral obligation was joined to civil law, within the authoritarian forms of constraint.[59]

As Robert Burton noted, "We have excellent laws enacted, you will say, severe statutes, houses of correction, etc., to small purpose it seems; it is not houses will serve, but cities of correction." (Everyman ed., "Democritus to the Reader," I, 92–93). The notion of the "Great Confinement," though shared in Britain, was not put into fullest practice.

Melancholy Anatomized: Burton, Willis, Sydenham, and "Hysteric Diseases," 1621–1682

To seek to define "melancholy" — or to "anatomize" it as Robert Burton so magnificently tried from the first plump quarto of the *Anatomy of Melancholy* in 1621 to its last lank folio version of 1676, a reprint of the sixth edition of 1651—is to seek to hold the wind in a net:

> What physicians say of distinct species in their books it much matters not, since in their patients' bodies they are commonly mixed. In such obscurity, therefore, variety and confused mixture of symptoms, causes, how difficult a thing it is to treat of several kinds apart; to make any certainty or distinction among so many casualties, distractions, when seldom two men shall be like affected *per omnia* [in all respects]![60]

Like Burton, I shall nonetheless "adventure through the midst of these perplexities, and, led by the clue or thread of the best writers, [seek to] extricate myself out of a labyrinth of doubts and errors."[61] I thus proceed to the species or kinds of melan-

[59] *Madness and Civilization*, pp. 47–48.

[60] *The Anatomy of Melancholy*, Pt. I, sec. 1, mem. iii, subsec. 4, "Of the Species or Kinds of Melancholy" (Everyman ed.), I, 175.

[61] Among the "best authors" who treat of the Renaissance phenomenon of melancholy or of Burton, the English encyclopedist of what was known as "The English Malady (Melancholy)," are the following: Raymond Klibansky, Edwin Panofsky, and Fritz Saxl, *Saturn and*

choly so abundantly illustrated from authority and from observation by Robert Burton.

Quite aware that melancholy was a masking or symbolizing affliction, Burton follows "the most received division" of the disease into three types. The first type, "head-melancholy," or corrupted blood in the brain: from an innate humour or from "distemperature adust"; from excess of venery, or defect; from agues, or some other precedent disease; or from fumes arising from the stomach. Its outward causes include such factors as excessive heat from the sun; a blow on the head; overmuch use of hot wines, garlic, onions, or spices; and excessive indulgence in hot baths. Idleness, solitariness, overmuch study, and "vehement labour" are listed among the "inward causes' of head melancholy, together with "passions" and "perturbations."

Burton's second type proceeds sympathetically from the whole body ,"when the whole temperature is melancholy." He is quite aware that "the Body works on the Mind," for "as the distraction of the mind, amongst other outward causes and perturbations, alters the temperature of the body, so the distraction and distemper of the body will cause a distemperature of the soul, and 'tis hard to decide which of these two do more harm to the other" (Pt. I, sec. 2, mem. v, subses. 1).

Hypochondriacal or "windy" melancholy is the third main type of melancholy with which Burton concerned himself. In his opinion it is "the most grievous and frequent" variety, although his judgment of the severity of this type of melancholy runs counter to that advanced by such earlier authorities as

Melancholy: Studies in the History of Natural Philosophy, Religion and Art (London, 1964); Lawrence Babb, *Sanity in Bedlam: A Study of Robert Burton's "Anatomy of Melancholy"* (Lansing, Mich., 1959); and Bergen Evans (in consultation with George J. Mohr), *The Psychiatry of Robert Burton* (New York, 1944). If authority be needed to observe Burton's own sense of deference and decorum, one should cite Sir William Osler, "Burton, the Man, His Book, His Library," in *Proceedings of the Oxford Bibliographical Society*, I (1925), 163–190, and Joseph L. Miller, Burton's *"Anatomy of Melancholy,"* *Annals of Medical History*, n.s., VIII (1936), 44–53.

Bruel and Laurentius (Pt. I, sec. 2, mem. v, subsec. 4). Windy melancholy is conceived of as arising from the bowels, liver, spleen, or the membrane caled mesenterium, from "heat and obstruction."

The causes so far cited as underlying the three types are merely "particular causes" to Burton, who distinguished them from general causes, subdividing these in turn into supernatural or natural causes. Supernatural causes stem from God immediately or arise by second causes in the punishment of sin or the satisfaction of his justice; or from the devil immediately (Burton here digresses on the nature of spirits, corporeal, mortal, fiery and aerial, watery and terrestrial [lares, genii, fauns, satyrs, wood nymphs, trolls, Robin Goodfellow, hobgoblins]), or mediately, through witches and magicians, via knots, amulets, words, and philters—not that "there is any power at all in those spells, charms, characters and barbarous words; but that the devil doth use such means to delude them, *ut fideles inde magos . . . in officio retineat, tum in consortium malefactorum vocet* [that he may keep the Magi true to their allegiance, and then summon them to join the company of evildoers]."

Natural causes of a general nature he traces back to congenital defects or old age and to outward adventitious or inward contingent events. For example, if a parent eats garlic or onions in excess or fats overmuch, or if he studies too hard or is over-sorrowful or "defected" in his mind or perplexed in his thoughts, his childern will be subject to madness and melancholy, "for if the spirits of the brain be fuzzled or misaffected by such means at such a time, [the] children will be fuzzled in the brain; they will be dull, heavy, timorous, discontented all their lives." Or if husbands "pay their debt (as Paul calls it) to their wives remissly, by which means their children are weaklings, and many times idiots and fools."

Similarily, bad diet, Burton believes, can be a general cause of melancholy: all venison he considers to be "melancholy" and a begetter of bad blood; and hare, a black meat hard to digest, like venison causes fearful dreams. So, too, fenny fowl, such as ducks, geese, swans, herons, cranes, coots, didappers, water hens, teals, currs, sheldrakes, and "peckled fowls, that come hither in winter, out of Scandia, Muscovy, Greenland, [and] Friesland," for though they be fair of feather and white of plume, their flesh is "hard, black, unwholesome, dangerous, melancholy meat." Similarly he would have his readers avoid gourds, cucumbers, coleworts, melons, and especially cabbage, for the latter causes "troublesome dreams and sends up black [melancholic] vapours to the brain." Likewise, nurses, terrors, affrights, scoffs, calumnies, honesty and want, servitude and imprisonment, and "a heap of other accidents"—the death of friends—can serve as outward or adventitious causes of melancholy.

Burton is indeed alert to the fact that it is difficult to distinguish "these three species one from the other, to express their several causes, symptoms, cures," since "they are so often confounded amongst themselves, having such affinity that they can scarce be discerned by the most accurate physicians, and so often intermixed with other diseases that the best experienced," as he colloquially remarks, "have been plunged." Nonetheless he finds the summum genus of the disease to be "anguish of the mind," thus distinguishing it from such diseases of the outward sense as cramps and palsy and differentiating it from its near kin, folly and madness, in that it is a "depravation" [*sic*] of function, not an abolition. Burton further defends it as being "without an ague" or fever, to separate it from frenzy; marked by fear and sorrow, "the true characters and inseparable companions of most melancholy," to separate it from madness; and "without cause," to specify it from "all other ordinary passions of 'fear and sorrow.' "[62]

Burton, as noted earlier, at times extends his definition of melancholy to include madness and acknowledges that it touches on dotage. After all, he asks, "who is not a fool, who is free from melancholy? Who is not touched more or less in habit or disposition?" (Everyman ed., I, 39). He admits that his authorities frequently confuse madness and melancholy and

[62] See Burton's "Definition of Melancholy, Name, Difference," *Anatomy*, Pt. I, sec. 1, mem. iii, subsec. 1 (Everyman ed.) I, 169–170.

that the symptoms of the two diseases sometimes overlap and that, in a psychological sense, one can incline or decline into the other. He well knows, incidentally, the "outward voyage" pursued in the search for the cure or riddance of madness, talking of it somewhat contemptuously and antipapistically in several places. The best example of his outlook on this matter occurs under the heading "Whether it be lawful to seek Saints for Aid in this Disease" (Pt. II, sec. 1, mem. iii [Everyman ed.], II, 11–13). While Burton would grant the efficacy of prayer as one of the cures of melancholy, he derisively notes that the "papists on the one side stiffly maintain how many melancholy, mad, demoniacal persons are daily cured at St. Anthony's Church in Padua, at St. Vitus' in Germany, by our lady of Loretto in Italy, our Lady of Sichem in the Low Countries," and sardonically comments that the Virgin not only cures the halt, the lame, and the blind, and all diseases of body and mind, but even commands the devil himself. Citing Jodocus Sincerus's *Itinerarium Galliae* (1617), he further mentions that in his own time madmen were brought to Saint Hilary's at Poitiers, there to sleep in the saint's bed and "after some prayers and other ceremonies" to wake up recovered: "'It is an ordinary thing in these parts [France] to send all their madmen to St. Hilary's cradle."

We should not linger over the issue of whether "black bile," as such, was a medically observable diagnosis arising from the swelling of the spleen in blackwater fever, thus accounting for the theory that the spleen was itself the source of black bile.[63] Nor should we more than mention Galen's monograph on black bile or the Galenic tradition, particularly as transmitted by the Arabs. Nor shall I discuss the way that the Empedoclean theory of the four elements and its expression in the macrocosm and microcosm helps to develop a "humoral" psychology in which melancholy is described as a "liquid or fluent part of the body" which is "cold and dry, thick, black, and sour, begot-

[63] For a recent review of modern attempts to "trace the origin of the teachings on melancholia to medical observations," see R. F. Timken-Zinkann's summary in *Medical History*, XII (1968), 288–292.

ten of the more feculent part of nourishment, and purged from the spleen" (Pt. I, sec. 1, mem. ii, subsec. 2). I shall merely mention the pseudo-Aristotelian Problem (xxx, 1) in which melancholy is linked with the complex notions of a fine frenzy derived from Plato, or perhaps (also) from Greek tragedy, and becomes—as a physical set of symptoms—a common, distinctive quality of lunatic, lover, poet, and man of genius. Klibansky, Panofsky, and Saxl have made all this abundantly clear in their book *Saturn and Melancholy*. For our purposes, however, I note in passing that the contents of that influential pseudo-Aristotlian problem were made accessible to the West through a Latin translation by Bartholomew of Messina. Twelve codices of his version are listed as of the thirteenth century, and ten codices of his translation date from the beginning of the fourteenth.[64]

By the fifteenth century, then, melancholy had been established as a mental illness characterized by anxiety, depression, and fatigue and stemming from an imbalance of the humours. In adjectival form the word also described a clearly recognizable physical type, disposed to the particular kinds of mental anguish assigned the disease. Late in medieval times, moreover, the significance of the term was attenuated to the point that "melancholy" could refer to a temporary state of mind, at times pensive, at times depressive, in either instance without apparent cause.

In an even larger process of diffusion and dilution, "melancholy" occupied a prominent niche in middlebrow parlance, comparable perhaps to the modern "neurosis," and took on certain actual popular representations. In "acquiring the psychological content of notions originally applying only to mental states, [it] inherited also their pictorial form"[65] or their verbal imagery. Thus such personifications of medieval poetry as "Despair" and "Sorrow," which embodied elements of psychological anguish, as "Despair" and "Sorrow" disappeared

---

[64] See Peter Dronke's review of Klibansky, Panofsky, and Saxl, *Saturn and Melancholy*, in *Notes and Queries*, CCX (1965), 354–356.

[65] Klibansky, Panofsky, and Saxl, *op. cit.*, p. 221.

at times behind the new mask of "Melancholy." In Alain Chartier's *Espérance ou Consolation des Trois Vertus* (1428), "Dame Mérencolye" takes over certain of the outward aspects as well as many of the inner functions of the allegorical character "Tristesse" of Guillaume de Loris's thirteenth-century poem, the *Roman de la Rose*. Similarly the "Melencolie" of the second half of the fifteenth century takes on the thin, disheveled, wrinkled appearance of Sadness, although also presenting the pensive qualities of one form of Melancholy as she broods profoundly by the fire.[66]

The most important extension of melancholy for which the late Middle Ages was responsible was the connection between the affliction and Saturn, as both god and planet. As early as the ninth century Arab astrologers had linked humours, organs, elements, and stars and had paved the way for the association of melancholy with Saturn, the cold, bitter, black planet. Yet the confusion of the Roman Saturn with the Greek Kronos, particularly as developed in Neoplatonic thought, had given the planet a dual potentiality, for good as well as for evil, for benevolence as well as for malignance, for creativity as well as for destruction:

> It was not only the combination of cold and dryness that linked black bile with the apparently similar nature of the star; nor was it only the tendency to depression, loneliness and visions, which the melancholic shared with the planet of tears, of solitary life and of soothsayers; above all, there was the analogy of action. Like melancholy, Saturn, that demon of the opposites, endowed the soul both with slowness and stupidity and with the power of intelligence and contemplation.[67]

Whether or not the notion that melancholy was the peculiar affliction of the great, the creative, and the contemplative is an innovation of the physician, priest, and philosopher, Marsilio Ficino, as expressed in *De vita triplici* (1489), or the recru-

[66] Both these examples are cited in *ibid.*, pp. 221–222.
[67] *Ibid.*, pp. 158–159.

descence of the concept resulting from a reinterpretation of the pseudo-Aristotelian Problem (XXX, 1), melancholy in Renaissance art, both pictorial and literary, became a central point of reference. By personifying it artistically one could present an awareness of life's sufferings, particularly the anguish of thought and contemplation and combine it with acknowledgment that the sovereignty of reason so much desired by Renaissance humanists meant slavery as well as freedom and involved the problem of choice among many different directions and alternatives. Ficino's "natural magic," a link between astrology and medicine, was used to convert the malevolent power of Saturn into redemptive strength. The highly gifted melancholic who suffered from the physical torment imposed by the astrological sign as well as the psychological vexations of fear, depression, and grief might, through the knowledge of occult stellar virtues, convert the blinkers of Saturn into the probes of creative contemplation.

Through the expansion and development of certain elements of Ficino's thought by the noted Henry Cornelius Agrippa of Netttesheim, whose *De occulta philosophia* was completed by 1510, although not actually published until 1533, melancholy could become high abstract contemplation through talismanic manipulation. The means of attaining this darkened source of creative genius by avoiding the "obscure doom" of melancholy might have been pictorially portrayed had Dürer completed a *Melencolia II* to match his *Melencolia I* (c. 1514–15). Dürer was apparently predisposed to accept Agrippa's extension of Ficino and what I shall call "Saturnine melancholy," perhaps as a result of his two Italian trips, more likely as a result of his own penchant for melancholy. In his youth he had painted himself in the attitude of a melancholic visionary. In addition, in a sketch (Bremen L130; Klibansky, Panofsky, and Saxl, *op. cit.*, pl. 145) of about 1512–13, made just before he had began *Melencholia I* and perhaps intended for a doctor's rush diagnosis or an apothecary's return prescription, Dürer represents himself as a sufferer from an irritation of the hypo-

chondria. With right index finger pointing to an encircled and
colored spot just below the bottom of the left half of the rib
cage, he presents his complaint in a superscription: "Do der gelb
fleck ist vnd mit dem / finger drawff dewt, do ist imr we."[68]
Perhaps he is pointing to the spleen or left hypochondria, "from
which is denominated hypochondriacal melancholy" (Burton,
Anatomy, Pt. I, sec. 1, mem. ii, subsec. 4). He is thus adapting a
conventional sign of the disease to his own description.

As Burton notes, citing Baptista Porta (*Caelistis Physiog-
nom*, lib. 10), "if a spot be over the spleen, 'or in the nails, if it
appear black, it signifieth much care, grief, contention, and
melancholy.' " In his verses to the frontispiece illustrations of
the *Anatomy*, Burton seems almost to describe Dürer in the
seated Hypocondriacus:

> *Hypocondriacus* leans on his arm [left arm]
> Wind in his side doth him much harm,
> And troubles him full sore, God knows,
> Much pain he hath and many woes.
> About him pots and glasses lie,
> Newly brought from's apothecary.
> This Saturn's aspects signify
>   [astrological symbols above seated figure]
> You see them portray'd in the sky.

It is vexing that one can not linger over Dürer's engraving to
give some sense of its peculiar power. It would be presumptuous, on the other hand, to attempt to do so after Klibansky,
Panofsky, and Saxl have pooled their genius in a full-sized book
to interpret the work. Perhaps we shall have to content ourselves here with mentioning its reputation as a symptom of the
Renaissance preoccupation with the disease of melancholy.

In speaking of the extreme symptoms of those who suffer
from melancholy—"anxious ever and very solicitous, distrust-
ful and timorous, envious, malicious, profuse one while, sparing

[68] See *ibid.*, p. 349, for a summary of the argument over the significance of the Roman numeral "I" in the title of Dürer's painting.

another"—Burton refers to Dürer's print as characteristic of the *cogitabundi* or the very intent, "as Albertus Dürer paints Melancholy, like a sad woman leaning on her arm with fixed looks" and wearing a "neglected habit" (Everyman ed., I, 392). The motives of the drooping head, the "dark" face; the loose, idle hand (in Dürer a tense, clenched near-fist); the geometric symbols, tools, and objects indicating not only how creative contemplation can measure things, how pathological melancholy frustrates creativity, but also how re-creation of the mind, to use Burton's phrase, can "expel idleness and melancholy" ("he that shall but see that geometrical tower of Garisenda at Bologna in Italy, the steeple and clock at Strasburg [*sic*], will admire the effects of art, or that engine of Arachimedes, to remove the earth itself" [Pt. II, sec. 2, mem. iv]); the seascape associated with Saturn—all these, or some of them, recur in the paintings, drawings, and engravings that form the artistic legacy of *Melencolia I*. Such persistency is not only a tribute to Dürer's power but also to the tough vitality of the "new" concept of melancholy—the strange case of frustrated gifts, of creativity in bonds, of genius in solitary isolation. One could mention Lucas Cranach's three paintings of Melancholy, dated 1528, 1532, and 1533. One could cite the anonymous West-German master "A. C." with his engravings *Geometria* (1526) and *Melancholy* (after 1526) or the fully allegorical *Melancholia* (1558) of Matthias Gerung. The tradition of portraits of Melancholy as a single female figure in the manner of Dürer can in fact be traced into the plastic arts of the seventeenth century and into the verbal arts of the eighteenth and early nineteenth centuries (if we may go so far afield as to include Keats's implicit portrait of Veiled Melancholy "seen of none save him whose strenuous tongue / Can burst Joy's grape against his palate fine").

We shall rather seek to trace discontinuity than continuity, although "Saturnine melancholy," as I have shown, was in itself a break with the "ordinary" melancholy of the earlier medieval past. In the analytical terms of Timothy Bright, whose *Treatise of Melancholy* (1586) preceded Robert

Burton's *Anatomy* by almost thirty-five years, I may have shut up the heart of my argument, as it were, in a dungeon of obscurity. Lest the reader sit comfortless, I turn now to mid-seventeenth-century developments in the diagnosis and prognosis of certain aspects of the all too embracing disease of melancholy. Particularly in "hypochondria" and "hysteria" do we find new medical metaphors, new styles of analysis.

I have earlier alluded to Blackmore's *Treatise of the Spleen and Vapours* (1725) as demonstrating that after the "discoveries" of Thomas Willis and Thomas Sydenham in the 1670s and 1680s, a new style of medical diagnosis of melancholy had been effected. To be sure, elements of the old views persisted, as reflected in Timothy Rogers's *A Discourse Concerning Trouble of Mind and the Disease of Melancholy* (lst ed., ? 1691; 2d, corr. ed., 1708). Nonetheless, the fact that in 1733 George Cheyne could write of melancholy under the title, *The English Malady: or, a Treatise of Nervous Diseases of all Kinds, as Spleen, Vapours, Lowness of Spirits, Hypochondriacal and Hysterical Distempers*, clearly shows by its distinctive references in the subtitle that the old all-encompassing affliction of melancholy had been splintered into more specifically identifiable diseases and now connoted a wider but still more specific variety of explanations and approaches.

Burton, when addressing himself to the "Causes of Hypochondriacal or Windy Melancholy" (Pt. I, sec. 2, mem. v, subsec. 4), had contented himself with summarizing and conflating the views of his authorities, which more or less agreed that the inward cause of "flatuous melancholy" lay in defective, obstructed, or inflamed inner organs or in an interaction of "misaffected parts," such as a hot liver and a cold stomach, which affected the blood and sent gross vapors to the heart and brain. Among the "outward" causes, they concur, are "bad diet, care, griefs, [and] discontents." Burton concluded his section by repeating this interpretation: "... most commonly fear, grief, and some sudden commotion or perturbation of the mind begin it, in such bodies especially as are ill-disposed."

In another section of the *Anatomy* here pertinent, "Symptoms of Maids', Nuns', and Widows' Melancholy" (Pt. I, sec. 3, mem. ii, subsec. 4), Burton discusses the melancholic afflictions of widows, nuns, "more ancient maids," pregnant women, and barren wives. Their physical symptoms were a burning of the midriff and heartstrings, an almost perpetual "beating about the back," an alternation of pain in breasts, hypochondria, belly, and sides, and an equally noticeable alternation of mood from pleasant sociability to distracted solitariness. The underlying cause of this special brand of melancholy, it seemed, lay in the vicious vapors that come from menstrual blood, from inflammation, and putridity, black smoky vapors that trouble the brain "not in essence, but by consent."

Fifty years after the first edition of Burton's *Anatomy of Melancholy*, in 1671, Dr. Thomas Willis (1621–1675) published an essay whose title itself reveals a changed metaphor of diagnosis and analysis: *Affectionum quae dicuntur hystericae et hypochondriacae pathologica spasmodica*, translated in 1684 as "On the Passions commonly called Hysterical, or Fits of the Mother."[69] The term "hypochondria" which appeared in Willis's Latin title was, incidentally, a seventeenth-century invention, having first been used in a work by Smollius, written in 1610. After summarizing the symptoms of these distempers, among them "a motion in the bottom of the belly, and an ascention of the same as it were a certain round thing, then a belching, or a striving to Vomit, a distention, a murmur of the *Hypochondria*, with a breaking forth of blasts of wind," Willis proceeds to the causes of what Burton had called "flatuous Melancholy" in women.[70]

Whereas most of the ancient and many of the contemporary theorists believed that hysteric seizure was caused by an actual

[69] In *Dr. Willis's Practice of Physick, Translated out of Latin by S[amuel] P[ordage]* (London, 1684).

[70] Although I have relied on my own layman's reading of Willis's "Of Convulsive Diseases," in the *Practice of Physick*, I have found most useful as a guide Dr. Hansruudi Isler, *Thomas Willis, 1621–1675, Doctor and Scientist* (New York and London: Hafner, 1968).

ascension of the womb (note Willis's "as it were," above), or by vapors arising from it, Willis, from his own observations, objected that in maids and widows the womb is so small and so firmly attached that it could not move from its nexus. He further argued that the descent or prolapsus of the womb, not infrequently observed, rarely caused hysteria, and that displacement of the womb to one side or the other, as occurred in child-bed, did not result in hysteria.

One of the fresh elements Willis advanced was the notion of a definite relationship or "commerce" between brain and spleen combined with the theory that what we might term "reflex action" is caused by an "explosive *Copula*," an "explosion of the spirits," "after the manner of gunpowder":

> ... we may suppose, that to the spiritous Saline particles, for the spirits inhabiting the interwoven *fibres* in the muscle, other nitrous sulphureous particles, of a diverse kind, do come, and grow intimately with them. . . . Then as often as the particles of either kinde, as *Nitre* and *Sulphur* combined together, by reason of the instinct of motion brought through the nerves, are moved, as an inkindling of fire, forthwith on the other side bursting forth, or being exploded, they suddenly blow up the Muscle, and from thence cause a most strong drawing together.[71]

Willis's vivid sense of spasms, explosive copulas, and convulsive motion in general is marked by an intensely bellicose imagery of "old Soldiers" and "unbridled Horses, pushed forward with Spurs," of "previous [nervous] skirmishing" and "light companies" of spirits in readiness for explosion. Willis, as Isler remarks, was convinced that hysteria or female melancholy was

[71] "Of Consulsive Diseases," in *Dr. Willis's Practice of Physick*, p. 2. For Willis's treatises, "The Anatomy of the Brain" and "The Description and Uses of the Nerves," see *The Remaining Medical Works of that Famous and Renowned Physician Dr. Thomas Willis (The First Part, though last Published), Englished by S. P. Esq.* (London, 1681).

chiefly, and in the first place, convulsive and most probably depended upon an affected brain and nervous system.[72]

Similarly, in speaking of the windy melancholy that seizes certain men, Willis developed a theory out of the notion that "spirits" or "most subtle vapours," as Burton calls them (*Anatomy*, Pt. I, sec. 1, mem. ii, subsec. 3), were expressed from the blood and tied together body and soul. Traditionally three sorts of spirits—natural, vital, and animal—were thought to populate the liver and veins, the heart and arteries, and the brain, respectively. The animal spirits, formed of the vital spirits, diffused through the nerves to the subordinate members, giving "sense and motion to them all" (*ibid.*). Willis, on the other hand, posits certain irregularities in the regimen of the animal spirits affixed by sudden fears or great sadness, from which women contract the disease named "the Mother," and men, "the Hypochondriack." He subordinates the older mechanical and metaphysical image of the animal spirits in the sinews or nerves to the image "more strictly physical but of an even more symbolic value, of a tension in which nerves, vessels and the entire system of organic fibre were subject."[73] Hence his explanation of "windy melancholy":

> For it seems that when the black bile or melancholic tumour in the Spleen, grows turgid, or swells up of its own accord, or is moved by some evident cause, its particles enter into the nervous *fibers*, thickly distributed to the same, which disturb the animal Spirits flowing in them, into explosions, or at least into some disorder: then the Spirits being so disturbed, infect those next to them, and they others; till by their continued series, the passion begun within the Spleen, is propagated even to the brain, and there produces inordinate Phantasms, such as happen to hypochondriacks.[74]

[72] *Thomas Willis, 1621–1675*, p. 130. Isler notes (p. 118) that some of Willis's metaphors are still being used in physiology textbooks in the twentieth century and that Bergson had taken up a goodly number of "Willisian Analogues," including that of the "explosive cause" of muscular spasms.

[73] Foucault, *Madness and Civilization*, p. 108.

[74] Willis, "Of the Distempers commonly called Hypochondriac," in *Practice of Physick*, p. 86.

To reverse the process, Willis's explanatory system can accommodate to a disturbance of the mind incurred through a distempered "Phantasy," the imbalance then being communicated to the spleen through a series of spirits planted in the nerves and intercostals. Its natural "ferment being put more into commotion," a sense of physical convulsion is thus stirred up and a psychosomatic upset can only ensue.

Approximately ten years after Willis's views on hysteria and hypochondria were first presented in Latin, Dr. Thomas Sydenham's essay "Of the Small-pox and hysteric Diseases" appeared. The second part of Sydenham's essay concerns us more than the first; it has generally been regarded as the century's "newly classical" description of hysteria.[75] It represents, on the one hand, the new empirical spirit of observation, and on the other the rapid acclimization, and even attenuation, of Willis's medical metaphors.

As Dr. William Cole noted in his epistle to Sydenham explaining the occasion, he had learned that Sydenham had made "some curious observations concerning *hysteric diseases* . . . demonstrating by this how unsafe it is to trust to our reason in philosophical matters, except in such things, as are manifest from the testimony of the senses."[76] Sydenham himself proclaimed that the cures he had worked out for hypochondria and hysteria through chalybeate medicines (iron therapy) to strengthen the ravaged blood came "rather from [his] own experience than from reading." It would be difficult to deny, nonetheless, that there are in Sydenham's treatise several parallels to Willis's notions, ideas, and expressions For example,

[75] For Sydenham's biography, see Kenneth Dewhurst, *Dr. Thomas Sydenham (1624–1689): His Life and Original Writings* (Berkeley and Los Angeles, 1966). See also Jerome M. Schneck, "Thomas Sydenham and Psychological Medicine," *Amer. J. Psychiatry*, CXII (1957), 1034–1036; and Ilza Veith, "On Hysterical and Hypochondriacal Afflictions," *Bull. Med. Hist.*, XXX (1956), 233–240. I have relied on the eighteenth-century translation of Sydenham's writings, *The Entire Works of Dr. Thomas Sydenham, Newly Made English from the Originals . . . by John Swan, M.D.* (London, 1742).

[76] *Entire Works of Sydenham*, p. 367.

hysterical cough was to Willis *casus . . . oppido rara* and to
Sydenham *species . . . oppido rara.*[77] And, in the common front
that he made with Willis against the adherents of the uterine
source of hysteria, Sydenham seems to have availed himself of
the Willisian notion of the disorders of the animal spirits without finding it necessary to argue the doctrine quite so vigor-
ously. Notice, for example, how Willis's militaristic "companies" and "squadrons" have been accepted but toned down
in Sydenham's explanation of the coldness of the external parts
in hysteric disorders: such coldness "arises from the spirits
forsaking their station, and crowding too much to some particular part (p. 381). Or notice in Sydenham's section on "the
curative" that he recommends the application of opiates "to
compose the tumultuary motion of the spirits and keep them in
their proper places."

Like Willis, Sydenham compares the hypochondriac complaints of men with the hysteric symptoms of women and finds
"a great similitude between them" (p. 368). Following Willis
and indirectly such encyclopedists of melancholia as Burton,
despite his focus on hysteria and hypochondria as distinct and
identifiable diseases, Sydenham remarks that "hysteric" disease
"is not more remarkable for its frequency, than for the numerous forms under which it appears, resembling most of the distempers wherewith mankind afflicted." He notes that it
sometimes attacks the head, causing an apoplectic-like fit which
may terminate in *hemiplegia*; he notices that it sometimes
causes epileptic-like convulsions. At times, he records, it occasions violent headache pains between the pericranium and the
cranium, "not exceeding the breadth of the thumb," or palpi-
tations of the heart so violent that "the patient is persuaded
those about her must needs hear the heart strike against the
ribs."

As I have already suggested, Sydenham, following Willis,
although a Willis toned down in language, believed that the
disorders termed hysteric in women and hypochondriac in men
"arise from *irregular motions* of *the animal spirits*, whence they

[77] Isler, *Thomas Willis*, p. 138.

are hurried with violence, and too copiously, to a particular part, occasioning convulsions and pain, when they exert their force upon parts of delicate sensation" (p. 376). What had earlier been attributed to "strangulation of the womb" or "fits of the mother," Sydenham, in Willisian notions, naturalized so to speak, attributes to spirits copiously collected in the lower belly, derived with violence to the fauces, occasioning convulsions in all the parts they pass through, and puffing up the belly like a ball. Externally, he adds, the process is marked by a coldness of the flesh and extremities—"dead bodies are not colder."

It is not entirely irrelevant to conclude this long section on melancholy anatomized into two specific afflictions, hysteria and hypochondria, by mentioning Sydenham's curatives. If violent disorders of the blood and nerves bring on hysteria, then the blood must be purged or the "tumultuary motion of the spirits" must be composed. If a dislocation of the spirits brings on depression, then through the prescription of chalybeate medicines the drooping spirits (as in female depression) might be roused. To strengthen the blood, Sydenham prescribes a "hysteric julep," consisting of 3 ounces each of distilled water of black cherries, rue, and bryony; and ½ dram of castor tied up in a piece of linen and suspended in a vial, mixed with enough fine sugar to sweeten the whole. Four or five teaspoons of the remedy were to be taken when the woman felt faint or low-spirited, "dropped into the first dose, if the fit be violent, 20 drops of spirit of hartshorn." Or filings of iron or steel were prescribed in Rhenish wine, left to settle, then to be strained off and the wine with a sufficient quantity of sugar boiled to the consistency of a syrup.

Something new had almost literally been added. Sydenham incidentally pioneered in the use of quinine for the fever and liquid laudanum in place of the old solid pill. He introduced a cooling regimen in the treatment of smallpox as well as using iron or steel filings in the treatment of hysteria and chlorosis. And yet, even as things change, we are still connected with older and not necessarily purely bookish observations on melancholy. Just as Sydenham's comment that hypochondria occurs in men "who lead a sedentary life and study hard" (p. 368) echoes Burton's subsection on the causes of melancholy, entitled "Love of Learning, or overmuch. With a Digression of the Misery of Scholars, and why the Muses are Melancholy" (Pt. I, sec. 2, mem. iii, subsec. 15), so his prescription of a wine cordial, touched with steel, does not totally differ from Burton's recommendation of wine. Calling to mind Matthiolus's praise of a deep cup as "a famous cordial," Burton had mused that wine "makes a good colour, a flourishing age, helps concoction, fortifies the stomach, takes away obstructions, provokes urine, drives out excrements, procures sleep, clears the blood, expels wind and cold poisons, attenuates [and] dissipates all thick vapours and fuliginous humours" (Pt. II, sec. 5, mem. i, subsec. 5).

To conclude our survey of the period 1350–1650 with a sense of the instauration of a different kind of "rationality," we must not underestimate the contributions made in the 1670s and 1680s to a new anatomy of melancholy, toward the concept of neurotic disease and the shaping of a "psychodynamic interpretation of . . . this concept." Out of the older notions of melancholy, in our study of the changing concepts of folly, madness, and melancholy, thanks to Willis and Sydenham, we find emerging, in Foucault's terms, a medical "dynamics of organic and moral penetration"; a "physiology of corporeal continuity": and, ultimately, "an ethic of nervous sensibility."[78] To this triad—to account for the hysteria-hypochondria alternation—we should add a fourth and final principle, a new organizing image or metaphor, that of chemical explosion. We have come a strange and meandering way in our metaphorical journey from the late fourteenth century. And we have seen notable shifts in social, psychological, and medical perceptions of the various forms of irrational behavior, derived from changing views of human nature as crystallized in "professional" metaphors, which in greatly simplified form illuminate new practices.

[78] Foucault, *Madness and Civilization*, p. 123.